Archaeology in the Avebury Area, Wiltshire:
Recent Discoveries Along the Line of the Kennet Valley Foul Sewer Pipeline, 1993

by Andrew B. Powell, Michael J. Allen, and I. Barnes

with contributions from
Rowena Gale, Mary Iles, Rosina Mount, Robert G. Scaife, Rachael Seager Smith, and Sarah F. Wyles

Illustrations by
Karen Nichols and John Hodgson

Wessex Archaeology Report No. 8

Wessex Archaeology 1996

Published 1996 by the Trust for Wessex Archaeology Ltd
Portway House, Old Sarum Park, Salisbury, England, SP4 6EB

British Library Cataloguing in Publication Data

A catalogue record for this book is available from the British Library

ISBN 1–874350–15–9
ISSN 0965–5778

Produced by Wessex Archaeology
Printed by Henry Ling (Dorset Press) Ltd, Dorchester

Editor: Melanie Gauden
Series Editor: Julie Gardiner

The publication was funded by Thames Water Utilities Ltd

Front cover: Work progressing along the route of the pipeline in Area B, looking south with Silbury Hill in the background

Back cover: Archaeological inspection of the pipeline trench, looking west with Silbury Hill in the background (photo: Thames Water)

Contents

List of Figures vii
List of Plates vii
List of Tables vii
Acknowledgements viii
Foreword, *by John Sexton* xi
Abstract xi

1. Introduction

Project Background 1
Environmental History, Topography, and Geology 2
Archaeology of the Avebury Area 2

2. Methods and Presentation of the Results

Methods 5
  Stage 1 Assessment 5
  Stage 2 Evaluation and Monitoring 6
  Environmental Sampling and Analysis 7
Results 7
  Presentation of Results 7

3. The Prehistoric Periods

Archaeological Background 10
  Mesolithic 10
  Neolithic 10
  Bronze Age 11
  Iron Age 13
Results of the Watching Brief 15
  Beckhampton Barrow 4 15
  The 'Stukeley' Barrow, Waden Hill 18
  Pound Field Barrow, West Overton 18
  Bronze Age Finds, *by Rachael Seager Smith* 19
  Environmental Analysis: Bronze Age 19
Discussion 26

4. The Romano-British Period

Archaeological Background 27
Results of the Watching Brief 30
  The Winterbourne Romano-British Settlement 31
  Romano-British Finds, *by Rachael Seager Smith* 39
  Environmental Analysis: Romano-British, *with contributions from Mary Iles,*
  Robert G. Scaife, and Rowen Gale 48
Discussion 56

5. The Saxon and Medieval Periods

Archaeological Background 59
  Saxon Period 59
  Medieval Period 59
Results of the Watching Brief 63
  Saxon Period 63
  Medieval Period 63
  Medieval Finds, *by Rachael Seager Smith* 66
  Environmental Analysis, *with contributions from Rosina Mount, Sarah F. Wyles,*
  Michael J. Allen, and Robert G. Scaife 67

6. The Post-Medieval Period

Archaeological Background 74
Results of the Watching Brief 74
  East Kennett Manor 74
  Post-Medieval Finds, *by Rachael Seager Smith* 76
Discussion 77

7. Undated Features

Beckhampton... 78
   Desk-Based Study Data.. 78
Butlers Field, Avebury.. 78
   Results of the Watching Brief.. 78
Winterbourne Romano-British Site.. 79
   Desk-Based Study Data.. 79
   Results of the Watching Brief.. 79
Waden Hill to West Kennett.. 79
   Desk-Based Study Data.. 79
   Results of the Watching Brief.. 80
East Kennett.. 80
   Desk-Based Study Data.. 80
   Results of the Watching Brief.. 80

8. Conclusions

The Contribution of Pipeline Archaeology to Our Understanding of the Environment, Farming,
and Settlement Patterns of the Winterbourne and Kennet Valleys, *by Michael J. Allen,
and Andrew B. Powell*.. 82
   Introduction.. 82
   Neolithic... 82
   Bronze Age.. 83
   Iron Age... 83
   Romano-British.. 83
   Saxon.. 84
   Medieval... 84
   Landscape Taphonomy.. 84
   Settlement Patterns... 84
Appraisal of the Methods.. 86
Conclusion.. 87

Bibliography.. 89
Index... 94

List of Figures

Figure 1   Location of the study area
Figure 2   Avebury World Heritage Site
Figure 3   Key to plans and sections
Figure 4   Area A: air photographs and geophysical surveys
Figure 5   Area B: air photographs and geophysical surveys
Figure 6   Area D: air photographs and geophysical surveys
Figure 7   Sections through the Beckhampton, 'Stukeley', and Pound Field barrows and the medieval lynchet
Figure 8   Mollusc histogram from the Beckhampton and 'Stukeley' barrows
Figure 9   Area B geophysical survey
Figure 10 Area B air photographic survey
Figure 11 Romano-British buildings I–V

Figure 12 Romano-British pits
Figure 13 Romano-British ditches
Figure 14 Copper alloy and worked bone objects
Figure 15 Romano-British pottery
Figure 16 Winterbourne Valley mollusc histogram
Figure 17 Medieval features, Butler's Field, Avebury, Area B surveys
Figure 18 Medieval features from Butler's Field, Avebury and post-medieval features from West Kennett
Figure 19 Medieval pottery
Figure 20 Mollusc histogram from Butler's Field, Avebury
Figure 21 Area C: geophysical survey
Figure 22 Archaeology of the Avebury area showing recently discovered sites

List of Plates

Plate 1   View of West Overton from the A4
Plate 2   'Stukeley' barrow ditch 71 and negative lynchet 72 on Waden Hill
Plate 3   View of the pipeline trench from Waden Hill
Plate 4   Building II, robbed wall foundation trench 190
Plate 5   Pit 158, Winterbourne Romano-British Settlement

Plate 6   West-facing section of Romano-British ditch 164
Plate 7   Medieval foundation trench 334, in Butler's Field, Avebury
Plate 8   Post-medieval feature north of East Kennett Manor
Plate 9   Conducting the geophysical survey at Pound Field, West Overton

List of Tables

Table 1   Number of known sites recorded in the study area
Table 2   Charcoal from the possible Bronze Age buried soil at Pound Field Barrow, West Overton
Table 3   Mollusca from the Pound Field barrow and Beckhampton barrow 4 ditch
Table 4   Mollusca from the 'Stukeley' barrow and the medieval lynchet on Waden Hill
Table 5   Probable Romano-British worked stone roof tile
Table 6   Fragments of worked stone with polished surfaces
Table 7   Romano-British pottery vessel forms by fabric type
Table 8   Romano-British pottery quantification by fabric and context

Table 9   Mollusca from Winterbourne alluvial edge terrace
Table 10 Animal bone from the Winterbourne Romano-British settlement
Table 11 Charred plant remains from the Winterbourne Romano-British settlement
Table 12 Charcoal from the Winterbourne Romano-British settlement
Table 13 Medieval pottery quantification by feature/layer and fabric type
Table 14 Mollusca from the alluvial sequence in Butler's Field
Table 15 Animal bones from medieval contexts
Table 16 Charred plant remains from medieval and post-medieval ditches

Acknowledgements

Wessex Archaeology would like to thank Mike Hall and Juliet Roper of Thames Water Utilities and David Skinner and Emma Bruton of Kennet District Council for their cooperation throughout this project.

The assistance, during the Stage 1 Assessment, of Chris Place of Wiltshire County Council Archaeological Service, and the staff of Geophysical Surveys of Bradford, and the Royal Commission on the Historical Monuments of England Air Photographic Unit, is also acknowledged.

In addition, Wessex Archaeology is grateful to Rosina Mount for the environmental consultancy and the use of her unpublished Ph.D. thesis; the Royal Commission on the Historical Monuments of England for permission to reproduce their recent survey of earthworks at Avebury and Avebury Trusloe; and the following people who provided information about recent research in the Avebury area: Andrew David, English Heritage, Ancient Monuments Geophysical Laboratory; John Evans, University of Wales College of Cardiff; Chris Gingell, National Trust; Robin Holgate, Luton Museum; Mike Pitts, Avebury; Gill Swanton, Wiltshire Archaeological and Natural History Society; Peter Ucko, University of Southampton, and Alasdair Whittle, University of Wales College of Cardiff. Michael Allen and Andrew Powell wish to thank Peter Fowler, University of Newcastle, for discussing the results and overview of his Fyfield–Overton Down project and for his encouraging comments on the Discussion.

The assistance, during the watching brief, of Barry Duncan of Kennet District Council, Robert Hope, of Hope and Clay Construction Ltd, and their site agent John Abraham is also acknowledged. Finally, the fieldwork could not have been completed successfully without the enthusiastic cooperation of the Hope and Clay construction crew.

The project was managed for Wessex Archaeology by Ian Barnes. The archaeological background data was collected by Andrew Powell and the watching brief undertaken by Andrew Powell, Ian Barnes, and William Boismier. The drawings were completed by Karen Nichols and John Hodgson.

Foreword

Re-laying sewers in and around the Avebury World Heritage Site was a daunting prospect. The fact that this has been achieved at no detriment to the historic landscape, is a tribute to our skilled and enthusiastic team of archaeologists and engineers.

By utilising the most modern archaeological survey techniques and designing equally innovative construction procedures, the work was able to proceed with the minimum of interruption. Thus, rather than damaging the buried heritage, Thames Water and its partners actually contributed to the understanding of the area's history, particularly the little known Roman and medieval settlements.

The project was a model of cooperation and this report is a fitting tribute to all those who made the work possible.

John Sexton

John Sexton
Director of Environment and Science
Thames Water

Abstract

The replacement of 4 km of sewer pipeline around Avebury provided an opportunity to cut a slice through a landscape rich in archaeological remains. This report, which combines the findings of the watching brief undertaken during the engineering works with the results of earlier desk-based research and air photographic and geophysical surveys, demonstrates the high potential of that landscape, not just for the ritual and mortuary monuments of Neolithic and Bronze Age date for which Avebury is famous, but also the archaeology of other periods, in particular for Romano-British and medieval settlement.

One aim of the desk-based study had been to identify which route for the replacement pipe would have least impact on the archaeological resource. However, the high potential of the entire Avebury landscape, as indicated by the study, suggested that there was unlikely to be any lower impact alternative to the existing pipeline route. It was, therefore, decided to abandon the usual techniques employed in the laying of pipelines in favour of those causing minimal damage to undisturbed ground. Instead of stripping soil from the working easement and cutting a new trench, no soil was stripped and the new pipe was laid within the existing trench along its entire route. All engineering works were archaeologically monitored.

Despite passing through the centre of a Neolithic 'ritual' landscape, no archaeological features of Neolithic date were recorded. The earliest features cut by the pipe trench were three Bronze Age round barrow ring-ditches,

one in the Beckhampton barrow cemetery, and two in dispersed locations. The barrow at the south end of Waden Hill had been recorded by William Stukeley but had since been plough levelled. There was, however, no previous record of the other barrow at West Overton. Environmental data from the barrow ditches show that the monuments were built in established grassland.

Evidence for an extensive Romano-British settlement along the east bank of the Winterbourne, south of Avebury, was discovered during the watching brief, adding to the known Roman material from around Silbury Hill. A number of features adjacent to the line of the Roman Road at the south end of the site are dated to the 1st and 2nd centuries AD but the site was occupied, possibly continuously, until the 4th and perhaps the 5th century AD. Wall foundation trenches for up to five buildings, as well as numerous pits and ditches, were recorded.

Previously recorded evidence of medieval settlement to the south-west of Avebury village was added to by the recording of medieval features, including a wall foundation trench, pits, and ditches of 12th–14th century date in Butler's Field. Post-medieval features were recorded at East Kennett, possibly associated with East Kennett Manor.

In addition to the dated features, numerous undated features were also recorded in the pipe trench and it is likely that many of these are closely associated with the Romano-British, medieval, and post-medieval sites within which they were located.

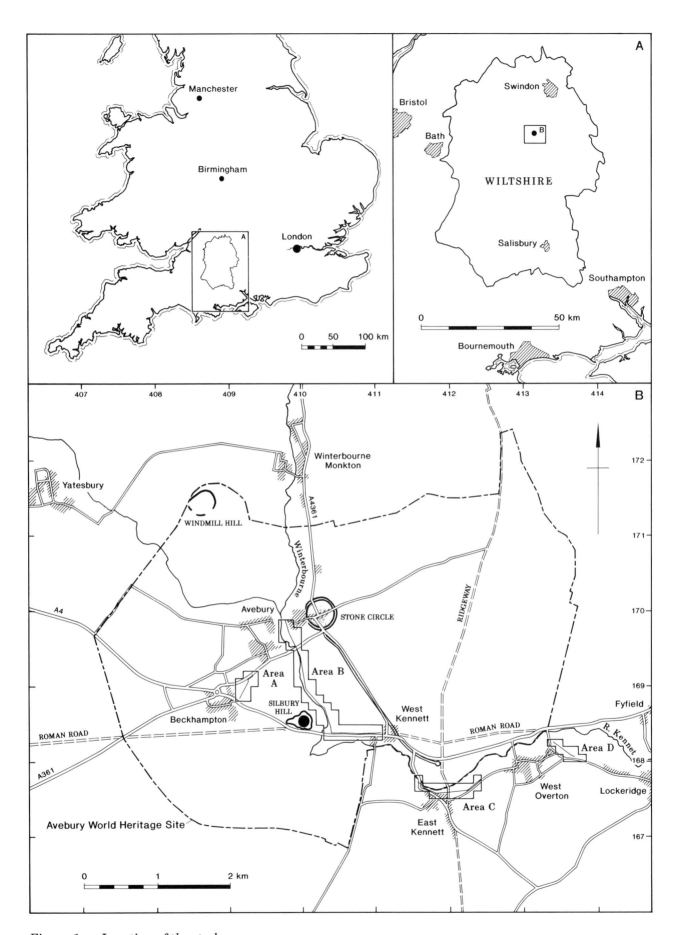

Figure 1   Location of the study area

1. Introduction

Project Background

In 1992 Thames Water Utilities was faced with the need to replace four sections of rising sewer main, with a combined length of approximately 4 km, in the vicinity of Avebury, Wiltshire and to undertake renovations at four accompanying pumping stations (Fig. 1, Areas A–D). The sections of existing sewer, which ran through Beckhampton, Avebury, West Kennett, East Kennett, and West Overton, had been laid during the 1960s, at which time certain archaeological deposits had been noted by Faith Vatcher of the Alexander Keiller Museum, Avebury. The dilemma faced by Thames Water, and Kennet District Council's Technical Services Group which undertakes waste management on their behalf, was that much of the preferred route lay within the Avebury World Heritage Site, a designation which recognises the international importance of the Avebury landscape with its concentration of closely associated archaeological monuments. If traditional sewer laying techniques were used then archaeological deposits within a 20 m wide easement along the entire 4 km route would have been threatened.

In order to mitigate the effects of the works and to ensure compliance with the Water Industry Environmental Code of Practice, a Stage 1 Assessment strategy was formulated jointly by Mike Hall, then Thames Water's Archaeologist and Chris Place, then Wiltshire County Council's Assistant Archaeological Officer. Its aims were to identify any archaeologically sensitive areas, within a defined corridor of interest around the preferred route, which might be disturbed by the excavation of new trenches, and to determine the feasibility of diverting the trenches around those areas. The project design took account of the County Council's guidelines for archaeological assessment as defined in their Acquisition and Presentation Standards of Archaeological Data (1992).

The assessment strategy consisted of two elements undertaken concurrently. The first was a desk-based study in which the Wiltshire County Council Sites and Monument Record air photographs and other sources, both published and unpublished, were consulted. The second was a geophysical survey, consisting of a magnetometer scan, with magnetic susceptibility sampling of almost the entire route, and a detailed magnetometer survey of those sections where previous finds had suggested a high archaeological potential. As a result of this two-fold assessment, 84 locations of archaeological and palaeo-environmental potential were identified within or impinging upon the corridor of interest. A report describing the results (Wessex Archaeology 1992a) was presented to Thames Water and Kennet District Council in May 1992.

The Stage 1 Assessment report indicated that the archaeological potential of the corridors of interest was high, particularly at Beckhampton and between Avebury and West Kennett, where the archaeological resource was reasonably well defined. At East Kennett and West Overton, however, the results were more ambiguous, the geophysical scan providing limited evidence of a number of possible sites but in insufficient detail to allow full mitigation proposals to be developed. A decision was made that these latter sites should be further evaluated and subsequent geophysical surveying of selected areas was undertaken as part of Stage 2 of the project. The results of these surveys confirmed that the archaeological potential of all four sections was such that the traditional engineering strategy needed to be revised so as to be more sympathetic to the archaeological resource by minimising any disturbance of new ground.

The choices facing Thames Water were: to find an alternative route for the replacement pipe, to undertake full scale excavation along the routes, or to re-excavate the existing pipe trench, remove the redundant pipe and lay the new pipe in its place. Other possible technical solutions, such as pipe busting were deemed unsuitable. The option of full scale excavation was ruled out on account of the Government's stated preference, in Planning Policy Guidance Note 16 (Department of the Environment 1990), for preserving nationally important archaeological remains *in situ;* by definition the archaeology of the World Heritage Site is an area of international importance. It was also clear that it would not be possible, given the apparent density of archaeological remains, to find a feasible alternative route for the pipeline which would not impinge to an equal degree to the preferred route upon the archaeological resource.

Thames Water and Kennet District Council, in consultation with Wiltshire County Council, decided that replacement of the sewer should, therefore, be laid along its entire length within the existing trench. Moreover, to complement the minimum disturbance policy, it was agreed that no easement stripping was to be allowed as would normally have been the case. However, because the re-excavation of the trench would re-expose any archaeological features cut when the original pipe was laid, a provision was made for an archaeologist to be in attendance at all times to record these features and any that, despite the mitigation strategy, might still be exposed by disturbance to new ground along the trench edge.

The brief for Stage 2 of the strategy, including the evaluation and the archaeological monitoring of the engineering works, was written by Thames Water and the County Archaeological Service and supplied to Wessex Archaeology in July 1992. After submitting its proposals for the project (Wessex Archaeology 1992b), Wessex Archaeology was commissioned to undertake the task of monitoring the engineering works. A watching brief was maintained throughout the trenching and associated excavations. Four sections of rising sewer main were replaced between February and June 1993, as follows:

- Area A: Beckhampton to Avebury (Fig. 4), 378 m.
- Area B: Avebury to West Kennett (Figs 5, 9, 10, and 17), 2286 m.
- Area C: East Kennett to West Overton (Fig. 21), 920 m.
- Area D: West Overton to Lockeridge (Fig. 6), 346 m.

The watching brief confirmed the high archaeological potential of the pipeline route, revealing a large number of archaeological features of Bronze Age, Romano-British, medieval, and post-medieval date, with evidence of settlement, economic and, in the Bronze Age, mortuary activity. A number of these features correspond to previously known archaeological sites, or to sites identified for the first time by the Stage 1 archaeological assessment and the Stage 2 evaluation. However, others add substantial new evidence to the archaeology of the Avebury area, including an extensive and previously unknown Romano-British settlement on the eastern bank of the Winterbourne, north of the A4 London–Bath trunk road.

Environmental History, Topography, and Geology

The landscape crossed by the four sections of pipeline consists of the valley floor and the adjacent lower slopes of undulating chalk downland in the upper Kennet valley. The River Kennet flows eastwards from Swallowhead Springs to the south of Silbury Hill towards West Overton. To the north of the springs the river is called the Winterbourne and is dry for part of the year. Recent research into the late Pleistocene and Holocene environmental history from the valley floor is fully described in Evans *et al.* (1993) and, therefore, only a general summary of the main results of the Postglacial environment is given here. The geology of the area is primarily Cretaceous Chalk, with localised surface concentrations of sarsen stone.

During the Mesolithic and Neolithic the valley floor at Avebury was a dry stable woodland with no evidence for a river, while down the valley floor at West Overton the ground was wetter with local streams and open marsh. There is evidence of woodland clearance resulting in localised alluviation during the Neolithic, followed by cultivation and the formation of a stable soil ('Avebury soil'). There was no regeneration of woodland on the valley floor as there was following clearance on the downs. From the later Neolithic into the Iron Age there was a major episode of alluviation ('West Overton Formation') caused by seasonal flooding along the whole of the study area, with the first evidence for a river upstream of Swallowhead Springs. This was possibly due to renewed clearance and cultivation on the downs. There was renewed soil formation during the Middle Ages ('medieval soil complex') during which time the valley floor was dry enough for settlement and cultivation but this was followed in the post-medieval period by a second episode of alluviation (Arion Clay), during

which time the management of the valley floor created the water meadow earthworks surviving along the Winterbourne and Kennet.

The Beckhampton to Avebury section of the pipeline (Area A) runs north-east from the pumping station in Beckhampton village (SU 0905 6883), crossing the A4 London–Bath trunk road immediately to the east of the Wagon and Horses public house. It runs up the side of the field, presently under arable cultivation, which lies to the east of the footpath between the A4 and the A4361, to the top of a low chalk spur called Folly Hill, crossing bands of Lower and Middle Chalk. It then runs along the south side of the A4361, before crossing to the north side.

The Avebury to West Kennett section (Area B) starts at the pumping station on the west side of Avebury village (SU 0979 6988) and runs south, to the east of the Winterbourne, through Butler's Field which is used for grazing. The trench crosses the A4361 to the east of the New Bridge and runs along the edges of arable fields on the east bank of the Winterbourne to the north side of the A4. Along this northern section the pipe trench cuts through alluvial deposits, as well as coombe rock and bands of Lower Chalk. From the point by the A4, the trench runs east over the southern end of Waden Hill, along the edges of the arable fields immediately north of the A4, crossing a band of Middle Chalk. The section ends north of Honeysuckle Cottage in West Kennett.

The East Kennett to West Overton section (Area C) starts at the pumping station at the west end of the village (NGR SU 1157 6772) and, cutting through river gravels, runs close to the River Kennet along the north edge of the main street through the village to a point east of The Cottage. It then runs along the north side of the farm buildings attached to East Kennett Manor and the Manor itself, before crossing the line of the Ridgeway. To the east of the Ridgeway it passes through a meadow before cutting through Middle Chalk across an arable field to the south side of the road to West Overton.

The West Overton to Lockeridge section (Area D) runs through Pound Field to the east of West Overton village (Pl. 1). It starts at the pumping station at the edge of the valley floor (NGR SU 1336 6827) and rises up the lower slopes of White Hill to the south-east, through bands of Middle and Upper Chalk, to a point east of Lockeridge Dairy.

Archaeology of the Avebury Area

The Beckhampton and the Avebury to West Kennett sections of the pipeline lie within the Avebury World Heritage Site, which covers some 22 km^2 around Avebury village, while the East Kennett and West Overton sections are sited immediately to the south and south-east. At the time of the study, a total of 345 archaeological sites were recorded within the World Heritage Site, of which 86 were Scheduled Monuments, and the following five were Guardianship sites:

- West Kennett Long Barrow
- Windmill Hill

- Avebury Circle and the associated West Kennett and Beckhampton Avenues
- The Sanctuary
- Silbury Hill

While the World Heritage Site is visibly dominated by the surviving ritual and mortuary monuments of the Neolithic and Bronze Age, creating the impression of a predominantly 'ritual' landscape, monument building was episodic (Whittle 1993), and a considerable amount of the archaeological and environmental evidence from the area relates to settlement and economic activity (Smith 1984). For instance, the Kennet valley floor, across which the pipeline cuts for much of its length, contains alluvial deposits providing a potentially rich source of information about human exploitation of the local environment from the early Post-glacial period to the present day (Mount 1991; Evans *et al.* 1993).

There is some evidence of occasional Mesolithic exploitation of the Avebury area, both from the valley floor and what would then have been the adjacent wooded downland (Whittle 1990), followed in the early Neolithic by localised clearance and low-density settlement and cultivation, such as the earliest evidence for the use of the plough in the British Isles, from under the South Street long barrow (Fowler and Evans 1967), and structural features on Windmill Hill from *c.* 3700 BC. Early monument construction, in the form of the early features at the Horslip, South Street and West Kennett long barrows (Ashbee *et al.* 1979), was also relatively modest and dispersed, with the more elaborate architectural features, such as the chambered tomb in the West Kennett long barrow being later in date.

Around 3250 BC, a causewayed enclosure, with concentric interrupted ditches enclosing an area of 8.5 hectares, was constructed on Windmill Hill (Smith 1965), with another at Knap Hill 8 km to the south-east. Such monuments would have been important sites of social, economic, and ceremonial activity for both the local and the regional populations. Finds at Windmill Hill of pottery and tools of stone, flint, and antler, as well as carved chalk figurines and phalli and human and animal bones, give some indication as to the range of communal activities undertaken there, with exotic materials, including stone axes from as far afield as Wales, Cornwall, and the Lake District, pointing to the wider social and economic networks into which the site was linked.

Some time around 2000 BC the Windmill Hill enclosure was abandoned, an event roughly contemporary with the blocking of the entrance to the West Kennett long barrow, effectively ending the monument's use as a tomb. However, the ritual activity in the Avebury landscape reached its peak in this period, with the construction of a sequence of monuments, which even individually would have required a massive increase in the scale of communal social endeavour. The Avebury henge, with a bank and ditch at least 15 m from

Plate 1   View of West Overton from the A4, with the pipeline excavation crossing Pound Field

the top to the base, has a circumference of 1.3 km. The construction of stone circles within the henge, and the 2.4 kilometre long West Kennett Avenue linking Avebury to the circular timber and stone structure, the Sanctuary, on Overton Hill, would have involved the dragging of some 600 sarsen stones, the largest weighing up to 60 tons, from the Marlborough Downs and the surrounding countryside. Silbury Hill, at 48 m high with its base covering 2 hectares, is the largest man-made mound in Europe, and the recently discovered palisaded enclosure at West Kennett adds a new dimension to this unique landscape. There is, however, little evidence as to the nature of local settlement in this period.

The earlier communal mortuary monuments were replaced in the later Neolithic by new forms of individual burial, associated particularly with a new artefact assemblage characterised by Beaker pottery. The association of individual graves under round barrows, often with an exclusive range of high status artefacts, was a feature that continued into the Early and Middle Bronze Age. Although the construction and use of the large ritual monuments ritual had ended by the start of the Bronze Age, elements of this unique landscape continued to exert their influence. Many of the Late Neolithic and Bronze Age round barrows which stud the skylines around Avebury are sited close or on top of to the earlier monuments, as on Windmill Hill and the 'linear cemetery' next to the Sanctuary on Overton Hill, others occupying elevated positions overlooking them, as at Beckhampton or on Waden Hill and Avebury Down.

The concentration of round barrows reflects the intensity of settlement and land division evident on the Marlborough Downs during the Middle and Late Bronze Age (Gingell 1992), patterns of exploitation of the landscape which continued during the Iron Age, the downs displaying a mosaic of settlements and fields (Fowler 1967). There was also continuity into the Romano-British period, with substantial evidence of settlement and agricultural activity on the downs around Avebury. More wealthy Roman settlements such as villas, however, appear to be relatively infrequent in north Wiltshire by comparison with neighbouring regions. Nonetheless, a possible 'villa' site to the west of Avebury and quantities of Roman finds and structural material found in the vicinity of Silbury Hill, close to the Roman road running between Mildenhall and Bath, do point to the emergence of a new settlement pattern on or close to the valley floors. Although a major Roman road passes through the centre of the study area, the evidence for these settlements has been intermittent and their nature has remained unclear.

Archaeological evidence for occupation during the post-Roman period is equally sketchy. The generally unsettled political nature of the period, however, is clearly evident in the construction of the Wansdyke across the North Wiltshire Downs to the south, and this may be reflected locally in the construction of a timber palisade on Silbury Hill, a coin of Ethelred the Unready being found in the upper recut terrace. There is evidence of Saxon settlement and a Saxon church at Avebury, but much of the information for this period is derived from documentary sources such as Saxon land charters. Excavations at Avebury have also revealed substantial evidence of medieval settlement to the south-west of the present village and medieval earthworks survive at both Beckhampton and West Overton. Strip lynchets on the lower slopes of the downland are also probably of medieval date.

The major river valleys, which provided the principal means of entry for the early Saxon settlers into Wessex, continued to be the preferred areas for settlement. Saxon and early medieval settlements in the upper Kennet valley, such as at West Overton, East Kennett, Beckhampton, and Avebury, are spaced at approximately equal distances along the valley floor, a pattern of settlement which has been preserved largely unchanged to the present day.

2. Methods and Presentation of the Results

Methods

This project has combined a series of different survey techniques in order to study the archaeology of the pipeline corridor. The methods employed for each stage are summarised below.

Stage 1 Assessment

Desk-based study
The aim of the desk-based study was to identify and catalogue any archaeological sites and areas of palaeo-environmental potential within four corridors of interest, each approximately 200 m wide as defined by Ordnance Survey hectares centred on the preferred route for the replacement pipeline.

The study was based on the Wiltshire Sites and Monuments Record (SMR), which is designed to list all recorded sites and findspots within the county. A complete catalogue listing all entries falling within the study corridor was obtained. Listed Buildings were excluded. The SMR contained 33 entries falling in the four areas as follows:

- Area A: Beckhampton to Avebury   11
- Area B: Avebury to West Kennett   13
- Area C: East Kennett to West Overton   6
- Area D: West Overton to Lockeridge   3

To supplement the information held in the SMR, a survey of all literature considered relevant and post-dating the last major revision of the SMR was undertaken. This involved consulting relevant volumes of the *Wiltshire Archaeological and Natural History Magazine (WAM)*, national archaeological journals, and monographs for any references to work in the Avebury area. In addition, in order to locate as many unpublished sources as possible, archaeologists known to have recently carried out fieldwork or other research in the Avebury area were contacted in order to gain access to their reports, archives, or theses.

Devizes Museum and the Alexander Keiller Museum, Avebury were visited to check their catalogues for material not yet included in the SMR. Salisbury Museum was also contacted. The Royal Commission on the Historical Monuments of England (RCHME) office at Salisbury was approached in order to obtain the results of an earthwork survey recently undertaken in the Avebury area. The four routes were walked in order to identify any surviving earthworks in areas not covered by the RCHME earthwork surveys. These were measured and plotted onto 1:2500 maps.

Air photographic survey
An air photographic survey was conducted by the RCHME Air Photographic Unit at Swindon (RCHME 1992b). Air photographs covering the four study corridors were examined in detail in an attempt to recognise potential archaeological sites not recorded on the SMR and to obtain information on those that had been. Photogrammetric plans were prepared at a scale of 1:2500 showing all archaeological features observed as plough-levelled crop or soil marks.

Sources include photographs held at the National Library of Air Photography (RCHME), particularly important among which were the vertical and oblique photographs in the O.G.S. Crawford Collection, many taken in the 1920s, those taken by Major G.W.G. Allen in the 1930s, and the results of recent RCHME) reconnaissance. Photographs held by the Cambridge University Committee for Air Photography (CUCAP) were also consulted, including a fine series of oblique photographs of the Beckhampton barrow cemetery taken from the 1940s onwards, and those held by the Wiltshire County Council's SMR.

Features were plotted using computer-aided photogrammetric rectification from oblique and vertical air photographs. Field control was derived from current edition OS 1:2500 plans, supplemented, for the earliest photographs, by earlier OS 6 inch maps, and, as a further check, known field boundaries were digitised from the photographs to allow checking against the base maps. As a result, the maximum error from any feature's true ground position was calculated at generally under 2.5 m.

Soils in the Avebury area give a relatively poor indication of buried archaeological features, with extensive mottled patches preventing the formation of a clear response. Moreover, features often have different appearances from year to year, round barrows, for instance, appearing as ring-ditches one year, chalky spreads in others, or not showing at all; the widths of features also varies. It is inevitable that there should be some differences between the results of the air photographic and geophysical surveys (*see* below) of the same feature.

Geophysical survey
A geophysical survey was conducted by Geophysical Surveys of Bradford (GSB) (1992a). It consisted of two parts: a detailed survey of limited areas of the route, and a less intensive scanning of the whole route.

Detailed survey
Detailed surveys were undertaken at five locations along the preferred pipeline route. These were over either known archaeological sites or where previous individual but unassociated finds (listed in the Wiltshire SMR) pointed to a high archaeological potential. These locations were: Beckhampton barrow cemetery (Fig 2), Butler's Field, Avebury (Fig 14), east of the Winterbourne at Silbury Hill (Fig 7), and Waden Hill and West Kennett (Fig 3).

Detailed magnetometer surveys were undertaken at these locations, with a combined total area of approximately 5.75 hectares. The survey involved taking readings at 0.5 m intervals along traverses 1.0 m apart, with a density of 800 readings per 20 m grid. The grids for the areas surveyed were tied in to OS 1:2500 maps. The results were displayed using X–Y traces, dot density plots, and full interpretation diagrams, the latter being used in this volume.

Scanning

A 50 m wide corridor centred on the preferred route, was scanned along the whole length of the route, with the exception of those areas where detailed survey was undertaken, with a combined total area of approximately 17 hectares. The corridor was subdivided into 10 fields, of which nine were part scanned by magnetometer. This involved walking the corridor in a zigzag pattern at approximately 10 m intervals. Any areas of possible archaeological interest, as defined during the magnetic scan, are indicated in the figures by stars.

All 10 fields were sampled to obtain background magnetic susceptibility readings, with 50 g soil samples collected from below the surface, being taken at 20 m intervals along the route. The soils were dried and, after being crushed and having stone and organic matter discarded, were measured in the laboratory on an AC Susceptibility Bridge. The results acted as a control for interpreting the results of the scanning survey. The magnetic susceptibility data is displayed on the figures as proportional circles, the larger the circle the higher the reading.

Stage 1 report

The results of the Stage 1 Assessment were combined in a report (Wessex Archaeology 1992a). The report listed in a Gazetteer all the archaeological sites, and sites of palaeo-environmental potential, identified by the desk-based study and the geophysical survey, in a form compatible with the Wiltshire SMR. They were also plotted at 1:2500 on an Ordnance Survey base supplied by Kennet District Council.

By the end of the Stage 1 Assessment the number of known sites within the study area had increased to 84 from the 33 previously recorded on the SMR (Table 1).

Table 1   number of known sites recorded in the study area

	Sites recorded on the SMR	Numbers of sites known by end of Stage 1 Assessment
Beckhampton to Avebury	11	25
Avebury to West Kennett	13	46
East Kennett to West Overton	6	9
West Overton to Lockeridge	3	5
Total	33	84

Stage 2 Evaluation and Monitoring

Further evaluation

Because of the ambiguity of some of the geophysical survey results, which provided limited evidence of possible sites but not in enough detail to allow full mitigation proposals, further magnetometer surveys were undertaken in two areas where the magnetometer scan had detected strong discrete geophysical anomalies corresponding to high magnetic susceptibility readings, one at East Kennett and the other at West Overton. The same procedures were followed as in the earlier survey (GSB 1992b).

Engineering mitigation

As a result of the conclusions of the desk-based study and the subsequent further evaluation, it was clear that there was little chance of finding an alternative to the preferred route for the replacement of the pipeline, as any other route would be likely to impinge to a similar degree upon the archaeological resource of the Avebury landscape. It was decided, therefore, that the replacement pipe should be laid, where possible, within the existing pipe trench for the whole of its length. In order to keep the sewer line in service while the existing pipe was removed, the sewage was to be over-pumped above ground, so bypassing sections of the pipe and allowing their replacement. Small excavations were necessary in order to find the existing pipeline but these caused minimal interference to previously undisturbed ground.

Of a total of 3930 m of new pipeline, all but 235 m was laid within the existing trenches, with new trenches being cut only where machine access was not possible, or where technical considerations prevented over-pumping. Where possible, the machine's excavating bucket did not stray outside the line of the existing trench. However, the requirement to lay the replacement pipe for much of its length deeper into the ground and the consequent need, given the varied ground conditions, to recut the trench to an adequate width for safety reasons, meant that the trench sides were almost always fully exposed. Nonetheless, in places, unexcavated trench backfill remained against the sides of the trench and it is possible that archaeological features may have been obscured at these points.

As a further mitigation measure to preserve the archaeological resource, it was decided that, contrary to normal practice, the topsoil would not be stripped from the working easement, as its removal and reinstatement would have disturbed the distributions of artefacts within the topsoil, hampering any future analysis of surface artefact collections. Furthermore, the exposure by topsoil stripping of any archaeological features and deposits would inevitably have subjected them to a degree of weathering and disturbance by machine traffic. Instead, the excavated topsoil and existing trench backfill were deposited separately on textile sheeting in order to prevent contamination of the underlying soil and were reinstated in sequence as soon as the new pipe had been laid.

Watching brief

The main engineering contract for the project included clauses detailing the role of the on-site archaeologist, who was written into the project team on a parity with the Site Engineer, with the power, if needed, to temporarily suspend work in order to record deposits.

All excavations undertaken during the course of the engineering works were monitored. These included the excavations to locate the existing pipeline for the purposes of over-pumping, the excavation of the existing pipe trench, and any excavations in areas of new ground undertaken in the course of renovations at the pumping stations.

All archaeological features showing in section were cleaned by hand and recorded using Wessex Archaeology's standard recording system which consists of a full written, drawn, and photographic record. Feature positions were recorded on 1:2500 plans based on a contract drawing provided by Kennet District Council, their locations being recorded with reference to the engineer's chainage points as measured in metres from each pumping station. Because of the problems of taking levels over long distances from infrequent Ordnance Survey bench marks, the levels are based on the ground surface levels recorded in the Kennet District Council's contract drawings which are at 10 m intervals along the lines of the pipeline. The levels for individual features referred to in the text relate to the tops of the features.

Any artefacts exposed during the cleaning of the sections of features were retained. Finds recovered unstratified from spoil excavated by the machine were also retained and were recorded to the nearest 10 m on the basis of their chainage positions. In addition, soil and subsoil profiles were recorded at 50 m intervals along the route of the pipeline.

Environmental Sampling and Analysis

A series of 23 bulk soil samples of approximately 10 litres were taken from a range of sealed and dated archaeological features, including pre-barrow features, Romano-British pits, ditches, and wall foundations, and from a medieval ditch. They were processed for the recovery of both charred plant remains and charcoal by standard flotation methods with the flots retained on a 0.5 mm mesh and residues on a 1 mm mesh following Wessex Archaeology's standard procedures (Allen 1992). After assessment of the sampled archaeological contexts and the preservation and quantity of both charred plant remains and charcoal in the flots, samples were selected for total extraction and analyses.

Charred plant remains
Some 23 samples of approximately 10 litres volume were processed from the above mentioned features. These included 14 samples from nine selected sealed archaeological features which produced well-preserved charred plant remains. Identification and counting was carried out using a Wild M3 low power binocular microscope in conjunction with modern seed reference material. Nomenclature and taxonomy follows Clapham *et al.* (1952).

Charcoal
Bulk soil samples were taken from a range of archaeological features. Charcoal was identified from a Bronze Age buried soil and four Romano-British contexts, including pits and wall foundation trenches. Contexts including charcoal were relatively infrequent and, when present, the fragments were small and few in number. The samples were examined with a x20 hand lens and sorted into groups based on the anatomical features observed on the transverse surface. Representative fragments were selected from each group for further examination and fractured to expose clean, flat surfaces in the transverse, tangential longitudinal, and radial longitudinal planes. The fragments were supported in sand and examined using an epi-illuminating microscope at up to x400 magnification. The structure was matched to authenticated reference material.

Mollusca
A series of columns of contiguous samples for molluscan analysis was taken through ring-ditch fills and through the alluvial deposits which were encountered on the floor of the Kennet valley (Fig. 5). The sampled ditch sediments have been described following the terminology of primary, secondary, and tertiary fills as defined by Evans (1972, 321–332) and Limbrey (1975, 290–300). Methods of mollusc analyses were standard and followed those outlined by Evans (1972) and detailed elsewhere (Allen 1989; 1990). The results are presented in Figures 6, 13, and 17 as standard histograms of relative abundance with *Cecilioides acicula* being calculated over and above the assemblage. Some of the species have been grouped for this purpose. Zonatids include *Aegopinella nitidula*, *Oxychilus cellarius*, and *Vitrea contracta*; other shade-loving species include *Discus rotundatus*, *Clausilia bidentata*, *Cochlodina laminata*, and Clausiliidae; Punctum group follows Evans' Punctum group, *Cochlicopa* includes both *Cochlicopa lubrica* and *Cochlicopa lubricella*. Nomenclature follows Kerney (1976).

Results

Presentation of Results

In order to present the results of the desk-based study (including the air photographic survey and the two stages of geophysical survey) and the watching brief in a sensible form, the results from each stage of work have been combined below by period. For each period there is an initial background summary of known archaeological evidence from within the study corridor, followed by the results of the watching brief (if any). These are followed by descriptions of any finds and environmental evidence recovered during the watching brief and each period section concludes with a discussion of the new data.

The *Archaeological Background* section incorporates the data collected during the desk-based study and the air photographic and geophysical surveys, as well as general background information. All discrete archaeological evidence from within the study corridor, whether individual finds or whole sites, are assigned a unique catalogue number, with a letter prefix (A–D) identifying the section of the study corridor. These numbers, listed below, identify the features on the area plans (these numbers differ from those assigned during the Stage 1 Assessment – Wessex Archaeology 1992a).

The *Results of the Watching Brief* section consists of a full description of those dated archaeological features recorded in the pipe trench. The locations of the features are denoted with a letter prefix, indicating the section of the pipeline route and the engineer's chainage measurements (ie B.1516–26 m), as shown on the area plans. Fortunately, the main features from each period are, to a large degree, circumscribed either by form or location. Those of Bronze Age date (ie the round barrows at Beckhampton, Waden Hill, and West Overton) are readily identifiable and comparable units of study, the distribution of which reflects the range of clustering and dispersal displayed by round barrows within the wider landscape. Features from the Romano-British, medieval, and post-medieval period are also located in identifiable 'sites' (ie the Winterbourne and Butler's Field settlements) and that in the vicinity of East Kennett Manor, respectively.

Only those features from either the desk-based study or from the watching brief for which there is no artefactual or typological dating, are described under the section *Undated Features*. However, as it is likely that some of those features, located within identifiable and dated sites, are of comparable date to the dated features from the sites, the undated features, from all stages of the project, are considered by site or general area.

List of sites, features, and finds identified during the desk-based study

Area A: Beckhampton to Avebury (Figure 4)

A1   Beckhampton barrow 1

A2   Beckhampton barrow 2 (air photographic and geophysical surveys)

A3   Beckhampton barrow 3 (air photographic and geophysical surveys)

A4   Beckhampton barrow 4 (air photographic and geophysical surveys)

A5   Beckhampton barrow 5 (air photographic survey)

A6   Beckhampton barrow 6 (air photographic and geophysical surveys)

A7   Beckhampton barrow 7 (air photographic and geophysical surveys)

A8   Beckhampton barrow 8 (air photographic survey)

A9   Possible ring-ditch 14 (air photographic survey)

A10   Possible ring-ditch 15 (air photographic survey)

A11   Possible ring-ditch 16 (air photographic survey)

A12   Sub-rectangular ditch 11 (air photographic survey)

A13   Sub-rectangular ditch 10 (air photographic survey)

A14   Pit (geophysical survey)

A15   Pit (geophysical survey)

A16   Bronze Age flint distribution

A17   Iron chape from Beckhampton

A18   Romano-British horseshoes from Beckhampton

A19   *Bachentune* (*Domesday* Book)

A20   Medieval earthworks at Beckhampton

A21   Medieval field boundaries north of A4361 (air photographic survey)

A22   Bank in 'The Paddock'

A23   Strip lynchets (air photographic survey)

A24   North/south parallel ditches (air photographic survey)

A25   East/west parallel ditches (air photographic survey)

Area B: Avebury to West Kennett (Figures 5, 9, 10, and 17)

Figure 5

B5   West Kennett palisade enclosure and small ring-ditch

B6   Neolithic pottery from Waden Hill

B7   Bronze Age axe-hammer, West Kennett

B8   'Stukeley' barrow, Waden Hill (geophysical survey)

B9   Small ring-ditch on Waden Hill (geophysical survey)

B18   Roman coins from Waden Hill

B19   Roman coins from West Kennett

B24   *Chenete* (*Domesday* Book)

B31   Medieval settlement at West Kennett

B36   Undated grave on Waden Hill

B37   Group of linear features on Waden Hill (geophysical survey)

B38   Pit/shaft on Waden Hill (geophysical survey)

B39   Group of 5 anomalies around 'Stukeley' barrow, Waden Hill (geophysical survey)

B40   East–west linear feature on Waden Hill (geophysical survey)

B42   Area of anomalies (geophysical scan) east of 'Stukeley' barrow

B43   High magnetic susceptibility readings west of 'Stukeley' barrow, Waden Hill

B44   High magnetic susceptibility readings at Honeysuckle Cottage, West Kennett

B45   Bank south of A4, West Kennett

Figure 9

B13 Area of pits by Winterbourne (geophysical survey)

B14 Ditch by Winterbourne (geophysical survey and air photographs)

B15 Area of anomalies by Winterbourne (geophysical scan)

B16 Area of anomalies (geophysical scan) and high magnetic susceptibility readings by Winterbourne

B35 Area of anomalies by Winterbourne; recent dumping (geophysical scan)

B41 Area of anomalies (geophysical scan) east of Winterbourne site

Figure 10

B2 Neolithic flints collected north of Silbury Hill

B10 Roman road south of Silbury Hill

B11 Quern fragment near Silbury Hill

B12 Romano-British grave by Winterbourne

B30 Strip lynchets on Waden Hill (air photographic survey)

B34 Winterbourne water meadows

Figure 17

B1 Mesolithic flints from Butler's Field, Avebury

B3 Neolithic flints from Butler's Field, Avebury

B4 'Beckhampton Avenue'

B17 Romano-British pottery from Butler's Field, Avebury

B20 Saxon pottery from Butler's Field, Avebury

B21 Saxon settlement in Avebury carpark

B22 Sunken hut in Avebury carpark

B23 Saxon settlement in Avebury carpark

B25 Medieval features in Butler's Field, Avebury

B26 Medieval features in Butler's Field, Avebury

B27 Features (geophysical survey) and high magnetic susceptibility readings in Butler's Field, Avebury

B28 Avebury carpark (geophysical survey)

B29 Medieval settlement in Avebury carpark

B32 Post-medieval pottery from Avebury carpark

B33 Earthworks in Butler's Field (RCHME)

Area C: East Kennett to West Overton (Figure 21)

C1 Ridgeway ancient trackway

C2 Neolithic flint arrowhead from East Kennett

C3 Bronze chisel and axe from East Kennett

C4 *Chenete* (*Domesday* Book)

C5 Saxon loom weights from East Kennett

C6 Medieval settlement at East Kennett

C7 Medieval key, from East Kennett

C8 Watermeadows at East Kennett

C9 High magnetic susceptibility readings east of East Kennett Manor

C10 Anomalies east of East Kennett Manor (geophysical scan)

Area D: West Overton to Lockeridge (Figure 6)

D1 High magnetic susceptibility readings in Pound Field, West Overton

D2 Pound Field barrow (geophysical survey and air photographs)

D3 *Ofaertune* (Saxon Charter)

D4 Medieval earthworks at West Overton

D5 Strip lynchets in Pound Field, West Overton

D6 Blacksmith's Garden, West Overton

3. The Prehistoric Periods

Archaeological Background

Mesolithic

A number of Mesolithic finds have been made in the Avebury area (Whittle 1990, fig. 2), many of them from surface collections, although more recent finds have been made during a series of palaeo-environmental studies undertaken between 1983 and 1986 (Evans *et al.* 1993). Flints of Mesolithic type were recovered from early Post-glacial tufa deposits, during excavations at North Farm on the north side of the River Kennet at West Overton, and from within the study corridor 14 microliths and a number of waste flakes from microlith production (B1) were among 1296 flints recovered from a Late Mesolithic/Early Neolithic buried soil (the 'Avebury soil') in test trenches excavated in Butler's Field, Avebury (SU 0979 6982) (Mount 1991).

The paucity of evidence for Mesolithic activity in the upper Kennet valley has led Whittle (1990) to suggest that exploitation of the area was of a transient nature, possibly organised from base camps outside the area, such as from the Mesolithic sites at Cherhill on the edge of the chalk 6 km to the west, or Hungerford 25 km to the east. Mount (1991), however, has argued that biases in the survival and retrieval of evidence may paint a misleading picture and that the range of woodland and river valley environments would have provided varied resources for Mesolithic hunter-gatherers.

No finds of Mesolithic date were found during the watching brief.

Neolithic

There is very limited evidence of Neolithic settlement and agricultural activity from the study corridor which passes close to but bypasses a number of the major Neolithic ritual sites. At the beginning of the century, flints were collected from the area north of Silbury Hill (SU 100 690) by A.D. Passmore and surface artefact collection was carried out in the same area by R. Holgate and J. Thomas in 1983. The latter collection (B2) contained 200 flints and, because it included more than four different types of flint implement, it was interpreted as representing a later Neolithic domestic site (Holgate 1988, table 4, no. 56). Other evidence of Neolithic activity consists of Early Neolithic pottery and carbonised cereal grains recovered from the 'Avebury soil', and a Late Mesolithic/Early Neolithic buried soil identified in test trenches excavated in Butler's Field, Avebury (SU 0979 6982) (Mount 1991; Evans *et al.* 1993). The layer also produced, from a collection of 1296 flints, a large number of Early Neolithic pieces (B3), including a leaf arrowhead.

The Avebury to West Kennett section of the pipeline cuts through the heart of the Neolithic and Bronze Age 'ritual landscape'. It starts immediately west of the west entrance of the Avebury circle, cutting across the line of the suggested Beckhampton Avenue (B4). William Stukeley, convinced of the symmetrical arrangement of the Avebury monuments, postulated the existence of a second serpentine avenue of stones to mirror the West Kennett Avenue, running from the west entrance of Avebury to a 'temple', similar to the Sanctuary, at Beckhampton, the sole remnants of the avenue being the two standing sarsens called the 'Long Stones'. During the excavation of the original pipeline trench, Vatcher recorded a 'burning pit' in the section of a trench immediately south of the Avebury pumping station (Vatcher 1971a). Burning pits may indicate the former positions of sarsen stones and, although sarsens may be naturally occurring, Ucko has suggested that the area around this trench would be where a search for the Beckhampton Avenue might be profitable (Ucko 1991, 199). A buried sarsen found in the Paradise garden (SU 0988 6986) was interpreted by Vatcher as being part of the Avenue (Vatcher 1971b).

From Butler's Field, Avebury, the pipeline runs south along the east bank of the Winterbourne to within approximately 250 m of Silbury Hill, before turning east towards West Kennett, where the south-east corner of the study corridor (SU 110 683) impinges on the northern edge of the West Kennett palisaded enclosures (B5). The enclosures were first identified in air photographs and subsequently noted in a pipeline trench by F. Vatcher in 1971. Excavations by A. Whittle between 1987 and 1993 and by Wessex Archaeology in 1989, revealed a complex of palisades set in backfilled ditches running in large concentric arcs. These features form part of an extensive Late Neolithic enclosure complex (Whittle 1991). A small circular ditch *c.* 7 m in diameter, visible in aerial photographs at SU 1083 6831, may be part of this complex (RCHME 1992a).

The only other feature of possibly Neolithic date sited within the study corridor is the Ridgeway (C1), which passes north–south through East Kennett. Along its route between Salisbury Plain and the Chilterns the Ridgeway passes many prehistoric monuments, which has led to speculation that it may be prehistoric in origin possibly dating as early as the Neolithic (Malone 1989), although recent research suggests a post-Roman date (Fowler 1995).

Evidence of Neolithic activity from elsewhere in the study area is limited to a number of finds unassociated with any features:

- Neolithic pottery (B6) found at the south end of Waden Hill in the vicinity of SU 107 684 during the excavation of the original pipeline trench (SMR no. SU 16NW127).

- A hollow-based Neolithic flint arrowhead and a waste flake mounted as a spearhead (C2) found in the vicinity of SU 115 677 in East Kennett (SMR no. SU 16NW124).

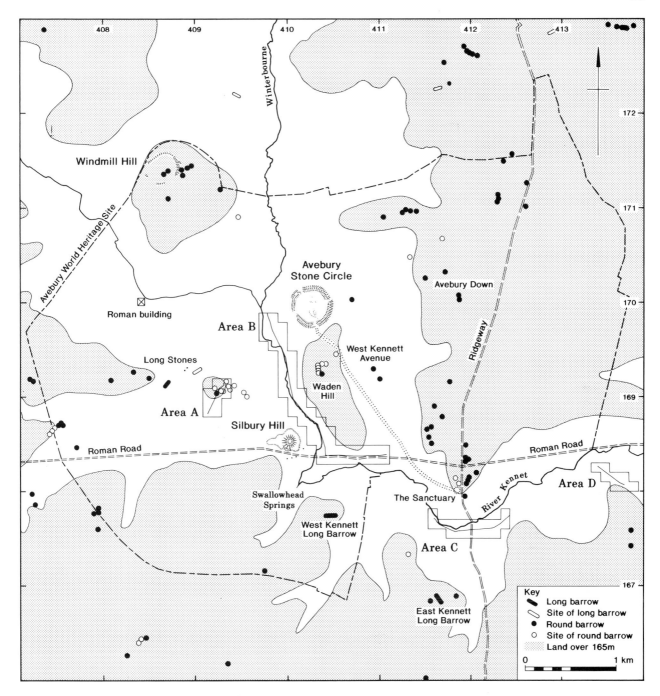

Figure 2   Avebury World Heritage Site

Despite the concentration of Neolithic monuments in the Avebury landscape, no features or artefacts of Neolithic date were recorded in the pipe trench during the watching brief.

Bronze Age

Bronze Age activity in north Wiltshire appears to have been concentrated on the high chalk downland and the only evidence for a Bronze Age presence in the study corridor consists of a number of individual finds and a series of round barrows. These are either clustered in groups, as in the Beckhampton and Overton Hill barrow cemeteries, or sited individually and while many survive

as upstanding mounds an unknown number, including all but one at Beckhampton, have been ploughed flat and are visible only as soil or crop marks in air photographs.

Beckhampton barrow cemetery

The Beckhampton barrow cemetery (Area A, Fig. 2) is situated on elevated ground to the north-east of the village of Beckhampton, between the A4 and the A4361 trunk roads. Most of the barrows had been ploughed flat by the time William Stukeley drew his panoramic views of the West Kennett and Beckhampton Avenues in the 1730s and by 1819 only one (presumably barrow 1, below), survived to appear in Crocker's plan of 'Abury and Silbury' (Hoare 1821, pl. x). The full extent of the barrow group, however, has recently been revealed in air photographs (RCHME 1992a). In addition, five of the monuments were also detected by the magnetometer survey. This largely confirmed the main features of their structure as revealed in the air photographs, although some of their details were interpreted slightly differently (GSB 1992a, fig. 5.7).

Most of the barrows are sited near the top of the field called Folly Hill, overlooking Avebury one kilometre to the north-east and Silbury Hill 1 km to the south-east. The cemetery contains approximately 12 barrows (possibly up to 16), 11 of which fall within the study corridor. The numbering of the barrows follows RCHME (1992a).

- Barrow 1 (A1) (SAM 678), centred on SU 0914 6906, is the only upstanding monument within the Beckhampton barrow cemetery. It is an oval turf covered mound, probably a bowl barrow, c. 20 m in diameter and up to 2 m high (SMR no. SU 06NE654). A flat riveted copper alloy dagger of Early Bronze Age date was recently found in spoil derived from disturbance to the barrow (Wessex Archaeology 1993b).

- Barrow 2 (A2) is a plough-levelled circular mound, c. 40 m in diameter, centred on SU 0918 6907. As interpreted from the air photographs, it had a large circular mound surrounded by a narrow inner ditch and a wide outer ditch. Marks within the mound suggest a probable central grave and several secondary burials, possibly of Roman or Saxon date as found in barrows on Overton Hill (Smith and Simpson 1964). On the east side of the mound, three ditches run out from the narrow inner ditch, perhaps forming a small secondary enclosure. The magnetic data revealed neither the internal features nor these radial ditches but provided a clearer picture of the concentric ring-ditches, seeming to indicate that they were approximately equal in width (SMR no. SU 06NE655).

- Barrow 3 (A3), a plough-levelled oval mound approximately 30 m in diameter, is centred on SU 0920 6903. As interpreted from the air photographs, the mound area contains a sub-circular narrow ditch with three gaps in its circuit, the gap on the south side having enlarged ditch terminals. The mound area is defined by a narrow ditch with traces of a narrow bank on its north-west side. This in turn is surrounded by a wider outer ditch. It may be a bell barrow or disc barrow with a pre-mound palisade or stake circle. The magnetic data, however, while showing neither the breaks in the inner ditch nor the ditch terminals, did indicate that both ditches were close to circular in plan. It also revealed the presence of a central anomaly, possibly a primary burial (SMR no. SU 06NE684).

- Barrow 4 (A4) is the most south-western of the Beckhampton barrows (SMR no. SU 06NE683). It is a large ring-ditch centred on SU 0913 6900 and was the only barrow in the Beckhampton group to be cut by the pipe trench (see below). Analysis of the air photographs suggested that there was a slight hollowing in the interior, possibly identifying it as a

disc barrow, a saucer barrow or even a pond barrow, a feature not suggested by the magnetic data and not revealed during the watching brief.

- Barrow 5 (A5), a ring-ditch 34 m in diameter, is centred on SU 0914 6912. The site, which is overgrown with scrub, has been damaged by the cutting of the A4361 on its south side and by a concrete structure over the site of the mound.

- Barrow 6 (A6), an elaborate barrow with ploughed out traces of a circular mound 27 m in diameter, is centred on SU 0922 6907. The mound area contains an ovoid ditch surrounding a central pit, possibly the primary burial, an interpretation supported by the magnetic data. It is possibly a bell or disc barrow or a multi-phase structure (SMR nos SU 06NE656–SU 06NE682).

- Barrow 7 (A7), a plough-levelled ring-ditch with clear traces of a central mound 22 m in diameter, is centred on SU 0927 6913. This barrow, which may be a bowl barrow, was also detected by the magnetometer survey.

- Barrow 8 (A8), a plough-levelled ring-ditch with clear traces of a central mound 22 m in diameter, is centred on SU 0929 6909. It may be a bowl barrow.

In addition, examination of the air photographs covering the Beckhampton barrow cemetery revealed a further five features, possibly associated with the barrow cemetery. Because of their location they are included in this section, although because they remain undated no certainty can be placed on their interpretation as Bronze Age barrows.

- Ring-ditch 14 (A9), a possible ring-ditch, approximately 10 m in diameter is centred on SU 0920 6900. Only the south-west half is faintly visible on air photographs.

- Ring-ditch 15 (A10), a possible ring-ditch, approximately 35 m in diameter is centred on SU 0916 6896. Only the north-eastern and south-western arcs are faintly visible on air photographs.

- Ring-ditch 16 (A11), a possible ring-ditch of which only the east half is faintly visible on air photographs, is centred on SU 0918 6820.

- A ditch surrounding a sub-rectangular area (A13) containing traces of a mound, centred on SU 0924 6917, was identified on air photographs (barrow 10). The enclosure is 42 m long, 32 m wide, and is cut by the A4361 at its south corner. The feature may be a barrow, as parallels are found associated with elaborate barrow groups (Soffe 1993). However, it is also possible that it is some other form of prehistoric enclosure (SMR no. SU 06NE688).

- A ditch surrounding a sub-rectangular area (A12) 20 m wide, centred on SU 0928 6917, was identified on air photographs (barrow 11). Only parts of the north, east, and west sides show on the north edge of the field against the A4361. As with barrow 10, this may be some other form of prehistoric enclosure.

The magnetometer survey of the Beckhampton barrow cemetery also detected two small anomalies, possibly pits associated with the cemetery, one (A14) at SU 0918 6903, the other (A15) at SU 0928 6913 (GSB 1992a, figures 5.5 and 5.3).

In 1983, a spread of predominantly Bronze Age flints was collected from the area between Beckhampton and Silbury Hill during fieldwalking undertaken by R. Holgate and J. Thomas (Holgate 1988, p. 92, fig. 6.13). The highest concentration (A16) was in the west of the area in the vicinity of the barrow cemetery, centred on SU 0925 6905.

Waden Hill

A number of round barrows have also been recorded at Waden Hill, most of which are located some distance from the study corridor at the north end of the hill overlooking the Avebury Circle (Fig. 2). A drawing by William Stukeley, however, entitled *A Scenographic view of the Druid temple of ABURY in north Wiltshire as in its original* (see frontispiece), shows a barrow, possibly a disc barrow, at the south end, bisected by the Roman Road (see below). Stukeley (1743) related that an urn was found in the barrow but the precise location of the barrow was not known (SMR no. SU 16NWU20).

Because a number of finds had been recorded from the south end of Waden Hill during the original pipeline excavation, including a polished perforated sandstone axe-hammer (B7) at SU 1103 6834. (Lawson 1989), it had already been decided, in formulating the Stage 1 Assessment strategy, to conduct a detailed magnetometer survey on the west facing slopes of the hill. Among the geophysical anomalies detected (GSB 1992a, figure 3.2) there were two features of probable Bronze Age date, one of them (B8) being the northern arc of a ring-ditch in the position of the 'Stukeley' Barrow (see below), centred on SU 1060 6830, the other being the eastern arc of a smaller circular feature (B9), possibly also a ring-ditch c. 10 m in diameter, centred on SU 1071 6840.

West Overton

A number of round barrows have been recorded in the area around West Overton (Area C, Fig. 2), both on the lower slopes north of the River Kennet in the vicinity of North Farm, one of which was excavated recently (Swanton in prep.) and to the south on the top White Hill. None had been recorded around the study corridor on the lower slopes of White Hill. However, during the Stage 1 geophysical survey in Pound Field on the east side of West Overton, a series of strong discrete anomalies (D1), centred on SU 1340 6822, was detected by the magnetometer scan, corresponding to high magnetic susceptibility readings (GSB 1992a, figure 12.1) and, in order to further evaluate the nature of the anomalies, a magnetometer survey of the area of the readings was undertaken. A feature, interpreted as the north and east sides of a ring-ditch (D2), c. 30 m in diameter (the Pound Field barrow, see below), was detected (GSB 1992b,

figure D5.4). This has since been identified in air photographs (Wiltshire County Council 1991, 97/91/175) where it appears to measure roughly 35 m in diameter. It is located approximately 100 m north-east of St Michael's Church and straddles the point where the shallow, north facing slope inclines steeply down into the Kennet Valley floodplain.

The only other Bronze Age finds from the study corridor were a bronze, broad-bladed tanged chisel and a socketed axe of Breton type with its clay core still in place (C3), both found in East Kennett at SU 1200 6750.

Iron Age

The Iron Age is poorly represented within the study corridor, with a single Iron Age find, part of the bronze chape of a scabbard or sheath (A17), found in Beckhampton in the vicinity of SU 0900 6880 (SMR no. SU 06NE204). This paucity of material is in marked contrast to the surrounding downland where there are traces of Celtic fields, earthworks, and enclosures indicating a high density of settlement and agricultural activity. On Overton Down, there is an Early Iron Age settlement overlain by Celtic fields cultivated before and during the early Romano-British period and an enclosed pre-Roman Iron Age settlement of Little Woodbury-type, containing timber structures (Fowler 1967). At a greater distance, there are the hillforts of Oldbury Castle near Cherhill and Barbury Castle south-east of Swindon.

No indisputably Iron Age finds were recovered during the watching brief. However, two sherds of pottery, one from the Pound Field Barrow ditch, West Overton, and the other from an undated feature, ditch 383, at East Kennett, are of either Iron Age or Saxon date. Their identification and interpretation are discussed in the section on the Saxon period (see below).

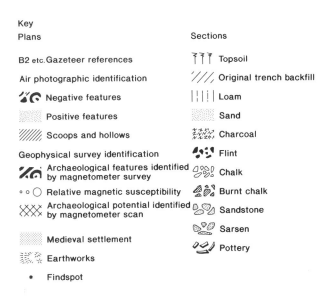

Key

Plans		Sections	
B2 etc. Gazeteer references		Topsoil	
Air photographic identification		Original trench backfill	
Negative features		Loam	
Positive features		Sand	
Scoops and hollows		Charcoal	
Geophysical survey identification		Flint	
Archaeological features identified by magnetometer survey		Chalk	
Relative magnetic susceptibility		Burnt chalk	
Archaeological potential identified by magnetometer scan		Sandstone	
Medieval settlement		Sarsen	
Earthworks		Pottery	
Findspot			

Figure 3   Key to plans and sections

14

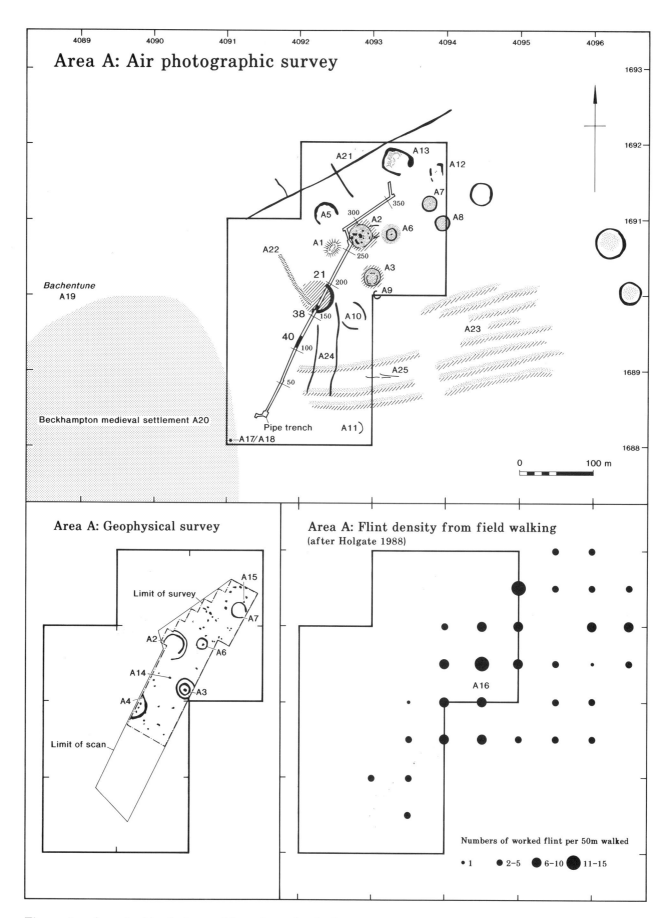

Figure 4   Area A: Air photographic and geophysical surveys

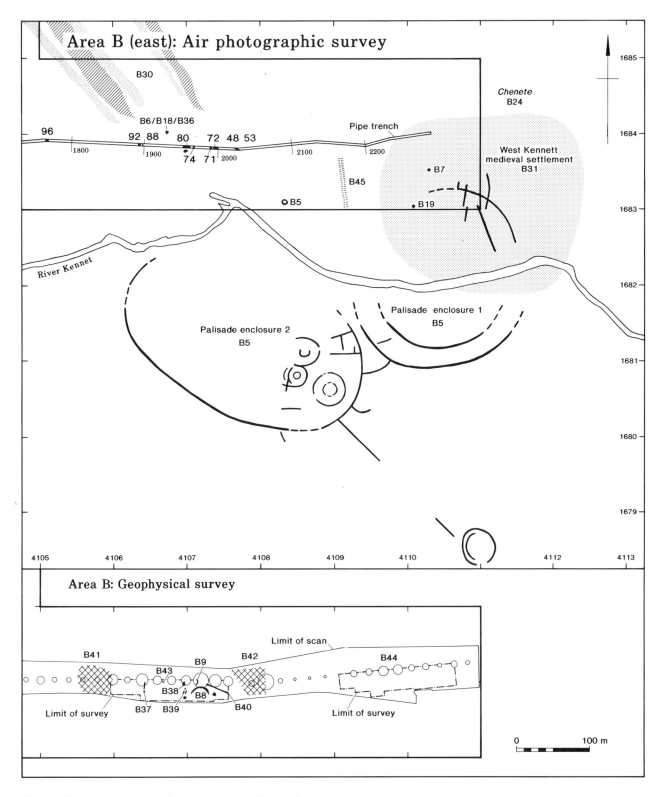

Figure 5   Area B: air photographic and geophysical surveys

Results of the Watching Brief

During the watching brief, the ring-ditches of three round barrows were bisected by the pipe trench in locations predicted by the air photographic and geophysical surveys. While all the ditch sections were recorded, no traces of burials were found and only the Pound Field barrow at West Overton held any material

of Bronze Age date, or any evidence (admittedly ambiguous) of a barrow mound.

Beckhampton Barrow 4

Ring-ditch 39 of barrow 4 (A4 above; Fig. 4) is centred on SU 0913 6900 and was cut by the trench on its

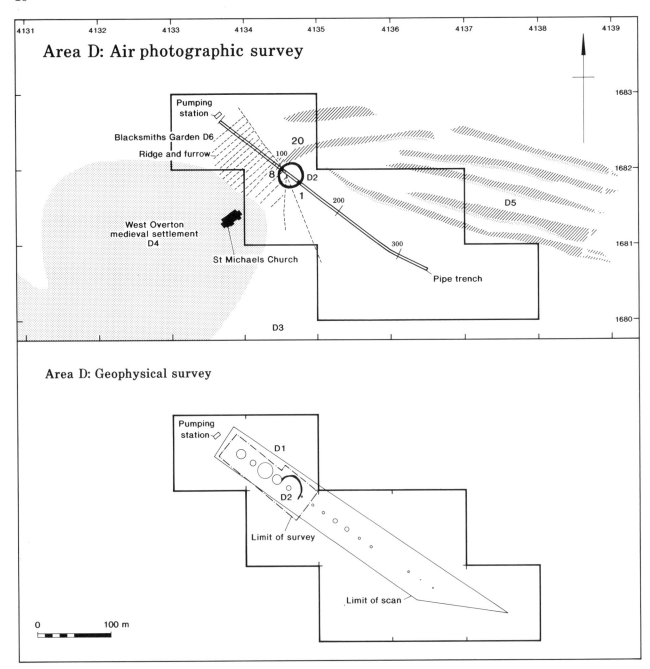

Figure 6   Area D: air photographic and geophysical surveys

north-east and south sides. It measured 41 m across on the line of intersection (A.159–200 m, 171.1–174.1 m OD).

Ditch 21 to the north-east was and 1.2 m deep and 3.55 m wide, with a flat base 2.0 m wide. The sides were steep towards the base, with a shallow lip on either side giving an overall width at the top of 5.0 m. The primary fill (22) consisted of loose chalk rubble and this was overlain by two further layers of chalk rubble in a very pale brown silty clay matrix (contexts 23–4), layer 23 containing a fragmented cattle mandible. The upper fills (contexts 26–7), which had a combined maximum thickness of 0.6 m, consisted of yellowish–brown silt loams.

Ditch 38 to the south was 3.05 m wide, with a flat base 2.2 m wide (Fig. 7). It was 1 m deep on the outer side and 1.5 m deep on the inner side. The outer side was vertical, while the inner side was moderately steep and stepped, with a wide shallow lip giving an overall width at the top of 4.7 m. The stratification of the lower fills (contexts 29–34) had been disturbed by tree root action but the primary fill (29) consisted of loose chalk rubble. The upper fills (contexts 35–6), which had a combined thickness of 0.7 m, consisted of brown/yellowish–brown silt loams.

There were no traces of a barrow mound and the profile of the site revealed no hollowing within the interior of the ring-ditch. No artefacts were recovered

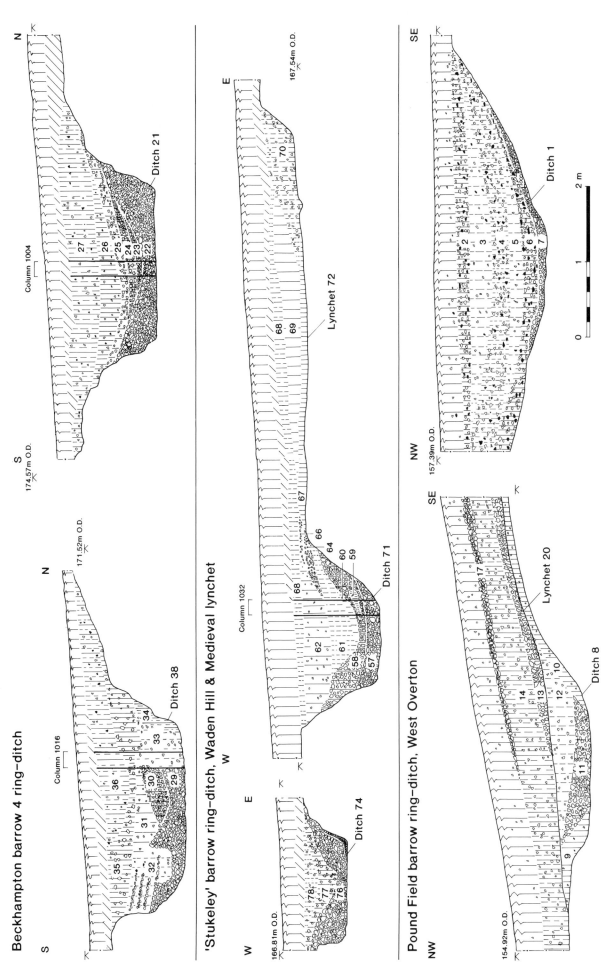

Beckhampton barrow 4 ring-ditch

'Stukeley' barrow ring-ditch, Waden Hill & Medieval lynchet

Pound Field barrow ring-ditch, West Overton

Figure 7 Sections through the Beckhampton, 'Stukeley', and Pound Field barrows and the medieval lynchet

Plate 2 *'Stukeley' barrow ditch 71 and (in the foreground) negative lynchet 72 on Waden Hill with a view of Silbury Hill to the west*

from either section of the ditch. Two mollusc columns were taken (sample series 1004) from the north- eastern ditch section and 1016 from the southern ditch section.

The 'Stukeley' Barrow, Waden Hill

The 'Stukeley' barrow ring-ditch (B8; Fig. 5) is centred on SU 1072 6838 and is sited immediately north of the A4 trunk road at a height of OD 166.3–167.3 m on a moderate south-east facing slope. Two sections of this ring-ditch were exposed and recorded during the watching brief.

The ring-ditch was cut by the trench on its east and west sides and was 27.5 m in diameter on the line of intersection (B.1964–91 m). Ditch 71 to the east, 2.6 m wide and 1.15 m deep, had a flat base 1.0 m wide (Pl. 2). The sides were steep, the inner (west) side being convex and the outer side being concave towards the base. The primary fill (57) consisted of loose chalk rubble, over which were further layers of chalk rubble in a chalky silt matrix (contexts 58–59), all with a maximum combined thickness of 0.6 m. These were overlain by layers of brown silt loam (contexts 60–62, 64, and 66). Adjacent

to the outer edge of the ditch was a shallow terrace cut into the slope. This represents the southern end of a negative lynchet (*see* 'below), the upper fill of which (68) extended over the ditch fills (*see* Pl. 2).

Ditch 74 to the west was 2.2 m wide, with a flat base 1.75 m wide (Fig. 7). It was 0.4 m deep on the outer side and 0.6 m deep on the inner side. The outer side was vertical, while the inner side was steep. The primary fills consisted of a thin layer of chalky silt (75) overlain by packed chalk rubble with a maximum depth of 0.45 m. The upper fills (contexts 77–8), with a combined thickness of 0.4 m, consisted of dark yellowish–brown silt loams.

There were no traces of a barrow mound and no finds were recovered from either section of the ditch. A mollusc column (sample series 1032 below), was taken from the eastern ditch section. One tiny body chip of a sandy coarseware pottery fabric, probably of Roman date, was extracted during the sorting of the mollusc sample from context 58, the second fill of the eastern ditch section 71.

Pound Field Barrow, West Overton

The barrow ring-ditch (D1; Fig. 6) is centred on SU 1346 6819, *c.* 100 m north-east of St Michael's Church. Two sections of the ring-ditch were exposed and recorded during the sewer pipe replacement. The ring-ditch was cut by the pipe trench on its south-east and north-west sides and was approximately 33.5 m in diameter on the line of intersection (D.101–34 m, OD 154.2–157.2 m). Ditch 1 to the south-east was 5.5 m wide and 1.2 m deep, with a flat base 1.2 m wide and shallow sides (Fig. 7). The primary fill (7) consisted of a brown, silty clay layer 0.1 m thick, which was overlain by a series of dark yellowish–brown clay loams containing moderate quantities of chalk and flint (contexts 6–2). These yielded small quantities of pottery (*see* below).

To the north-west, ditch 8 was *c.* 4 m wide with a shallow lip on the inner edge giving an overall width of *c.* 6.5 m (Fig. 7). It had a flat base 1.7 m wide and moderately steep sides and was 0.3 m deep on the outer side and 0.75 m deep on the inner side. The primary fills (contexts 9 and 10), lying against the sides of the ditch, consisted of brownish–yellow silty clay. These, and the base of the ditch, were overlain by a layer of dark yellowish–brown silt loam (11) containing moderate quantities of chalk and flint. The upper fill (12) was a largely stone free dark yellowish–brown silt loam. Overlying the ditch and cutting into its upper fills, was a shallow terrace representing the western end of an undated negative lynchet (20) (*see* below).

Below the topsoil and extending over the whole of the interior of the ring-ditch, was a layer of chalk rubble (17) on average 0.1 m thick. It did not extend beyond the ditch uphill of the barrow but did extend over the ditch to the north-west and was interpreted initially as barrow material spread down the hill by ploughing. Immediately below it was a very dark greyish–brown layer of compacted silty clay (16) up to 0.10 m thick and extending for approximately 4 m. This layer, which contained a broken flint blade and fragments of charcoal (*see*, below), appeared to represent a pre-barrow buried soil and was therefore sampled. Underlying it was an area of red, burnt subsoil (15).

However, layer 17 is now recognised to be the part of the original backfill of the pipe trench and not eroded mound material, and this must raise some doubts about the antiquity of the buried soil (16).

Bronze Age Finds,
by Rachael Seager Smith

Pottery
Seven sherds (37 g) of pottery were recovered from ditch 1 of the Pound Field barrow ring-ditch (Fig. 7). Six of them (31 g) are probably from a single vessel, a fairly thick-walled, slack-shouldered jar without any surface finish or decoration and with a hard, sandy, grog-tempered fabric (Fabric G1). They cannot be precisely dated but are likely to belong to the early 1st millennium BC and were found in the secondary fill of the ditch section. The results of full petrological analysis of this fabric by D.F. Williams of the Department of Archaeology, University of Southampton are presented in the archive.

Fabric G1   Hard, unoxidised fabric containing well-sorted, common angular quartz, <0.20 mm rare to sparse mica, and rare iron oxides. Also rare to sparse fragments of light-coloured sandy argillaceous material, probably grog. Handmade.

The seventh sherd (6 g) was found in tertiary fill 3 and may be of Saxon date (*see* below).

Environmental Analysis: Bronze Age

Charcoal from the Pound Field barrow,
by Rowena Gale
The sample from the possible buried soil (16) recorded at the Pound Field barrow included charcoal of oak (*Quercus*), hazel (*Corylus*) and a member of the Pomoideae (Table 2). However, the uncertainty as to this layer's antiquity should be borne in mind when considering the interpretation.

The most likely members of the Pomoideae to have thrived on the calcareous soils of the area are hawthorn and whitebeam, and possibly apple and pear, although the latter is considered doubtfully native (Clapham *et al.* 1952) and may have been introduced at a later date. Hazel typically grows as understorey with oak in often dense woodlands but the presence of a possible hazel nut shell suggests a more sparsely wooded vegetation or one with glades or open areas, since hazel requires sunny, well-lit sites for fruiting to occur. Moreover, hawthorn and whitebeam are colonisers of secondary woodland. The former (particularly *C. monogyna*) tolerates some shading in woodland but more often grows in marginal woodland or as scrub on exposed sites.

With such slender evidence it is only possible to speculate that the environment around the site con-

Table 2 charcoal from the possible Bronze Age buried soil (context 16) at the Pound Field barrow, West Overton

Context	Number	Species
Layer 16, possible buried soil at Pound Field barrow	7	*Corylus* sp., hazel
	5	family Rosaceae, subfamily Pomoideae*
	2	*Quercus* sp., oak, probably sapwood but not twiggy
	1	possible nutshell, probably *Corylus* sp., hazel
	1	seed

(The sample was made up of small fragments, mainly <3 mm in transverse section)

*Family Rosaceae, subfamily Pomoideae includes *Crataegus* sp., hawthorn, *Malus* sp., apple, *Pyrus* sp., pear, and *Sorbus* sp., rowan, whitebeam, and wild service. These genera cannot be distinguished from each other by their anatomical structure.

tained lightly wooded areas. The species are consistent with those identified from other Bronze Age sites associated with nearby areas around Stonehenge (Richards 1990) which, in all probability, recolonised following widespread land clearance in the Neolithic period. Chalk downlands, such as those around Avebury, frequently support a wide variety of trees and shrubs and the limited range named from this small sample of charcoal may not necessarily be fully representative. The range of species growing in the vicinity of the pipeline appears to have remained relatively stable throughout the Bronze Age and later Roman and medieval occupations.

Land Mollusca from Bronze Age features,
by Sarah F. Wyles and Michael J. Allen
A spot sample was taken from the possible buried soil at the Pound Field barrow. However, uncertainty as to the antiquity of this layer should be borne in mind when considering its interpretation.

Columns of continuous samples were taken through the ditch fills of both the Beckhampton 4 and 'Stukeley' barrows (Fig. 7; Tables 3 and 4). The sampled ditch sediments have been described following the terminology of primary, secondary, and tertiary fills as defined by Evans (1972, 321–32) and Limbrey (1975, 290–300). Methods of mollusc analyses were standard and followed those outlined by Evans (1972) and detailed elsewhere (Allen 1989; 1990). The results are presented as standard histograms of relative abundance (cf Evans 1972) in Figure 6. Some species have been grouped for this purpose and the nomenclature follows Kerney (1976).

Table 3 Mollusca from the Pound Field barrow buried soil and Beckhampton barrow 4 ditch

	OLS	ditch 38		Beckhampton barrow 4 — ditch 21										
Sample	1002	1029	1030	1005	1006	1007	1008	1009	1010	1011	1012	1013	1014	1015
Context	16	29	30	22	23	24	25	25	26	26	26	27	27	27
Depth (cm)	spot	spot	spot	140–150	130–140	120–130	110–120	100–110	90–100	80–90	70–80	60–70	50–60	40–50
Wt (g)	1000	1950	1000	1500	1000	1000	1000	1000	1000	1000	1000	1000	1000	1000
MOLLUSCA														
Terrestrial														
Pomatias elegans (Müller)	–	1	+	+	7	3	–	+	2	+	+	2	1	1
Carychium tridentatum (Risso)	2	–	2	–	–	–	5	15	15	3	1	–	–	–
Carychium spp.	–	–	–	–	–	–	–	10	8	3	1	1	–	–
Cochlicopa lubrica (Müller)	–	–	–	–	6	–	–	–	–	7	4	6	9	–
Cochlicopa lubricella (Porro)	–	–	–	–	–	12	4	2	12	8	7	5	2	–
Cochlicopa spp.	–	+	1	1	24	19	7	7	13	29	26	29	14	7
Vertigo pygmaea (Draparnaud)	1	–	–	–	13	13	1	6	14	42	38	42	17	1
Vertigo spp.	1	+	–	1	–	–	–	–	–	–	–	–	–	–
Pupilla muscorum (Linnaeus)	4	6	12	4	94	47	6	52	119	192	269	273	166	68
Vallonia costata (Müller)	3	1	4	3	122	99	25	145	186	160	117	81	53	10
Vallonia excentrica (Sterki)	5	8	13	6	139	159	32	87	218	259	258	228	186	55
Acanthinula aculeata (Müller)	–	–	–	–	–	–	–	–	–	–	–	–	–	–
Ena obscura (Müller)	–	–	–	–	–	–	–	–	–	–	–	–	–	–
Punctum pygmaeum (Draparnaud)	–	2	1	–	9	9	5	29	33	20	11	9	5	–
Discus rotundatus (Müller)	+	–	–	–	–	2	1	–	–	–	1	–	–	–
Vitrina pellucida (Müller)	–	–	–	1	–	–	–	1	7	3	4	2	–	–
Vitrea crystallina (Müller)	–	1	–	–	–	–	–	–	–	–	–	–	–	–
Vitrea contracta (Westerlund)	1	–	–	1	–	7	4	–	–	11	–	1	–	–
Nesovitrea hammonis (Ström)	–	–	–	–	–	–	–	26	41	–	–	–	–	–
Aegopinella pura (Alder)	–	–	–	–	–	–	–	–	–	–	–	–	–	–
Aegopinella nitidula (Draparnaud)	–	1	1	–	–	–	–	2	–	–	8	–	–	–
Oxychilus cellarius (Müller)	2	–	1	–	–	–	–	–	–	–	–	1	–	–
Limacidae	4	5	5	2	25	18	3	42	38	87	72	72	61	17

Table 3 continued

	OLS	ditch38	ditch38	Beckhampton barrow 4 — ditch 21										
Feature Sample	1002	1029	1030	1005	1006	1007	1008	1009	1010	1011	1012	1013	1014	1015
Context	16	29	30	22	23	24	25			26			27	
Depth (cm)	spot	spot	spot	140–150	130–140	120–130	110–120	100–110	90–100	80–90	70–80	60–70	50–60	40–50
Wt (g)	1000	1950	1000	1500	1000	1000	1000	1000	1000	1000	1000	1000	1000	1000
MOLLUSCA contd														
Terrestrial														
Euconulus fulvus (Müller)	–	–	–	–	–	–	–	–	–	–	–	–	–	–
Cecilioides acicula (Müller)	32	–	–	–	–	–	–	–	–	3	2	–	28	17
Cochlodina laminata (Montagu)	–	–	–	–	–	1	–	–	–	–	–	–	–	–
Clausilia bidentata (Ström)	–	1	–	–	6	6	–	1	1	–	–	1	–	1
Clausiliidae	–	–	–	+	–	–	–	–	–	–	–	–	–	–
Candidula gigaxii (L. Pfeiffer)	–	–	–	–	–	–	–	–	–	–	–	–	–	–
Cernuella virgata (Da Costa)	–	–	–	–	–	–	–	–	–	–	–	–	–	1
Helicella itala (Linnaeus)	8	4	3	1	26	38	19	61	88	119	119	100	69	38
Trichia hispida (Linnaeus)	1	5	9	2	5	38	28	142	213	253	163	131	107	16
Arianta arbustorum (Linnaeus)	–	–	–	–	–	–	–	–	–	–	–	–	–	–
Cepaea hortensis (Müller)	–	–	–	–	–	–	–	–	–	–	–	–	–	–
Cepaea / Arianta spp.	–	2	1	–	10	2	–	–	3	2	–	–	1	–
Helix aspersa (Müller)	–	–	–	–	–	–	–	–	–	–	–	1	–	–
Fresh-water/brackish-water species														
Lymnaea peregra (Müller)	–	–	–	–	–	–	–	–	–	–	–	–	–	–
Lymnaea truncatula (Müller)	–	–	–	–	–	–	–	–	–	–	–	–	–	–
Anisus leucostoma (Millet)	–	–	–	–	–	–	–	–	–	–	–	–	–	–
Taxa	11	11	12	10	12	15	12	14	15	15	14	17	12	12
Shannon index	2.16	2.14	2.06	2.07	1.95	2.06	2.12	2.14	2.14	2.09	2.00	1.99	1.92	1.79
TOTAL	32	36	53	22	486	473	140	628	1011	1200	1099	985	691	216

Note; the burrowing species *C. acicula* is not included in the totals

Table 4 Mollusca from the 'Stukeley' barrow ditch and the medieval lynchet on Waden Hill

	'Stukeley' barrow ditch 71								lynchet 72	
Feature Sample	1033	1034	1035	1036	1037	1038	1039	1040	1041	1042
Context	58	60	61	61		62		68	67	69
Depth (cm)	98–110	88–98	78–88	68–78	58–68	48–58	38–48	30–38	spot	spot
Wt (g)	1000	1000	1000	1000	1000	1000	1000	1000	1000	1000
MOLLUSCA										
Terrestrial										
Pomatias elegans (Müller)	4	5	9	5	4	5	+	1	6	5
Carychium tridentatum (Risso)	7	6	35	31	1	–	1	–	–	–
Carychium spp.	7	9	19	14	1	2	–	–	–	–
Cochlicopa lubrica (Müller)	1	2	4	3	3	1	–	–	–	–
Cochlicopa lubricella (Porro)	–	–	–	–	–	–	–	–	–	–
Cochlicopa spp.	2	10	16	17	7	3	2	–	3	2
Vertigo pygmaea (Draparnaud)	12	14	19	11	6	8	10	6	37	52
Vertigo spp.	–	–	–	–	–	–	–	–	–	–
Pupilla muscorum (Linnaeus)	88	113	121	120	185	130	72	34	71	135
Vallonia costata (Müller)	64	63	99	83	43	13	17	13	90	112
Vallonia excentrica Sterki	35	46	57	57	63	58	28	15	83	118
Acanthinula aculeata (Müller)	–	–	–	10	2	–	–	–	–	–
Ena obscura (Müller)	1	1	8	–	–	–	–	–	–	–
Punctum pygmaeum (Draparnaud)	1	3	5	4	1	4	–	–	22	25
Discus rotundatus (Müller)	–	–	1	5	–	1	2	–	4	–
Vitrina pellucida (Müller)	–	1	–	2	–	–	–	–	–	–
Vitrea crystallina (Müller)	1	5	7	2	2	–	–	–	–	–
Vitrea contracta (Westerlund)	2	–	16	19	2	–	–	–	21	1
Nesovitrea hammonis (Ström)	4	8	11	8	1	–	–	–	1	–
Aegopinella pura (Alder)	1	1	2	3	–	1	–	–	–	–
Aegopinella nitidula (Draparnaud)	3	7	8	38	3	–	–	–	1	–
Oxychilus cellarius (Müller)	–	–	1	2	–	–	–	–	1	–

Table 4 continued

MOLLUSCA		'Stukeley' barrow ditch — ditch 71 —								lynchet 72	
Sample		1033	1034	1035	1036	1037	1038	1039	1040	1041	1042
Context		58	60	61	61	61	62		68	67	69
Depth (cm)		98–110	88–98	78–88	68–78	58–68	48–58	38–48	30–38	spot	spot
Wt (g)		1000	1000	1000	1000	1000	1000	1000	1000	1000	1000
Terrestrial											
Limacidae		24	35	39	50	53	41	34	13	24	24
Euconulus fulvus (Müller)		–	–	–	–	–	–	–	–	–	–
Cecilioides acicula (Müller)		3	–	1	1	–	7	9	17	5	1
Cochlodina laminata (Montagu)		–	–	2	3	–	1	–	–	1	2
Clausilia bidentata (Ström)		5	12	18	29	5	4	8	2	4	6
Clausiliidae		–	–	1	–	–	–	–	–	–	–
Candidula gigaxii (L. Pfeiffer)		–	–	–	–	–	–	–	3	–	6
Cernuella virgata (Da Costa)		–	–	–	–	–	–	–	1	3	6
Helicella itala (Linnaeus)		28	48	61	56	68	37	14	13	23	15
Trichia hispida (Linnaeus)		40	48	90	131	71	52	15	17	42	67
Arianta arbustorum (Linnaeus)		–	–	+	–	–	–	–	–	–	–
Cepaea hortensis (Müller)		–	–	–	–	1	1	–	–	–	–
Cepaea / Arianta spp.		2	6	9	7	2	1	1	1	5	3
Helix aspersa (Müller)		–	–	–	–	–	+	–	+	–	1[m]
Fresh-water/brackish-water species											
Lymnaea peregra (Müller)		1	2	5	6	1	–	–	–	–	–
Lymnaea truncatula (Müller)		–	–	–	–	–	–	–	–	1	–
Anisus leucostoma (Millet)		–	–	1	–	–	–	–	–	–	–
Taxa		20	19	24	25	20	17	12	12	20	16
Shannon index		2.25	2.38	2.58	2.63	2.00	1.95	1.94	2.06	2.30	2.08
TOTAL		333	444	656	724	525	363	204	119	443	580

[m] = modern. Note: the burrowing spcies *C. acicula* is not included in the totals

23

Pound Field barrow
The buried soil (16) under the barrow mound consisted of a very dark greyish–brown (10YR 3/2) clay loam.

Beckhampton barrow 4

Ditch fills
0–0.3 m   ploughsoil.
0.3–0.4 m (28)   white chalk rubble. The remains of backfill of the original pipe trench.
Tertiary fill
0.4–0.8 m (27)   light yellowish–brown (10YR 6/4) silt loam with c. 5% chalk and flint.
Upper secondary fill
0.8–1.1 m (26)   yellowish–brown (10YR 5/4) silt loam with c. 5% chalk and flint.
1.1–1.2 m (25)   pale brown (10YR 6/3) sandy silt with c. 40% chalk (pea grit) and occasional flint.
1.2–1.3 m (24)   very pale brown (10YR 8/3) clayey silt with c. 80% chalk. Packed chalk rubble.
Lower secondary fill
1.3–1.4 m (23)   very pale brown (10YR 7/3) clayey silt with c. 70% chalk.
Primary fill
1.4–1.5 m (30)   very pale brown (10YR 8/3) sandy silt with c. 80% packed chalk rubble to (22 and 29) white loose chalk rubble.

'Stukeley' barrow

Ditch fills
0–0.27 m   ploughsoil.
0.27–0.3 m   white chalk rubble. The remains of backfill of original pipe trench.
Tertiary fill
0.3–0.38 m (68)   dark brown (10YR 3/3) silt loam with c. 5% chalk inclusions up to 100 mm.
Upper secondary fill
0.38–0.68 m (62)   dark yellowish–brown (10YR 4/4) silt loam with c. 5% chalk and flint inclusions with larger pieces being 0.02–0.05 m.
Lower secondary fill
0.68–0.88 m (61)   light yellowish–brown (10YR 6/4) silt loam with rare chalk pieces up to approximately 0.02 m.
0.88–0.98 m (60)   yellowish–brown (10YR 5/6) silt loam with rare chalk pieces up to 0.02 m.
Primary fill
0.98–1.10 m (58)   white (10YR 8/2) silt with 90% chalk. Packed chalk rubble.

Shell numbers were generally high to very high and preservation was good. All the assemblages were dominated by open country species and the two histograms have been divided into common mollusc assemblage zones (Fig. 8) for clarification, as similar local changes can be seen in both the 'Stukeley' and Beckhampton barrows. These zones represent minor but significant fluctuations in local landuse and coincide with the ditch fill sequences.

Biozone 1: possible buried soil
(Pound Field barrow)
This zone is characterised by an open country assemblage with a significant (c. 15%) shade-loving element

comprised of *Carychium tridentatum* and the Zonatids. As the mollusc numbers in this zone are low (32 shells) caution must be exercised in interpretation. This zone is characterised by *Helicella itala* and *Vallonia excentrica* with *Pupilla muscorum,* and *Vallonia costata.*

Biozones 2–4: barrow ditches (Beckhampton 4 and 'Stukeley' barrows)
Zone 2, from the primary fills of both barrow ditches and the lower secondary fills of the Beckhampton ditch, is characterised by open country species dominated by *Pupilla muscorum, Trichia hispida,* and *Vallonia costata,* with *Vallonia excentrica* and *Helicella itala.* The shade-loving element is limited. A few freshwater shells were recovered from the 'Stukeley' ditch (Tables 4).

Zone 3, from the lower secondary fills of the 'Stukeley' ditch and upper secondary fills of the Beckhampton ditch, is characterised by an increase in the shade-loving element *(c.* 20–25%), particularly the Punctum group but also the Zonatids and Clausiliidae. The open country element is dominated by the *Vallonias* and *Pupilla muscorum* with both *V. excentrica* and *V. costata* in increased numbers. A few freshwater species occur in the 'Stukeley' ditch.

Zone 4, from the upper secondary fills of the Beckhampton ditch and tertiary fills of both ditches, is characterised by *Pupilla muscorum* becoming dominant and the shade-loving elements virtually non-existent. Minor variations in the composition of the open country group are seen between the two barrows (Fig. 8) but *Helix aspersa* and the Introduced Helicellids occur in both.

Interpretation
In the interpretation of these assemblages it has been borne in mind that in previous studies in the Avebury area (Waden Hill), *Vallonia excentrica* has been found to behave more like *Vallonia costata,* in that of the two, *Vallonia costata* normally prefers the shorter grazed grassland, but in this area seems to prefer longer grass than *Vallonia excentrica* (Evans 1972).

The pre-monument and contemporaneous environment, as shown by the possible old land surface at the Pound Field barrow (zone 1) and the primary ditch fills at the Beckhampton 4 and 'Stukeley' barrows (zone 2), appear to be that of short grazed grassland as preferred by *Pupilla muscorum* and (here) *Vallonia excentrica.*

The secondary fills (zone 3) indicate that the ditches became rapidly overgrown by long grassy vegetation which was colonised by the specialised ditch mollusc fauna. These assemblages, with *Carychium tridentatum, Trichia hispida,* and the Punctum group, indicate fauna exploiting the shade provided by longer grass at the ditch edge and within the ditch itself. The occurrence of true rupestral species, albeit in small numbers, may well indicate the proximity of a small amount of scrub. Although the overall landscape history is the same at the Beckhampton and 'Stukeley' barrows, the occurrence of this zone in the lower secondary fills of the Beckhampton 4 ditch, but in upper secondary fills of the 'Stukeley' ditch, indicates a degree of local or temporal variation.

A return to short grazed grassland and arable habitats is seen in the upper secondary and tertiary fills

25

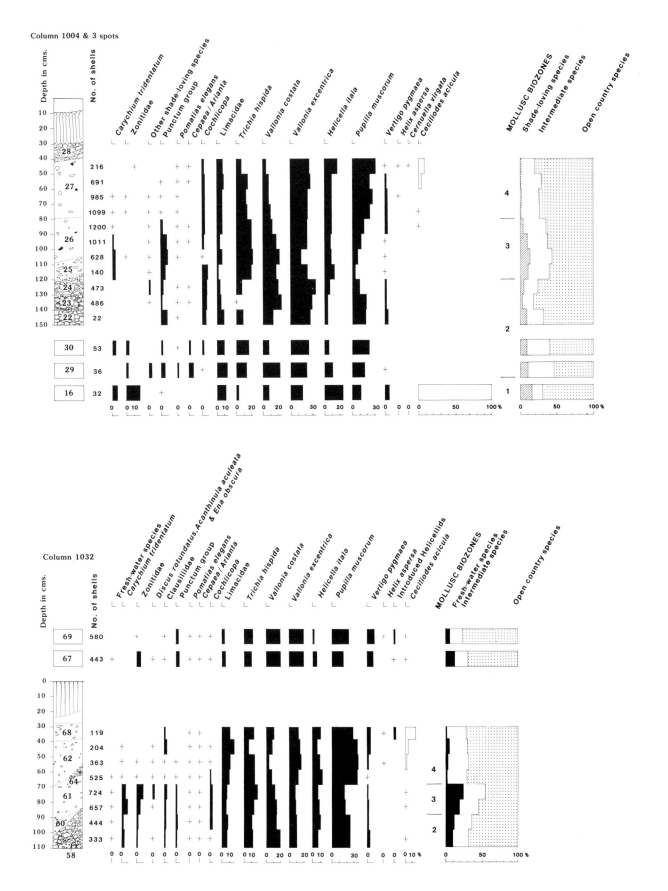

Figure 8   Mollusc histogram from the Beckhampton 4 (upper histogram) and 'Stukeley' barrows (lower histogram).

(zone 4). The occurrence, initially, of *Helix aspersa* and then of the Introduced Helicellids indicates that these fills were deposited during the post-Roman, medieval, or later periods (Kerney 1966; 1977).

A small but consistent number of freshwater shells were present in the 'Stukeley' barrow assemblages, being found throughout the ditch fills. Their presence appears to be accidental, and they cannot be seen as part of the ditch assemblages and do not reflect the local environment. Rather, they may have been incorporated inadvertently, possibly deriving from the River Kennet *c.* 500 m to the south, although, in view of the location of the barrow, their presence cannot be a result of the river having flooded. Their incorporation here may be as a result of natural agencies, such as on the foot of a bird as commonly suggested, but in view of their persistent occurrence, they can perhaps be seen as being the result of manuring or mulching local arable fields with vegetative material from the Kennet Valley (cf Allen 1994, 359; Allen in Smith *et al.*)

Summary

Both the Beckhampton 4 and 'Stukeley' barrows, and possibly also the Pound Field barrow, were constructed in an established Bronze Age grazed downland. The ditches became fairly rapidly colonised with long grass and possible scrub. In the Roman or later periods, the overgrown ditches were cleared and the area around, and possibly the barrows themselves, were in open grazed downland pasture. The change from this Roman and post-Roman pastoral landscape to an agricultural one in the region of the 'Stukeley' barrow can be seen in the medieval and later periods in both the tertiary fills and in the presence of the negative lynchet. Analysis (*see* below) of Mollusca from the negative lynchet on the field edge, however, reflects a localised grassy verge.

The Beckhampton and 'Stukeley' barrows follow the same basic environmental episodes which individually reflect localised changes, but together form a basis from which the general landscape history may be summarised.

The localised environments suggested by the molluscs are consistent with those put forward in previous work. Although there has been evidence for earlier woodland on the valley bottom (Evans *et al.* 1993) and for earlier clearance and cultivation at Avebury and South Street (Evans 1972), the valley sides appear to have been pasture over much of the area. The well established nature of this pasture is emphasised locally by the absence of woodland regeneration in the barrow areas (*see* Allen, and Mount, this volume).

Discussion

While the pipeline's bisection of three round barrows cannot be dismissed, the fact that it did not cut through any internal or mortuary features means that the primary evidence from the watching brief relates to the environmental potential of the ditch fills at Beckhampton barrow 4 and the 'Stukeley' barrow, and the possible buried soil at the Pound Field barrow. In general, this evidence, primarily molluscan, confirms the known environmental sequence for the Bronze Age and later periods in the Avebury area.

The siting of round barrows on the lower slopes of the Marlborough Downs suggests that by the Bronze Age the downland above the valley floor must have been largely cleared of extensive woodland. Certainly by the time the 'Stukeley' and Beckhampton 4 barrows were constructed, the adjacent downland had long been cleared and had become established pasture, presumably for grazing cattle and/or sheep and probably remained so through the Bronze Age, although with some small secondary woods of hazel, hawthorn, and oak. While the local mollusc assemblages from the two barrow ditches show that neither barrow was maintained, their ditches being allowed to become colonised with scrub, this was a local phenomenon relating solely to these monuments and not to the surrounding downland.

This contrasts with the more intensive and organised exploitation of the upper downland, which have evidence for long term settlements and extensive associated field systems (Gingell 1992). This pattern, which may have started on a small scale in the Late Neolithic/Early Bronze Age, reached its peak in the Middle Bronze Age, although by the Late Bronze Age /Early Iron Age upland cultivation had been abandoned.

Although the geophysical survey identified two ring-ditches not previously recorded in the SMR, their locations are not untypical and, given the concentration of round barrows in the landscape, simply reinforce a well established distribution pattern.

The geophysical and air photographic surveys of the Beckhampton barrow cemetery (Fig. 4) have added substantially to our knowledge of one of the major groupings of round barrows in the Avebury area. The cemetery, defined by Fleming (1971) as a 'nucleated cemetery', is situated at the north-east corner of an extensive zone of fairly regular barrow distribution extending to the south-west, with another similar zone on the Marlborough Downs to the east. The detail which these surveys have added to the barrows in the cemetery, with their wide range and complexity of forms, has reinforced the pattern, noted by Fleming, for barrows in the Avebury area, as around Stonehenge, to include a high proportion (14.5%) of special barrow types. In addition, the two sub-rectangular ditched features, barrows 10 and 11, have parallels associated with other elaborate barrow groups (Soffe 1993), such as at Woodhenge.

4. The Romano-British Period

Archaeological Background

The Roman Road, which branches off Ermin Street to the west of *Spinae* (Speen, Berks), and then passes through *Cunetio* (Mildenhall near Marlborough, Wilts) on its way to *Aquae Sulis* (Bath, Somerset), passes through the study corridor to the east of Silbury Hill (B10) (Margary 1955). The road, a small section of which is a Scheduled Monument (AM93), was aligned on Silbury Hill but its line had to be diverted to the south in order to skirt around it. To the west, where part of the road is visible in air photographs, it is then aligned on the southern spur of Calstone Down and bisects a large ring, possibly a disc barrow, close to the Beckhampton to Devizes road.

A well preserved section of its *agger* survives, 12 m wide and up to 1 m high, where it crosses Overton Hill but between there and Silbury Hill its line cannot be traced. William Stukeley's conjectural plan of the completed Avebury monuments (*see* frontispiece), however, shows the road, marked as *Via Badonica*, bisecting a disc barrow at the south end of Waden Hill. This is the 'Stukeley' barrow (*see* Bronze Age section, above) detected by the geophysical survey and subsequently recorded in the pipe trench as a ring-ditch. No traces of the road, or of associated features such as flanking ditches, were identified by the geophysical survey or during the watching brief but, judging from the position of the ring-ditch, it appears to have run very close to the south edge of the field flanking the A4. Excavations and probing along the line of the road were undertaken by Reverend Wilkinson for the Wiltshire Archaeological Society in 1867 (Wilkinson 1869).

Although no buildings had previously been found in the area, there was substantial evidence of Romano-British activity, from both sides of the Roman Road in the vicinity of Silbury Hill, although the nature and extent of that activity has remained unclear. During the 1867 excavations, two sections were cut through the line of the road to the east of Silbury Hill, on the east side of the river and north of the road. According to the report, many coins were found at a spot where irregularity in the ground surface marked a possible building. The precise location of this building is not recorded but it is likely that it relates to either Building I or Building II identified during the watching brief (*see* below). A large rubbish pit was also excavated which yielded sherds from some 80 vessels, including samian, an iron *stylus*, nails, and shears, as well as bones from sheep, cattle, deer, horse, and boar. In the same general area, during the excavation in 1926 of a water pipe trench running down the south-west slope of Waden Hill, M.E. Cunnington recorded, on the north side of the Roman Road, patches of dark soil containing tiles and Romano-British pottery, including samian (Cunnington 1932). Evidence of occupation has also been found on the south side of the Roman Road, two pits containing debris having been excavated at SU 1017 6830 and SU 1011 6821 (Brooke and Cunnington 1897).

A number of wells have been recorded in the vicinity of Silbury Hill, two of which at SU 1015 6838 (Brooke and Cunnington 1896, fig, 1) and SU 1000 6835, (Brooke 1910) on the south side of the road, have been excavated (Fig. 10). The former was approximately 9 m deep and contained ceramic tiles, a quern fragment, dressed stone blocks, and the base of a stone column as well as a bronze finger ring, iron *stylus*, hook, and shear blade, pottery, and coins of Arcadius (AD 383–395) and Theodosius (AD 408–450). Other wells are recorded at SU 1009 6848, SU 1013 6813, and SU 1008 6837.

More recently, during the 1968 excavations at Silbury Hill, large quantities of Romano-British finds were recovered from the upper fills of the Silbury Hill ditch (Whittle forthcoming) and, in 1971, roof tiles and 3rd and 4th-century pottery were found in an oil pipeline trench cut in the bend of the river near Swallowhead Springs. A fragment of a flat quern (B11) was found between the Winterbourne and Silbury Hill at SU 1020 6860 (*WAM* 1990) and quantities of pottery have been found eroding from the bank of the Winterbourne during dredging of the river channel by Thames Water.

A Romano-British grave (B12) was also found in the eroded river bank, during the investigation of geological deposits by J.G. Evans in 1964 (Evans 1966). The grave is 180 m north of the A4 at SU 1037 6855, it was 1.5 m long (but was truncated at the west end), 0.65 m wide, and 0.55 m deep and was sealed by a 0.5–0.6 m thick layer of hillwash containing quantities of animal bone, building debris, and abraded Romano-British pottery. The grave contained an extended supine male skeleton aged approximately 25 years, incomplete at the shoulders but with his head to the west. The left leg was crossed over the right below the knee and the left arm flexed over the chest with the hand near the throat. In the grave fill there were bones of cattle, sheep/goat and horse, oyster shells, crude flint flakes, and pieces of limestone, sandstone, and roofing tile, as well as 30 iron hobnails at the feet. The pottery, unabraded unlike that from the hillwash, included a variety of wares as well as undatable samian fragments and a single rim of a wall-sided mortarium, and a cooking pot rim decorated with narrow horizontal grey painted bands, suggesting a date for the burial late in the Roman period.

Because of the location of this burial it was decided, in formulating the Stage 1 Assessment, to undertake a geophysical survey in the area to the east of Silbury Hill, in addition to the geophysical scan. During the survey, a large number of geophysical anomalies were detected, centred on SU 1036 6859 (Fig 7), which were subsequently shown to be associated with the Winterbourne Romano-British settlement (*see* below). These included an area of low level anomalies interpreted as pits, centred on SU 1035 6860 (B13). The clearest feature was a 30 m long linear response running approximately east–west at SU 1036 6852 (B14, *see* ditch 164 below). This feature is also visible in an aerial photograph (Wiltshire County Council 1991, 169/92/049) where it can be seen to extend for over 100 m to the

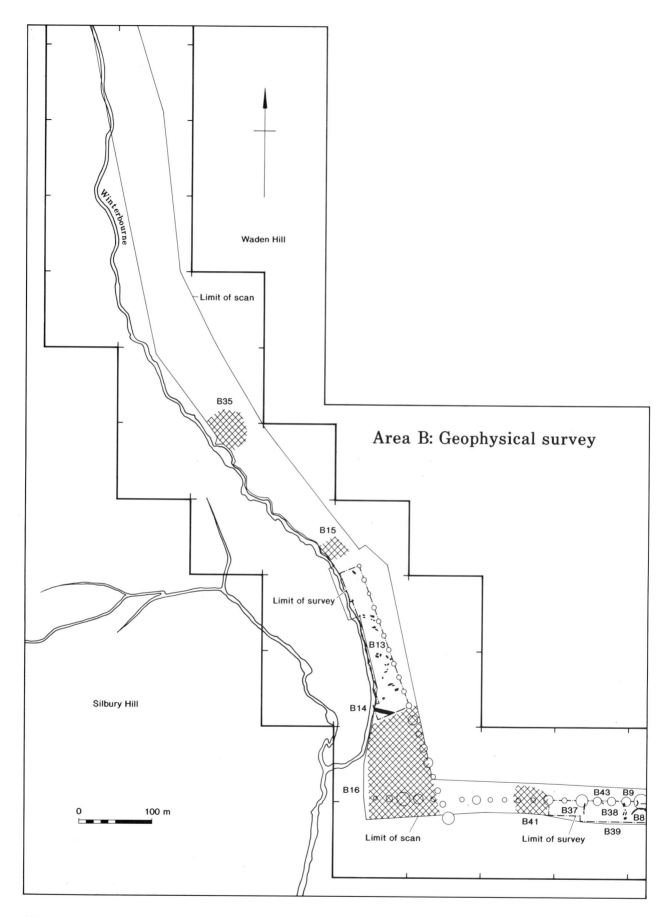

Figure 9   Area B geophysical survey

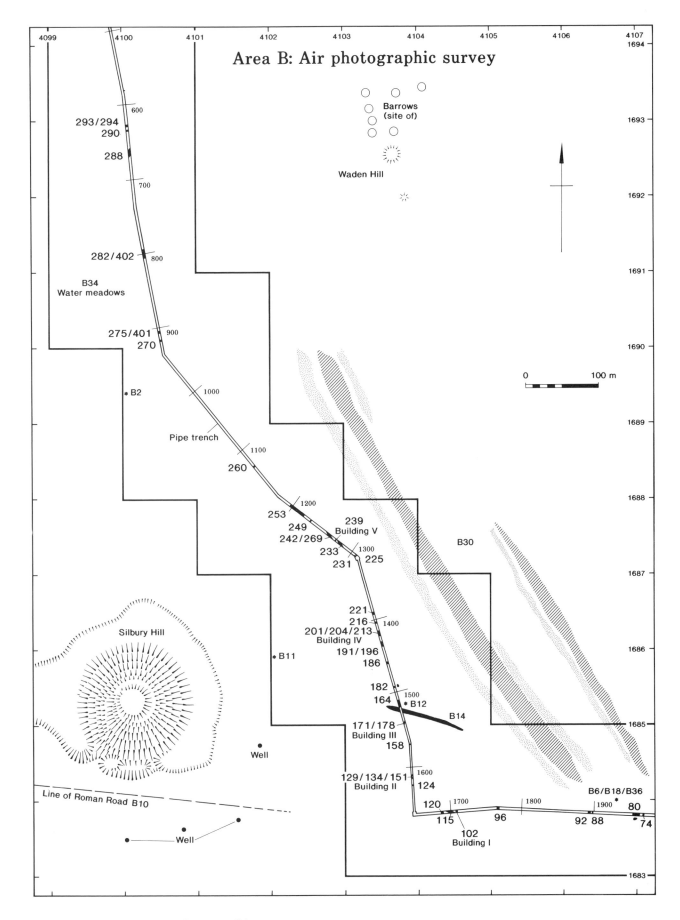

Figure 10   Area B air photographic survey

east-south-east. Any continuation of this line would take it over the south end of Waden Hill on the line of the linear feature detected by the geophysical survey (*see* B40, below). In addition, two general areas of anomalies (B15 and B16) were detected by magnetometer scan, centred on SU 1030 6873 and SU 1039 6845 (GSB 1992a, figures 2.1–3, 8.1 and 9.1).

Evidence of Romano-British activity from elsewhere in the study area is limited to the following individual finds unassociated with features.

- Two Romano-British horseshoes (A18) found at Beckhampton in the vicinity of SU 0900 6880 (SMR no. SU 06NE300).

- Five sherds of Romano-British pottery (B17), probably residual, found in Butler's Field, Avebury, during excavations by R. Mount in 1985 (Mount 1991). The pottery includes Savernake ware, dating from the 1st–2nd century AD.

- Isolated finds of Romano-British pottery and five Roman coins (B18) found at the south end of Waden Hill at *c.* SU 1070 6840. The coins were in very bad condition but one had discernible features of a head,

identified as Valentinian I (AD 363–375) (SMR no. SU 16NW318).

- Eleven coins (B19), including two barbarous radiates (dated to *c.* AD 270), a follis of Crispus (AD 317–326), and four 4th-century AD coins found in West Kennett in the vicinity of SU 1100 6830 (SMR no. SU 16NW319).

Results of the Watching Brief

During the watching brief, further evidence of Romano-British settlement activity was recorded in the trench in the vicinity of Silbury Hill. While, as described below, the Roman features were distributed over a considerable distance, the material is of sufficient quality and density for it to be treated as a single settlement site, here referred to as the Winterbourne Romano-British settlement.

Apart from this site, little Romano-British material was recovered during the watching brief and all of it can be considered as residual. Two sherds of pottery were found, in association with 13th–14th-century pottery, in Butler's Field, Avebury, one (Fabric Q100, *see* below)

Plate 3   View from Waden Hill, showing the pipeline trench running parallel to the Winterbourne and cutting through the site of the Romano-British settlement running down to the A4, with Silbury Hill in the background

recovered from a bulk soil sample from a medieval feature, the other (Fabric E101) from the layer of post-medieval alluvium (350) at the north end of the field. A single unstratified sherd of sandy coarseware was recovered from south of the Pound Field barrow, West Overton.

The Winterbourne Romano-British Settlement

The Romano-British settlement site identified by the watching brief is situated on the east side of the Winterbourne, on the lower slopes and flat ground to the west of Waden Hill, looking across to Silbury Hill (Fig. 10; Pl. 3). Features were recorded in the pipe trench between B.796 and B.1768 (880 m as the crow flys), indicating that the Romano-British settlement around Silbury Hill, of which the Winterbourne site must be viewed as part, was far more extensive than previous finds had suggested.

Buildings

A number of robbed foundation trenches were recorded in the pipe trench and, because they are all spaced at least 75 m apart, these have been interpreted as representing five buildings, although it is possible that a number of the trenches form parts of the same structure.

Building I

Trench 102, a single foundation trench, was visible in the north side of the pipe trench at B.1708–11 m (SU 1045 6838, OD 151.8 m) (Fig. 10). It appeared to be aligned north–south and extended 0.4 m across the base to a roughly squared terminal. It was 1.4 m wide and 0.85 m deep, with near vertical sides and a flat base extending 0.17 m below the bottom of the pipe trench and contained numerous large chalk blocks in a very pale brown silt matrix, 0.6 m thick (103). The blocks towards the base appeared to be laid, although there were no traces of mortar, and must represent the *in situ* remains of the building's substantial foundations (Fig. 11).

Immediately to the west of the foundation trench were the remains of a wall constructed of chalk blocks (112), with traces of decayed mortar visible between them and in a thin layer under them. The wall was built at ground level resting on a 0.1 m thick chalky layer, 111. Both the trench and the wall were overlain by a layer of dark greyish–brown silt loam (contexts 104–5) containing further chalk blocks as well as traces of decayed mortar. This appears to be building rubble. Above this layer and filling a small steep-sided cut in it over the trench (110), was a layer of very dark brown silt loam (107) containing, animal bone, stone roofing tiles, and pottery, including three sherds of Central Gaulish samian dated to AD 100–200. This, in turn, was sealed by a 0.45 m thick layer of hillwash (114).

Building II

Building II was the only structure to be clearly represented by more than a single foundation, the western side of the pipe trench cutting the junction of two walls, one aligned east–west and the other north–south

Plate 4   Building II, robbed wall foundation trench 190, looking west towards Silbury Hill

(Figs 10 and 11). The combined features extended over 5 m (B.1612–7 m) at a height of OD 152.2 m (SU 1039 6843). While the north–south foundation, 134, crossed the pipe trench at a shallow angle, being elongated in section to 3.3 m, the east–west foundation, 146, crossed the pipe trench almost at a right-angle. At this point it was 0.73 m wide and 0.63 m deep with vertical sides and a flat base. Although it had been robbed of much of its stone footing, a few chalk blocks remained *in situ* on its south side, set in a light greyish–brown silty matrix (130) containing what appeared to be decayed mortar. Robber cut 129, was filled with layers of dumped material (contexts 131–3) containing broken chalk blocks and fragments of charcoal. Foundation material (153) also remained *in situ* in the cut, 190, visible on the west side of the pipe trench (Pl. 4).

The north–south foundation, although elongated in section by its angle to the pipe trench, had similar dimensions to the east–west foundation, but at this point had been completely robbed of stone. As visible on the west side of the pipe trench, robber cut 151 was filled with a series of dumped layers (contexts 152, 154–7). Near the base of the cut on the east side, 134, there was a layer of charcoal (137) up to 0.12 m thick containing burnt flint, fired clay, and a number of iron nails,

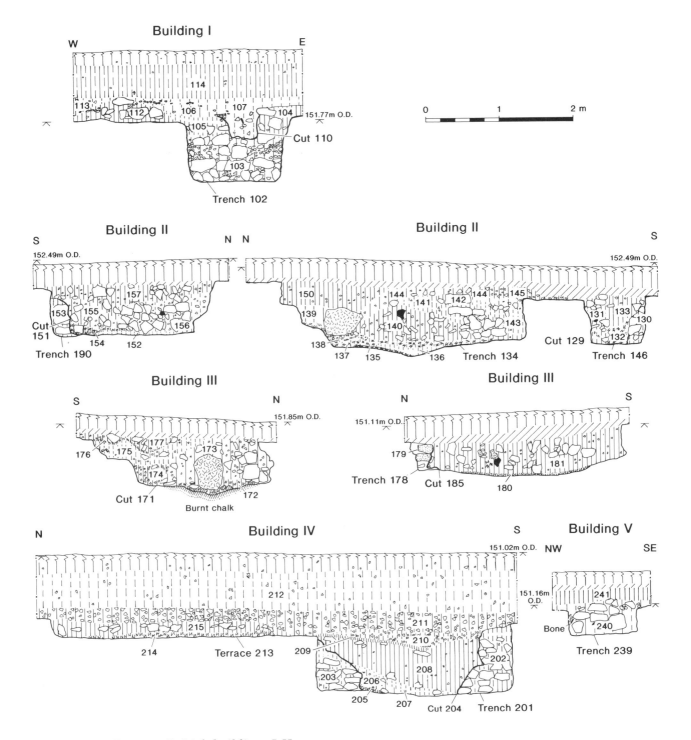

Figure 11   Romano-British buildings I–V

overlain by layers of dumped building debris (contexts 139–45, 150), including a large undressed sarsen block measuring 0.35 m by 0.5 m.

Building II was 75 m north-west of Building I, on a low rise in the ground. Its foundations, as recorded in the trench, were 25–30 m north of the expected line of the Roman Road. However, their alignments are at a slight angle to the road suggesting that the building was not constructed to front directly onto it. Instead, it is possible that the building was constructed facing west-

wards, in which case it would have looked directly towards Silbury Hill.

There was nothing from the trenches to provide a date for the building, although like Buildings III and IV (below), it had been extensively robbed and contained significant quantities of charcoal, possibly pointing to destruction by fire. Charcoal from foundation trenches 129 and 134 respectively, may have been the remains of burnt structures. It included fragments from an oak post at least 5 cm in diameter and an ash post at least 10 cm in diameter, as well as narrow roundwood or rods of hazel and alder.

Building III

The foundation trench, recorded at B.1532–7 m (SU1038 6850, OD 151.3–151.7 m), was also aligned approximately north–south, being visible in both sides of the pipe trench (Figs 10 and 11). It had vertical sides and a flat base but, because it crossed the pipe trench at a shallow angle, its width could not be determined. However, with a depth of between 0.58 m on the east side and 0.70 m on the west, the trench would have had similar dimensions to the Building II foundation trenches. On the east side, three courses of mortared sandstone blocks, at the north end of cut 178, was all that remained of wall foundation 179, most of it having been robbed. The robber cut, 185, had a thin layer of charcoal at its base, overlain by a layer of undifferentiated dumped building material (181) containing chalk blocks, flint, and sandstone.

The opposite section displayed no surviving *in situ* traces of the foundation but provided further evidence of the destruction of the building and the robbing of the foundation trench. Primary fill 172 of robber cut 171 again showed evidence of burning, containing burnt chalk blocks and substantial quantities of charcoal as well as a single iron nail. However, the natural chalk at the base of the cut also showed signs of scorching, indicating that this material had been dumped into the robbed trench while still hot. The upper fills (contexts 173–7) consisted of layers of dumped burnt and unburnt building material, including a second large sarsen block measuring 0.4 by 0.5 m, with two of the layers (contexts 173–4) producing sherds of greyware pottery of general Romano-British date. The evidence of burning from this trench and the use of sarsen as a building material, provide a further comparison with Building II.

Building IV

This structure, at B.1414–27 m (SU 1035 6862, OD 150.1 m), was represented by a wide trench containing a robbed stone foundation flanked to the north by a shallow terrace (Figs 10 and 11). A second small cut, possibly the remains of another small wall footing, 7 m to the south at the northern edge of ditch 191, may be part of the same structure (Fig. 13). The foundation trench was visible in both sides of the pipe trench. However, while it measured 2.65 m on the east side, it widened to 3.6 m on the west, suggesting that the pipe trench crossed the junction between two or more foundations. Only the east section was recorded.

Trench 201 was 0.9 m deep with vertical sides and a flat base. Much of the foundation survived *in situ* against both sides of the cut (contexts 202–3) and consisted of up to six courses of chalk blocks in a pale brown silt matrix. No traces of mortar were evident. The foundation stones in the centre of the feature, however, had been robbed, the lower fills of robber cut 204 appeared to have derived from the north side of the feature. They consisted of a thin spread of charcoal (205) at the base, sealed first by a layer of brown silt (206) and then by a

black silty layer containing a substantial amount of charcoal (207), both layers containing frequent chalk blocks. The main fill of the robber cut was a layer of pale brown silt (208) up to 0.7 m thick, largely stone free apart from a few pieces of chalk at the top. It was overlain by a thin layer of very dark greyish brown silt (209), also spread from the north side, and a 0.2 m thick stony silt layer (210).

The top of the foundation trench on the north side was 0.17 m lower than on the south, as the feature was flanked to the north by terrace 213, 3.65 m wide. This was 0.25 m deep at its north end with a flat base, its side being vertical at the top and concave at the base. Over much of its base was a very dark greyish brown silt layer, 214, containing a large amount of charcoal. The layer above it (215) consisted of a greyish–brown silt loam and contained frequent chalk building blocks up to 0.2 m in length, which extended to within 0.3 m of the foundation trench.

Seven metres to the south of the foundation trench was a third feature, 196 (Fig. 13), also possibly a robbed wall footing. The cut was 0.75 m wide and 0.4 m deep with vertical sides and a flat base stepped down in the centre. Its primary fill (197) was a 0.06 m thick layer of black silt containing a considerable quantity of charcoal. This was overlain by a greyish–brown silt loam (198) containing frequent chalk blocks.

The proximity of the three features suggest they are related, although the lack of any stratigraphical relationship makes them hard to interpret. The level base of the terrace suggests that it may have contained a laid surface, possibly a floor since robbed. The large foundation trench is considerably deeper than those of Buildings II and III, although similar to Building I, and is entirely different in nature to the smaller wall footing to the south. Building IV is the only structure to fall within the area of the geophysical survey undertaken along this section of the Winterbourne. Although a number of the discrete and localised low level anomalies which were detected (B13) in this area were interpreted as possible pits, some of the anomalies in the general area of Building IV have a more linear appearance and may, therefore, represent foundation trenches or other structural features associated with it (GSB 1992a, fig. 2.1).

The small wall footing was situated at the northern lip of a wide ditch, 191 (*see* below), and was cut into the ditch's primary fill which reached to the top of the ditch on the north side. It may also have cut the upper fills, although the stratigraphic relationship was not entirely clear. As a result, it is at least possible that the ditch was almost completely silted when this feature, and possibly also the other Building IV features, were constructed. There is no date for the ditch, but the only pottery from the immediate vicinity consisted of sherds of Romano-British fineware, dated no later than the 2nd century AD, from the charcoal layer at the base of the robbed wall footing, and from layer 199 sealing both it and the ditch.

The entire length of the structure(s) represented by these three features was overlain by hillwash. The lower stonier layer 199/211 was a greyish–brown silt loam averaging 0.25 m thick. The upper layer 200/212, which was largely stone free, was a brown/dark brown silt loam up to 0.85 m thick.

Building V
A robbed wall foundation trench, 239, at B.1273 m (SU 1028 6874, OD 150.7 m), was visible in the north-eastern side of the pipe trench but did not extend across it (Figs 10 and 11). It was 0.93 m wide and 0.35 m deep with vertical sides and a flat base and was filled with a brown silt loam (240) containing large chalk blocks and traces of mortar. The feature was sealed by a layer of brown– dark brown clay loam hillwash soil, which was 0.2 m thick (241).

Pits
The distribution of the buildings recorded in the pipe trench corresponds largely to that of the pits, the significant concentration of which, between B.1229 and B.1264, was predicted by the results of the magnetometer survey and scan (B13) (GSB 1992a, figs 2.3 and 9.1). Eight pits were recorded, distributed over *c.* 400 m, the most southerly being sited immediately south of Building II, the most northerly *c.* 45 m north-west of Building V.

Pit 124
This pit, cut by the east side of the pipe trench, was sited 6 m south of Building II at B.1623–4 m (OD 152 m) (Fig. 12). It was 0.83 m wide at the top and 0.6 m at the base, and 1.64 m deep. Its basal fills all slope down from north–south. The primary fill, 125, was a brown silt, up to 0.7 m thick, containing patches of clean chalk rubble, with large chalk lumps and pieces of sandstone building material concentrated towards the base. This was overlain by a 0.12 m thick layer of very dark brown, fine sand (126) containing fragments of charcoal. A sample (1047) from the layer produced sherds of Romano-British coarseware and some animal bone. This was sealed by

a layer of brown sandy silt (127) up to 0.18 m thick, also containing charcoal. The pit's upper fill, 128, 1.17 m thick, was a brown/dark brown silt loam from which was recovered oyster shell, animal bone, an iron nail, and a sandstone roof tile with a diamond-shaped perforation, probably a peg-hole. It also yielded pottery, including sherds of Romano-British fineware and Central Gaulish samian, both of late 1st–early 2nd century AD date.

Pit 158
The eastern edge of pit 159 was cut by the west side of the pipe trench, approximately midway between Buildings II and III at B.1571 m (OD 151.7 m) (Fig. 12). As it appeared in section it was 1 m wide at the top narrowing quickly to 0.55 m and was 0.25 m wide at the base (Pl. 5). It was 2.65 m deep, with its primary fill (159) consisting of a 0.2 m thick layer of dark yellowish–brown sandy silt containing charcoal, bone, and sherds of Romano-British fineware and coarseware. This was overlain by three layers (contexts 160–2) of stony silt averaging 0.15 m thick. The main pit fill, 163, was 2 m thick, consisted of a homogeneous, and largely stone free, brown silt loam from which animal bone was recovered. The fineware pottery has a date range of between the mid 2nd–early 3rd centuries AD, the later date from pit 124 possibly reflecting a gradual progression of settlement activity away from the Roman Road over time.

Pit 182
This pit was 45 m north of Building III, at B.1492 m (OD 151 m), and was visible in both sides of the pipe trench, although the unstable nature of the ground permitted only cursory recording. It was 1.6 m wide at the top, narrowing to 1.1 m at a depth of 2 m where it continued down below the base of the trench. Its lowest visible fill (context 183) was a dark greyish–brown loam at least 0.65 m thick. The upper fill, 184, was a very dark greyish–brown loam 1.35 m thick, both layers being almost completely stone free.

Pit 186
This pit was sited 32 m north of pit 182, midway between it and Building IV, at B.1460 m (OD 150.6 m). It was cut only by the east side of the pipe trench, and continued below its base. It was 1 m wide and over 1.5 m deep with straight vertical sides. The lowest visible fill, 187, consisted of a brown silt loam at least 0.7 m thick and contained a sherd of Black Burnished ware pottery, of general 1st–4th century AD date, and animal bone. The upper fill, 188, a dark greyish–brown silt loam, 0.8 m thick, yielded a potsherd, also of general Romano-British date, oyster shell, animal bone, and non-local stone.

Pit 216
The western edge of this pit, sited 10 m north of Building IV at B.1404 m (OD 150 m), was cut by the east side of the pipe trench. It was 0.8 m wide at the top with vertical sides, and extended below the base of the trench at a depth of 0.9 m. It was filled with two layers of dark greyish–brown silt loam, the lower, 217, which was at least 0.4 m thick, being stonier. The upper fill, 218 contained a range of pottery forms of general

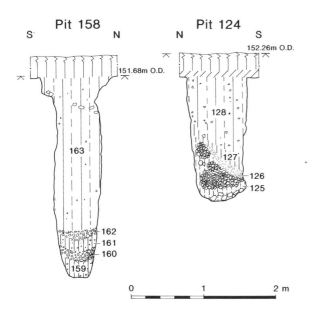

Figure 12   Romano-British pits

Plate 5   Pit 158, Winterbourne Romano-British settlement

Romano-British date as well as shell, animal bone, and non-local stone. The pit was sealed by layers of brown/dark brown silt loam hillwash, the lower stonier layer, 219, being 0.2 m thick, the upper layer (220), which was largely stone free, being 0.6 m thick.

Pit 225
This pit was sited 36 m south-east of Building V at B.1311 m (OD *c.* 151.8 m). The pipe trench at this point was over 3 m deep and cut into loose chalk requiring almost immediate shoring. As a result, only limited details could be recorded, with fill descriptions based largely on the observation of excavated material. The pit, which was visible in the east side of the pipe trench, was over 3 m deep and *c.* 1.5 m wide. Its lowest visible fill (226) was a dark brown, silty sand containing a number of large sarsen blocks. The layer produced animal bone and pottery, including two sherds of Romano-British fineware. Above this was a layer of yellowish–brown silty clay (227), with loose chalk rubble towards the centre of the cut, also containing pottery and bone, sealed by a thin layer of very dark greyish–brown silt (228) containing a substantial quantity of charcoal. The layer produced Romano-British fineware

and coarseware, animal bone, shell, and sandstone building material, as well as iron hobnails and a 3rd–4th-century AD copper alloy brooch (Fig. 14: 1). The pit's upper fill, 229, was a brown silt loam, as was the 0.4 m thick layer of hillwash (context 230) sealing the feature. The pottery from pit 225 gives a range of dates continuing up to the late 4th and even 5th centuries AD.

Pit 231
For the same reasons as pit 225, only limited records were taken. The pit was sited 2 m north-west of pit 225 at B.1309 m (OD *c.* 152 m), and was visible in the south-west side of the pipe trench. It was *c.* 1.2 m wide and over 1.8 m deep, and its fill(s) (232) contained a sherd of 3rd–4th-century AD pottery, as well as animal bone and sandstone building material.

Pit 249
The most northerly pit of Romano-British date recorded in the pipe trench was sited 43 m north-west of Building V at B.1229–30 m (OD 150.4 m). It was visible only on the north-east side of the pipe trench, and extended below its base at a depth of 1.3 m. The pit was 0.9 m wide at the top with a shallow lip on the south-east side giving an overall width of 1.7 m. Its lower visible fill (250) was a dark yellowish–brown silt loam at least 0.95 m thick from which was recovered a sherd of pottery of general Romano-British date. The upper fill was a brown silt loam 0.35 m thick. The feature was sealed by a 0.18 m thick layer of brown, silt loam hillwash.

Ditches
Seven ditches of Romano-British date were recorded extending over 970 m of pipe trench and distributed from the line of the Roman Road to *c.* 480 m north-west on Building V. A further six ditches, from which no direct dating evidence was recovered, were also recorded within the distribution of dated Romano-British features, and it is likely that at least some of these are of a similar date, particularly since there were no prehistoric features recorded in this area and, like many of the dated features, they are sealed by a layer of hillwash dated to the Romano-British period or later (*see* Allen, below). The ditches vary in size and in their apparent relationships to other features, including to the Roman Road and the River Winterbourne. In general, those located along the side of the Winterbourne are aligned either approximately parallel to it, or at a right angle to it, implying a possibly regular arrangement of land boundaries set out in relation to the course of the river.

Ditch 96
This feature with the profile of a ditch, at B.1765–8 m (OD 152.8 m), was visible only in the north side of the pipe trench as the south side of the existing trench was not exposed (Fig. 13). Its alignment, therefore, could not be determined. It was 2.8 m wide and 0.73 m deep with straight sides, shallow to the west and moderately steep to the east, and a concave base. The primary fill (97) was a 0.25 m thick layer of yellowish–brown silt, a sample from which produced an iron hobnail and a fragmentary triangular bone weaving tablet (Fig. 14: 2). The main fill, 98, consisted of brown, silt loam containing

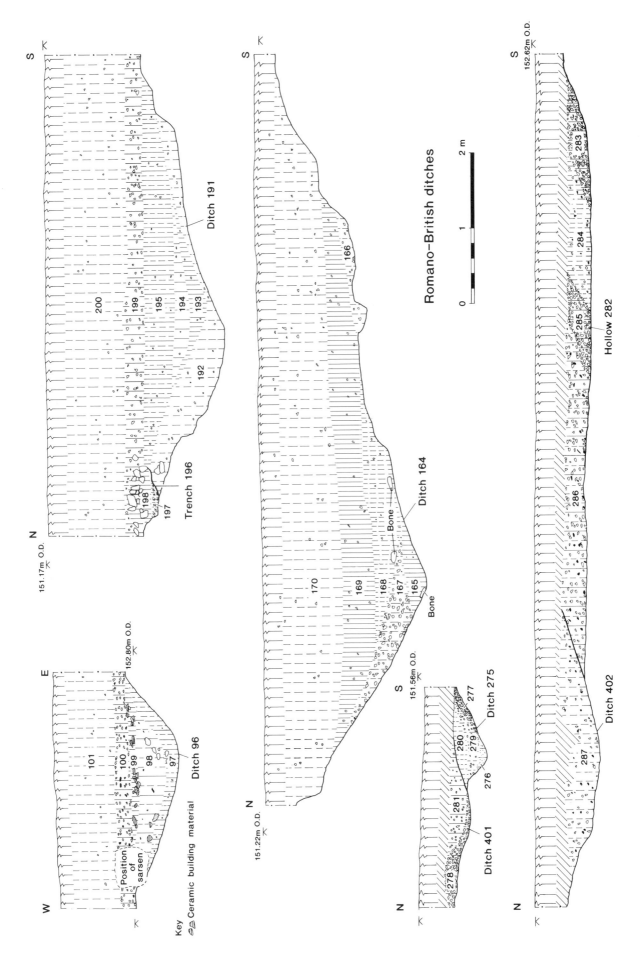

Figure 13 Romano-British ditches

a number of pieces of Roman brick as well as pieces of flat sandstone, probably also building material. During machine excavation of the pipe trench, a large sarsen block was removed from close to the top of the west side of the feature and appeared to derive from this layer. The upper fill, 99, a dark greyish–brown silt loam, contained further large quantities of sandstone, as well as animal bone, Romano-British fineware and coarse-ware pottery of late 3rd–4th century AD date, shale, slag, shell, and burnt flint. The ditch was sealed by hillwash, a lower stonier layer (100) consisting of brown/dark brown silt loam, 0.2 m thick, the upper layer (200/212) a largely stone free brown silt loam, 0.65 m thick.

Because this ditch was sited some 55 m to the east of Building I, the nearest structure recorded in the pipe trench, the quantity and range of building materials from this feature, including the only Romano-British ceramic building material from the Winterbourne site, as well as 35 % (by weight) of the sandstone, point to the likely proximity of some other, possibly substantial, structure.

Ditch 115

A ditch was recorded running between 3 m and 16 m to the west of Building I (B.1692–1705 m, OD c. 152.1 m). It was aligned approximately east–west, very close to the alignment of the pipe trench, crossing from the south side to the north side towards the west. As a result, its profile was very elongated, and it was not recognised until the trench had been fully excavated, when it was visible as a 0.3 m wide cut in the trench base. In section it was c. 0.5 m deep and appeared to be approximately V-shaped. Its primary fill, 116, was a light yellowish–brown silt, 0.15 m thick, containing a fired clay object and 17 sherds of Romano-British pottery. This was overlain by a 0.2 m thick layer of dark yellowish–brown silt loam (117), containing animal bone and further pottery. The upper fill (118) was a dark greyish–brown loam, from which was recovered pottery, bone, and a piece of ferrous material of no recognisable form. The ditch was overlain by a 0.5 m thick layer of brown/dark brown silt loam hillwash.

The location of this ditch, close to the line of the Roman Road, suggests that its east–west alignment may bear some relationship to the road, possibly as a roadside ditch. Moreover, the pottery recovered from its fills is of mid 1st–2nd century AD date and comprises, therefore, the earliest evidence of Romano-British activity from the Winterbourne site, with Building I immediately to the east, possibly representing the earliest construction phase.

Ditch 120

A small, shallow feature (0.6 m wide and 0.15 m deep), possibly a ditch, was recorded to the west of Building I at B.1698 m (151.5 m OD). It was visible only in the north side of the pipe trench, the southern side at that point not being exposed. It had moderately steep sides with a flattish base and contained a single fill, a dark greyish–brown silt loam, 121. It is undated and was sealed by 0.65 m of hillwash (contexts 122 and 123).

Plate 6　West-facing section of wide Romano-British ditch 164, also detected by the geophysical survey (B14)

Ditch 164

The magnetometer survey identified a linear geophysical anomaly running approximately east–west for some 30 m (B14). It crossed the line of the pipe trench, at B.1516–26 m (OD 151 m), 10 m north of Building III, and ran to the east bank of the Winterbourne (GSB 1992a, figure 2.3). As exposed in the pipe trench the ditch was 9.5 m wide and 2 m deep with a moderately steep, straight north side vertical at the top and a shallow stepped south side (Fig. 13, Pl. 6). Primary fill (165) was a light greyish–brown silt containing animal bone and pottery, some of late 1st–early 2nd century AD date. This was overlain by a stonier layer of greyish–brown silt (167) lying against the north side of the ditch, above which, on the south side, was a layer of pale brown silt (168) from which was recovered later pottery (from the mid 3rd century AD), plus shell, animal bone, and an iron nail. The primary fill in the irregular shaped step on the south side was a stony, pale brown silt (166).

The lower layers, which had a combined thickness of 0.7 m, were sealed by a layer of very dark greyish–brown silt loam (169), 0.48 m thick, containing pottery, animal bone, slag, and an unidentified lump of ferrous material. The upper fill of the ditch (170) was a brown/dark brown silt loam, 0.78 m thick. Bulk samples (1052 and 1053) were taken from layers 168 and 169, the latter yielding a sherd of late 2nd–4th-century AD Trier-type Rhenish ware. However, the flow of sewage from the existing pipe into the base of the trench at the time of recording prevented the primary fills being sampled.

Ditch 191

A substantial ditch, 6 m wide and 1.12 m deep, was recorded immediately south of Building IV (Fig. 13). It was aligned approximately east–west, at B.1427–33 m (OD 149.0 m) and had shallow irregular sides and a concave base. The primary fill (192) was a very pale brown, slightly stony silt extending up both sides of the cut but thickest on the north side (0.54 m). This was overlain by two layers filling up the centre of the cut, the lower (193) similar to 192 but less stony, the upper (194) consisting of a brown silt loam. The top fill of the ditch (195) was a dark yellowish–brown silt loam up to 0.4 m thick.

The ditch crosses the pipe trench 85 m north of the large Romano-British ditch 164. Although it has a similar general alignment, its precise course cannot be determined as, despite its size, it was not detected by the geophysical survey. The robbed wall trench 196, interpreted as forming part of Building IV, was cut into layer 192 at the top of the ditch's north side. Stratigraphically, therefore, the ditch is of prehistoric or Romano-British date, although it yielded no artefactual dating evidence. As with Building IV, the ditch was sealed by hillwash 1.1 m thick (contexts 199–200).

Ditch 221

This ditch, at B.1392 m (OD 149.5 m), ran east–west across the pipe trench, 22 m north of Building IV. It was 1.4 m wide and 0.45 m deep, with shallow sides at the top angling sharply to an approximate V-shape at the base. The primary fill 222 was a pale brown silt, the shallow upper part of the ditch containing a brown/dark brown silt loam, 223. The ditch was sealed by a 0.22 m thick layer of brown silt loam hillwash but provided no direct dating evidence.

Ditch 233

The north-west to south-east alignment of this ditch was close to that of the pipe trench, running to the north of the trench at the north-west end and to the south at the south-east end. Consequently, in section, its profile, which appeared to be U-shaped, was elongated to over 2 m in width. It was recorded between 3 m and 12 m south-east of Building V at B.1276–85 m (OD 150.7 m). In the north-east side of the trench it was 0.36 m deep, with a single fill, 234, of dark yellowish–brown clay loam. The ditch was overlain by a c. 0.2 m thick layer of brown/dark brown clay loam (235) which contained a fragment of fired clay. On the south side of the pipe

trench it was offset by c. 6 m to the south-east but had a similar stratigraphy and profile. The ditch provided no dating evidence.

Ditch 242/269

An 8 m long feature, aligned north-west to south-east, was recorded crossing the pipe trench between approximately B.1255 m and 1268 m (OD 149.9 m), immediately north-west of Building V. The ditch is elongated in section but by shortening the horizontal scale its true profile becomes clear, appearing as two cuts (242 and 269), the latter cutting the former. The feature runs approximately parallel to ditch 233 (above), but because the alignments of neither feature could be ascertained precisely, it was not possible to determine the distance between them. However, it is estimated that they were separated by only 2–3 m, suggesting that they may have bounded a trackway running approximately parallel to the Winterbourne, away from the main settlement area.

The earlier ditch 242, which was 0.57 m deep, appears to have had an approximately V-shaped profile with a narrow flat base. The primary fill, 243, was a 0.34 m thick layer of yellowish–brown silty clay, overlain by a 0.13 m thick layer of pale brown silty clay (244). There was a similar layer of brown silty clay (368) filling a shallow step at the top of the south-west side and another (345), which was truncated on the north-east side, by the later cut 269, filling the top of the ditch. Cut 269 was 0.5 m deep with an irregular V-shaped profile, shallower on its north-east side where it cut the upper fill of ditch 242. Its primary fill (246) was a yellowish–brown silty clay, 0.3 m thick, containing a substantial amount of chalk. This was overlain by a 0.3 m thick layer of brown silt (247), slightly less stony in content. Although neither cut yielded any direct dating evidence, both were sealed by a layer of brown silt loam hillwash (248) 0.2 m thick.

Ditch 253

A feature, which showed in the pipe trench as a long cut up to 0.55 m deep, is interpreted as a ditch running for 22 m (B.1196–1218 m) on the same alignment as the trench. It is aligned north-west to south-east, parallel to the River Winterbourne, approximately 90 m north-west of Building V, at a height of OD 150.1 m. Because of its alignment, its real profile could not be determined and the stratigraphy of its fills, which appeared to vary considerably along the cut's length, was difficult to ascertain precisely. In general, the primary fills towards the edges of the cut (contexts 254 and 263) consisted of yellowish–brown silty clay at the base of which, towards the south-east, was a thin spread of charcoal. These were overlain, at either end, by stonier layers of pale brown to brown silty clay (contexts 255 and 262) and towards the centre by a layer of chalk rubble, 256. Filling the centre of the cut were two layers of dark greyish–brown silt loam, the lower layer, 257, lying over natural, yielding a single sherd of late 1st–2nd-century AD pottery, the upper, 258, containing quantities of animal bone, Romano-British pottery with a range of dates, sandstone building material, as well as shell and fired clay. The whole feature was sealed by a 0.3 m deep layer of brown silt loam hillwash, 259.

The finds from the fills, including pottery forms dated to the 4th and 5th centuries AD, point to the presence of late settlement activity within the vicinity of this ditch and outside the distribution of buildings as revealed in the pipe trench. The absence of structural features in the pipe trench in this area may be explained by the fact that, for some 300 m to the north-west of Building V, the ground on the line of the pipe trench reaches its lowest level in Area B, with the original ground level, under the hillwash, falling to below OD 150.5 m. It is possible, therefore, that along this stretch of the Winterbourne any buildings would have been sited further away from the river on the higher and drier ground to the east.

Ditch 260

This ditch was recorded c. 150 m north-west of Building V at B.1126 m (OD 149.8 m), running north-east to south-west at a right angle to the River Winterbourne. It was 1.3 m wide and 0.35 m deep, with a shallow U-shaped profile, and its fill, 261, from which pottery of general Romano-British date was recovered, consisted of a brown clay loam.

Ditch 270

This ditch was aligned approximately east–west and crossed the pipe trench at B.918 m (OD 150.5 m). It was 1.15 m wide and 0.35 m deep with a shallow, U-shaped profile, rising slightly in the base. The primary fill (271), lying against the north side of the cut, was a 0.08 m thick layer of yellowish–brown silty clay containing a considerable quantity of chalk. The rest of the ditch was filled with a brown clay loam (272) containing animal bone. The ditch, which provided no direct dating evidence, was sealed by a 0.27 m thick layer of brown silty clay loam hillwash.

Ditch 275

A ditch, c. 365 m north-west of Building V at B.907 m (OD 151.1 m), was only visible in the north-eastern side of the pipe trench as the opposite side of the existing trench was not exposed (Fig. 13). Consequently, its alignment and true profile could not be ascertained but, as it appeared in section, it had a moderately steep V-shaped profile. It was truncated on its north-west side by an undated shallow cut, ditch 401, and was 1.3 m wide and 0.45 m deep (see below). The primary fill in the base of the ditch (276) was a yellowish–brown silty clay, 0.11 m thick, with a stony layer of brown silty clay (277), 0.12 m thick, lying against the south-east side. Overlying these was a layer of yellowish–brown silt loam (279), 0.17 m thick, containing a sherd of Romano-British pottery. The upper fill (280), cut by ditch 401, was a dark yellowish silt loam, 0.16 m thick.

Ditch 401

A ditch, at B.905–7 m (OD 150.7 m), ran east–west adjacent to Romano-British ditch 275, truncating its north side and its upper fill (Fig. 13). It was 1.9 m wide and 0.2 m deep, with a shallow U-shaped profile. It was filled with two layers of yellowish–brown silt loam, the lower stonier layer, 278, lying on the base and against the north side of the cut, the upper layer 281, 0.23 m thick, filling the rest of the cut.

Ditch 402 and hollow 282

As the most northerly Romano-British feature, at B.795– 9 m (OD 152.3 m), ditch 402 (Fig. 13) represents the northern limit of the Winterbourne Romano-British site as visible in the pipe trench. It truncates the north end of a wide feature, hollow 282, the two features having a combined width of over 10 m, and it is possible that their profiles, as they appear in section, have been elongated by their crossing the trench at a very shallow angle. Because the west side of the trench was only partly exposed, it was not possible to determine the alignment of these features. Ditch 402 had a shallow U-shaped profile in section and was was 4 m wide and 0.55 m deep. It was filled with a dark greyish–brown silt loam, 287, from which was recovered a piece of pottery of general Romano-British date, animal bone, and an iron nail.

Hollow 282, at B.798–806 m (OD 152.0 m), was approximately 8 m wide and 0.4 m deep, with a very shallow south side and a flattish base. It contained a series of brown/dark brown clay loam fills which all sloped in from the south side and, because they all rested on the base of the cut, appear to have been dumped. The primary fill 283, extending c. 2 m from the south side, contained a large quantity of chalk rubble. Over it, and extending for a further 2 m, was a less stony layer 284 but over that was a further layer containing chalk rubble, 285. The final fill 286, covering c. 5 m at the north end and truncated by ditch 402, was a brown/dark brown silt loam, also relatively stony. It contained pottery of possible Romano-British date.

Romano-British Finds,
by Rachael Seager Smith

Ceramic building material

A total of 55 pieces (5640 g) of ceramic building material was recovered from the fills of ditch 96. All are comparatively small and abraded and no complete lengths/widths are preserved. Their appearance and thickness (32–62 mm) suggest that they are all derived from Roman brick forms although these cannot be identified more specifically (cf Brodribb 1987, 34–62). Roman bricks were generally used as flooring, for bonding or lacing the courses of stone walls, or in the structure and capping of hypocaust *pilae*. It is likely that all these fragments were derived from the nearby structures but the absence of ceramic roofing tiles implies the use of stone tiles or organic roofing materials for these buildings. One short section of a curvilinear, double-finger, smeared signature was noted on one of the Fabric 1 fragments. Four fabric types were identified:

CBM Fabric 1

> Moderately hard, fine-grained, even textured fabric containing common to abundant quartz < 0.25 mm, rare to sparse iron oxides <2 mm and rare flint and soft, white calcareous particles, probably limestone, <3 mm across. Generally oxidised, some examples have an unoxidised core;

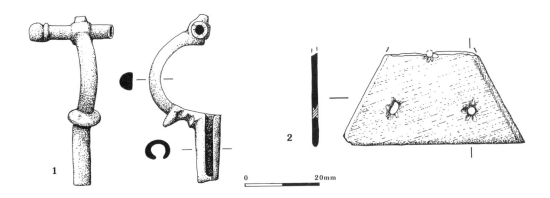

Figure 14 Copper alloy and worked bone objects

colour varies from yellowish–brown to brick red. 32 pieces, 3910 g.

CBM Fabric 2

Hard, smooth, poorly-wedged fabric containing rare to sparse quartz < 0.25 mm, sparse iron oxides < 4 mm and rare grog/clay pellets up to 2 mm across. Oxidised but with a highly laminated appearance due to the poor clay preparation; light orange–red with many horizontal off-white streaks. 4 pieces 290 g.

CBM Fabric 3

Hard, moderately fine-grained fabric with moderate amounts of quartz <0.5 mm and rare to sparse iron oxides <3 mm. Oxidised, pinkish–orange in colour, but with irregular off-white streaks and lumps due to poor clay preparation. 13 pieces 1040 g.

CBM Fabric 4

Hard fabric containing sparse grog / clay pellets up to 7 mm across, moderate to common quartz < 0.5 mm and iron oxides <2 mm. Oxidised; reddish–orange in colour. Surface of fabric often slightly pitted where the grog/clay pellets have eroded away; in fracture the fabric has a very lumpy appearance. 6 pieces 400 g.

Fired clay

One fragmentary fired clay object was recovered from ditch 115. The object, a flat fragment 26 mm thick, with one smoothed surface and the other with vegetable impressions, has a coarsely grog-tempered fabric and is probably part of a ceramic disc. Similar discs in locally produced, coarsely tempered fabrics have been found in Oxfordshire at Ashville, near Abingdon (Miles 1978, fig. 57, 32), Farmoor (Sanders 1979, fig. 28, 124–127), and Mill Street, Wantage (Wessex Archaeology 1993c), and at Shrewton in Wiltshire (Wessex Archaeology 1993d). Their function is uncertain, although various interpretations have been suggested, including components of ovens or other heating structures and storage con-

tainer or cheese-press lids. Associations with pottery of the later 1st or 2nd century AD from the same feature suggests a similar date for this object.

Fired clay Fabric 1

Moderately hard fabric; matrix composed of common to abundant microscopic quartz or mica with rare to sparse iron oxides <1 mm, rare quartz < 0.5 mm, and sparse poorly-sorted, off-white grog up to 10 mm across. Vegetable impressions on one flat surface. Well-prepared clay, pale brownish–grey with a grey core.

Iron objects

A total of 41 iron objects was recovered from the Winterbourne site and, with the exception of one fragment probably from a natural pyrites nodule found in ditch 164, all are likely to be of Romano-British date. One timber nail, with a round, flat head and a tapering shank, and 26 small, dome-headed nails, with clenched tips, were found in pit 225. Many of the dome-headed nails have mineralised wood or leather surviving to a depth of c. 6 mm immediately beneath the head. These may be hobnails from leather (or leather and wood) footwear, or they may be from decorative stud-work on leather and wood objects. A similar dome-headed nail was found in ditch 96.

Twelve nails or fragments of nails with round, flat heads and tapering shanks, subsquare in cross section, were also found, nine from the fills of the robbed wall foundation trench 134 of Building II, with further single examples from foundation trench 171 of Building III, pits 124 and 225, and ditches 164 and 402. These were presumably used for construction purposes. An unidentifiable, featureless lump of iron was recovered from the upper filling of ditch 115.

Copper alloy objects

A single copper alloy object (Fig. 14, 1), an undecorated brooch of crossbow type with a sheathed foot, was recovered from pit 225. Part of one wing, the hinge or possible spike on the head of the bow and the pin are missing. The type is dated to the 3rd–4th century AD

Table 5   probable Romano-British worked stone roof tile fragments

Fearure	Context	Number	Wt (g)	Description
Ditch 96	98	2	177	15–17 mm, medium-grained dark grey sandstone
"	99	8	2804	17–26 mm, medium-grained grey sandstone
Pit 124	125	3	2238	12–17 mm, coarse-grained sandstone
"	128	3 (joining)	304	15 mm, medium-grained pale grey sandstone with perforation
Pit 225	228	1	492	22 mm, medium to coarse-grained sandstone
Pit 231	232	3	1454	12–24 mm, 1 medium- and 2 coarse-grained sandstone
Ditch 253	258	1	366	26 mm, medium to coarse-grained sandstone

and is comparatively uncommon in Britain, although similar brooches are known from Cirencester (Macreth 1986, 105, fig. 77, 5), the Lankhills cemetery, Winchester, Hampshire (Clarke 1979, fig. 32, 532), and Colchester, Essex (Crummy 1983, fig. 13, 73).

Worked bone

One piece of worked bone, a triangular weaving tablet, was found in ditch 96 (Fig. 14: 2). The fragment is flat, c. 1.5 mm thick, with one corner broken off, the complete side measuring 50 mm. Three small perforations, one on the line of the break, are set at equal distances from the corners. The edges of the perforations are irregular where the movement of the threads has worn away the bone.

Weaving tablets could be made in different shapes, but the triangular form was especially popular during the Romano-British period (Wild 1970, 73–74). A similar weaving tablet, dated from the late 3rd–4th century AD, is known from Colchester (Crummy 1983, fig. 72, 2006) and two others, one made of copper alloy, are displayed in the Caerleon museum. Four square tablets from Cirencester (Wild and Viner 1986, fig. 84, 218–221) indicate a knowledge of this weaving technique in the north Wiltshire to south Gloucestershire area. Large areas of cloth could be woven using weaving tablets, but MacGregor (1985, 191) notes that they were more commonly used to produce braids, tapes, and the borders of textiles woven on a warp-weighted loom. Although weaving tablets were used over much of northern Europe until the 12th or 13th centuries, they are most commonly found in Romano-British contexts.

Unworked stone

Three fragments (120 g) of unworked, non-local (not available within 15 km of Avebury) stone were recovered. These were probably brought to the area as building stones. They comprise one fragment of fossiliferous limestone from 216 and two medium- to coarse-grained sandstone fragments, one from the fill of cut 110, above wall foundation trench 102, and one from the layer above ditch 120. No datable artefacts were recovered from the layer above ditch 120, but the other two fragments were all associated with pottery of Romano-British date.

Worked stone

A total of 28 pieces (9345 g) of stone showing signs of deliberate working was found, all in association with Romano-British pottery (Tables 5 and 6). All the objects consist of flat pieces of fine or medium/coarse grained sandstones, ranging from 12–26 mm thick. While no

Table 6   fragments of worked stone with polished surfaces

Feature	Context	Number	weight (g)	Description (and thickness)	Smoothed / polished surfaces
Ditch 96	98	1	230	medium-grained dark grey sandstone	one flat surface
Pit 186	188	1	94	fine-grained dark grey sandstone	one flat surface
Pit 231	232	1	113	14 mm, fine-grained sandstone	one flat surface and edge
"	"	1	591	19 mm, medium-grained sandstone	one flat surface
Ditch 253	258	1	308	14 mm, medium-grained sandstone	one flat surface
"	"	1	48	20 mm, medium-grained sandstone	one flat surface
Ditch 288	289	1	126	14 mm, fine-grained sandstone	both surfaces

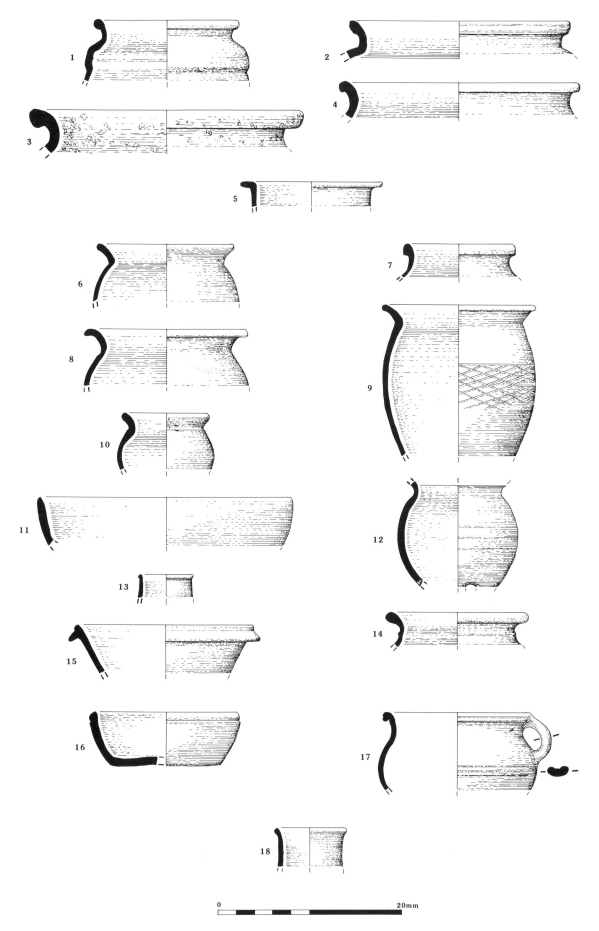

Figure 15 Romano-British pottery

Table 7 Romano-British pottery: vessel forms by fabric (number of occurrences recorded)

Fabric	Vessel Forms																	
	2	3	4	5	6	7	8	9	10	11	12	13	14	15	16	17	C51	Dr35
E304	–	–	–	–	–	–	–	–	–	–	–	–	–	–	–	–	–	1
E170	–	–	–	–	–	–	–	–	–	–	–	–	1	–	–	–	1	–
E101	2	–	2	–	–	–	–	–	–	–	1	–	1	–	–	–	–	–
G100	–	–	–	–	–	1	–	–	–	–	–	–	–	–	–	–	–	–
Q100	–	–	3	1	1	–	1	–	1	1	2	1	1	–	1	1	–	–
Q101	–	1	–	–	–	–	–	–	–	–	–	–	–	–	–	–	–	–
Q103	–	–	1	–	–	–	–	1	–	–	–	–	–	–	–	–	–	–
Total	2	1	6	1	1	1	1	1	1	1	3	1	2	1	1	1	1	1

Key to vessel forms

2	Everted rim jar (Fig. 15, 6 and 9)	11	Small jar with rounded shoulder and slightly everted rim (Fig. 15, 10)
3	Necked jar with slightly everted rim (Fig. 15, 7)	12	Shallow, straight-sided dish, 'dog-dish' (Fig. 15, 11 and 16)
4	Rim fragment too small to assign to a specific type (not illus.)	13	Round-bodied bowl/jar (Fig. 15, 12)
5	Wide-mouthed, necked jar with a well-defined shoulder and a girth groove (Fig.15, 1)	14	Beaded, slightly flaring beaker rim (Fig. 15, 13 and 18)
6	Wide-mouthed jar with an upright neck and a squared rim (Fig.15, 2)	15	Dropped-flange bowl/dish (Fig. 15, 14)
7	Large jar with slightly everted, rolled rim (Fig.15, 3)	16	Everted rim, thickened at tip and with a cordon on the neck (Fig. 15, 15)
8	Necked jar with a hooked rim (Fig.15, 4)	17	Necked bowl with at least one strap handle (Fig. 15, 17)
9	Small, flat-flanged bowl/dish (Fig.15, 5)	C51	Flanged bowl (Young 1977, 160, type C51)
10	Slightly everted rim jar (Fig.15, 8)	Dr35	Samian cup form (not illus.)

complete lengths or widths are preserved, most are likely to be from roof tiles, one fragment from pit 124 having a diamond-shaped perforation, probably a peg-hole. It is also possible, however, that they could have been used, in the same way as ceramic bricks, for lacing or bonding the courses of walls.

Seven fragments (Table 6) show some degree of surface smoothing and polish on one or both flat surfaces and, in one example, on the edges also. These may be fragments of floor tiles or possibly even flat whetstones. However, one piece from ditch 253, which has two groups of parallel cutmarks on its smooth polished surface, may best be interpreted as part of a working surface for cutting.

Pottery

A total of 211 sherds (4175 g) was recovered from the pipe trench in the area of the Winterbourne Romano-British settlement. The assemblage has been analysed in accordance with the standard Wessex Archaeology recording system for pottery (Morris 1992). It was divided into four broad fabric groups on the basis of dominant inclusion types: grog-tempered wares (Group G), sandy fabrics (Group Q), shell-tempered wares (Group S), and fabrics of known source or type (Group E). These groups were then further sub-divided into 16 different fabric types based on the range and coarseness of the inclusions present. The following terms are used to describe the quantity of inclusions present: rare, less than 2%; sparse, 3–7%; moderate, 10–15%; common, 20–25%; and abundant, 30%+. Each of the fabrics has been assigned a unique fabric code.

The pottery has been quantified using both the number and weight of sherds by fabric type for each context and details of vessel form, surface treatment, decoration, and manufacturing technique have been recorded. A site-specific vessel type series has been constructed (Fig. 15: 1–18) and, where possible, correlated with larger, more extensive collections (ie Rigby 1982a; Wedlake 1982; Seager Smith forthcoming) or published type series (ie Fulford 1975; Young 1977, Seager Smith and Davies 1993). Table 7 summarises the vessel forms present in each fabric type and pottery fabric totals by context are given in Table 8.

Imported finewares
Only two imported fineware fabrics were recognised (Table 7). Five sherds (42 g) of Central Gaulish samian (Fabric E304) include a base fragment from a platter from cut 110 above wall foundation trench 102 (Building

Table 8 Romano-British pottery quantification by fabric and context (number/weight in grams)

Feature	Context	Imports			British Finewares						Coarsewares						Amph.
		E121	E304	E162	E170	E171	Q102	Q104	E101	G100	Q100	Q101	Q103	Q105	Q106	S100	E256
Ditch 96	97	–	–	–	–	–	–	–	1/7	–	–	–	–	–	–	–	–
"	99	–	–	–	3/123	–	–	–	7/75	–	2/52	1/9	–	–	–	–	1/51
Cut 110	107	–	3/35	–	–	–	–	–	–	1/11	–	–	–	–	–	–	–
Layer	113	–	–	–	–	–	–	–	1/4	–	2/10	–	–	–	–	–	–
Ditch 115	116	–	–	–	–	–	1/11	–	–	10/548	4/136	–	2/106	–	–	–	1/115
"	117	–	–	–	–	–	–	–	3/7	1/68	3/25	–	–	–	–	–	–
"	118	–	–	–	–	–	1/3	–	–	–	1/25	–	4/7	–	–	–	–
Layer over Ditch 120	122	–	–	–	–	–	–	–	–	–	4/37	–	2/9	–	–	–	–
Pit 124	126	–	–	–	–	–	–	–	1/1	–	2/1	–	–	–	–	–	–
"	128	–	1/6	–	–	–	1/3	–	–	1/15	3/25	–	2/2	–	–	–	–
Pit 158	159	–	–	–	–	–	–	1/8	1/5	–	–	–	–	–	–	–	–
Ditch 164	165	–	–	–	–	–	1/2	–	1/1	–	–	–	–	–	–	–	–
"	168	–	–	–	1/20	–	–	–	–	–	–	–	–	–	–	–	–
"	169	1/1	1/1	–	3/5	–	–	–	7/73	1/8	2/33	–	1/3	–	–	–	–
Robber cut 171	173	–	–	–	–	–	–	–	–	–	1/70	–	–	–	–	–	–
"	174	–	–	–	–	–	–	–	–	–	2/11	–	–	1/14	–	–	–
Pit 186	187	–	–	–	–	–	–	–	1/33	–	1/7	–	–	–	–	–	–
"	188	–	–	–	–	–	–	–	–	–	–	–	–	–	–	–	–
Robber cut 196	197	–	–	–	–	–	2/17	–	–	–	–	–	–	–	–	–	–
Layer	199	–	–	–	–	–	2/19	–	–	–	–	–	–	–	–	–	–
Terrace 213	215	–	–	–	–	–	–	–	–	–	–	–	1/4	–	–	–	–
Pit 216	218	–	–	–	1/3	–	1/4	1/4	–	–	2/24	–	5/23	–	–	–	–
Pit 225	226	–	–	–	1/3	–	1/1	–	14/330	–	13/294	–	–	–	–	–	–
"	227	–	–	–	–	–	–	–	–	1/67	–	–	–	–	–	–	–
"	228	–	–	–	1/4	–	–	2/5	10/107	3/445	8/83	–	–	–	–	–	–
Pit 231	232	–	–	–	–	–	–	–	1/27	–	–	–	–	–	–	–	–
Pit 249	250	–	–	–	–	–	–	–	–	1/9	–	–	–	–	–	–	–

Table 8 continued

Feature	Context	Imports			British Finewares							Coarsewares					Amph.
		E121	E304	E162	E170	E171	Q102	Q104	E101	G100	Q100	Q101	Q103	Q105	Q106	S100	E256
Ditch 253	262	–	–	1/2	–	–	–	–	–	–	1/4	–	–	–	–	–	–
"	257	–	–	–	–	–	1/5	–	–	–	–	–	–	–	–	–	–
"	258	–	–	3/98	5/20	2/262	–	–	–	–	19/450	–	1/9	1/4	1/4	1/5	–
Ditch 260	261	–	–	–	1/1	–	–	–	1/2	–	1/10	–	1/1	–	–	–	–
Ditch 275	279	–	–	–	1/1	–	–	–	–	–	–	–	–	–	–	–	–
Hollow 282	287	–	–	–	1/1	–	–	–	–	–	–	–	–	–	–	–	–
Total		1/1	5/42	4/100	18/181	2/262	11/65	4/17	49/672	21/1195	69/1273	1/9	20/165	2/18	1/4	1/5	2/166

I), and a rim fragment from a Dr35 cup from pit 124. The remaining sherds are unidentifiable body chips from plain forms. All the sherds are likely to date from c. AD 100–200.

A single sherd of Trier-type Rhenish ware (Fabric E121) was recovered from an environmental sample taken from upper fill 169 of ditch 164. The sherd is very small but the fabric can be dated to the later 2nd or 3rd century AD (Greene 1978, 19), possibly continuing into the later 3rd or even the 4th century AD (Symonds 1992, 46).

British finewares

British fineware fabrics from known sources consist of New Forest colour-coated ware (Fabric E162), which can be dated to c. AD 270–400 (Fulford 1975, 24), and Oxfordshire red and brown colour-coated wares (Fabric E170), and white colour-coated ware (Fabric E171), which were produced c. AD 240–400 (Young 1977, 123, and 117 respectively). Most of the sherds were body fragments, although two of the New Forest colour-coated ware sherds from ditch 253 were from a handled, globular-bodied flagon or jug. In addition, the Oxford-shire white colour-coated ware sherds, from the same feature, were from the base of a mortarium (*ibid.*, 120–122, WC4–7). This vessel, the only mortarium to be recovered, is very worn, indicating considerable use. The only other recognisable vessel forms were a flanged bowl (*ibid.*, 160, type C51) in red colour-coated ware from ditch 96 and a beaker rim of indeterminate type (Fig. 15: 13) in brown colour-coated ware, from pit 225.

Two fineware fabrics (below) of unknown provenance were also identified, both likely to be of fairly local origin. In Fabric Q102, the use of a white slip to disguise an otherwise red firing fabric is a common feature of late 1st–2nd-century AD assemblages across southern England, although the production centres remain largely unknown. A variety of white-slipped red ware fabrics occur at Wanborough, in north Wiltshire (Seager Smith forthcoming, fabrics 10, 15, 22, 77, 96, and 97) and a local source is suggested for at least one of those found at Cirencester (Rigby 1982a, 154–155, fabric 9). No rim sherds were present, although it is likely that the majority of the sherds are from flagons, the most common vessel type produced in these wares. Only body sherds were present in Fabric Q104, but all of them are likely to be from closed forms, probably flagons or beakers.

Fabric Q102 Hard, fine-grained sandy fabric containing moderate sub-rounded quartz <0.5 mm and rare iron oxides <0.75 mm. Wheel-made. Generally oxidised with an off-white or cream slip on the exterior. White-slipped red ware.

Fabric Q104 Very hard, brittle, fine-grained ware containing a sparse sub-angular quartz <0.5 mm, rare iron oxides and soft, white, non-calcareous particles <1 mm. Also very rare elongated voids probably left by organic material, <15 mm long. Wheel-made.

Irregularly fired with streaky grey–brown surfaces and a grey core.

Coarsewares

Eight coarseware fabrics (below) were identified, including three which are 'catch-all' groups containing the products of more than one source.

Only the Black Burnished ware (Fabric E101) could be positively attributed to a known source. This ware comes from the Wareham/Poole Harbour region of Dorset and has a date range from the 1st–4th century AD, although all the recognisable vessel forms from the Winterbourne site (Types 2, 12 and 15; Figure 15: 6 and 9, 11, and 14 respectively) are characteristic elements of the late 3rd–4th-century AD industry. Vessels of these types are well known elsewhere in the area (Rigby 1982b, fig. 45, 95 and 96, 109, and fig. 46. 115–123; Keely, 1986, 171; Seager Smith forthcoming fig. 99, 448 and 449, fig. 100, 463–467 and fig. 101, 481–489). Black Burnished ware represented 24% of all the pottery recovered from the Winterbourne site.

The grey wares (Fabric Q100) are numerically dominant within the total pottery assemblage (Table 7), representing 33% of all sherds recovered. Sandy grey fabrics are known to have been produced to the west of Swindon from the early 2nd century AD until the end of the 4th century AD (Anderson 1979). Greyware wasters and kiln furniture have been found at Westbury (Rodgers and Roddham 1991, 51) and it is likely that other kilns have yet to be identified in the area. It is also possible that New Forest (Fulford 1975, 89–103) and Oxfordshire (Young 1977, 202–230) grey wares may be included within Fabric Q100. The greyware fabrics present vary from comparatively soft, coarse, dark brownish–grey wares imitating Black Burnished ware (ie Fig. 15: 9, 12, 15, and 16), to much harder, fine-grained, blue–grey fabrics (ie Figure 15: 10 and 17). Almost all are wheel-made, including those imitating the handmade Dorset BB1.

Vessel forms indicate that these wares span the entire Roman period. The wide-mouthed, necked jar with a girth groove (Fig. 15: 1), for example, is a typical mid 1st–2nd-century AD form in the region, occurring in a range of fabrics including sandy grey wares (Wedlake 1982, fig. 105, 23–25; Seager Smith forthcoming, figs. 85, 86, 91, and 95). Also notable are the sherds from the round-bodied jar/bowl form (Fig. 15: 12). Although incomplete, it is possible that this vessel is a local copy of a later 4th–5th-century AD Black Burnished ware form (Seager Smith and Davies 1993, 233, type 18). A similar vessel, also in an imitation BB1 fabric, is, however, known from Cirencester and dated to c. AD 380 to early 5th century (Keely 1986, fig. 109, 155). The closely spaced horizontal rilling on a body sherd of a slightly calcareous sandy greyware fabric from ditch 253, can be paralleled on jar forms found in 4th–5th-century AD groups at Cirencester (Keely 1986, fig. 111, 197) and Nettleton (Wedlake, 1982, fig. 110, 436).

Only one sherd of the sand and flint tempered coarseware fabric (Fabric Q105) was identified, while the oxidised sandy coarsewares (Fabric Q103) represent 10% of all sherds recovered (Table 7). These fabrics form part of the standard range of wares found on most Romano-British sites but little is known of their provenances, although they are likely to be of fairly local origin. All the sherds in this group were wheel-made and are mostly derived from closed forms, probably flagons. Such fabrics probably provided slightly better quality wares fulfilling a role between the coarse cooking and storage vessels and the fine tablewares.

The grog-tempered wares (Fabric G100) represent 10% of all sherds recovered (Table 7), and also include the products of more than one centre. A thin-walled jar base from ditch 115, is almost certainly Savernake ware. This highly variable fabric was produced near Mildenhall in the Savernake Forest and possibly other areas of north Wiltshire from the immediate post-conquest period well into the 2nd century AD (Annabel 1962, 142–55; Hodder 1974, 67–84; Swan 1975, 36–47; Rigby 1982a, 154). The remaining sherds are principally derived from large storage jars (Fig. 15: 5) or other thick-walled kitchen wares. These wares can be paralleled in the south of the county (Mepham 1993; Lehmann in prep; Seager Smith in prep.) and also belong to the later 1st–2nd centuries AD.

Fabrics Q101, Q106, and S100 are each represented by a single sherd (Table 7). It is possible that Fabric Q101 might be an example of the coarser oxidised ware produced in the Oxfordshire region (Young 1977, 185). The form (Fig. 15: 7) is broadly paralleled among these wares and is likely to date from the late 3rd century AD onwards (ibid., fig. 71, type O10 or O11). However, the Avebury area lies well beyond the known distribution zone (ibid., fig. 70).

The shell-tempered wares (Fabrics S100 and Q106) are both represented by small featureless body fragments from ditch 253. The sand-free fabric (Fabric S100) can be paralleled at Cirencester (Rigby 1982b, 1/5 D10; Keely 1986, 163, fabric 115), Shakenoak (Brodribb et al. 1971, I, 68ff and 1972, III, 54), Nettleton (Wedlake 1982, 250) and Wanborough (Seager Smith forthcoming, fabric 85). These sites all indicate a late Romano-British date for the ware but the absence of shell-tempered ware from the make-up levels at the Beeches, Cirencester suggests an appearance after the middle of the 4th century AD (Keely 1986, 163).

Fabric E101 Black Burnished ware. Wareham/Poole Harbour region of Dorset. 1st century BC – 4th century AD.

Fabric G100 Hard, coarse-grained fabric containing a selection of the following inclusion types in variable amounts: grog/clay pellets, quartz, flint, organic material, soft, white calcareous and non-calcareous particles and iron oxides, generally between 0.5–4 mm across. Handmade. Soapy texture and a lumpy appearance, although surfaces frequently slurry coated which can be matt, rilled or smoothed to a fairly glossy finish. Oxidised, unoxidised and variable fired examples all occur. 'Catch-all' fabric group for grog-tempered wares.

Fabric Q100 Hard to very hard fabric containing sparse to common sub-rounded quartz < 0.75 mm and rare iron oxides < 0.5 mm. Very rare grog, flint, organic material, and soft, white calcareous or non calcareous particles can also occur in some sherds. Wheel-made. Unoxidised, grey or greyish–brown in colour. Surface treatments include smoothing, burnishing and slipping, often in combination. A 'catch-all' fabric group for sandy grey coarsewares.

Fabric Q101 Hard gritty fabric containing moderate to common sub-rounded quartz 0.25–2 mm across, and rare, red iron oxides < 0.5 mm. Wheel-made. Oxidised with unoxidised core. The larger quartz inclusions closely resemble the coloured quartz trituration grits characteristic of mortaria from the Oxfordshire region.

Fabric Q103 Soft to very hard, moderately fine-grained fabrics containing moderate to common quartz < 0.5 mm, rare iron oxides < 1 mm and rare limestone fragments < 0.75 mm. Wheel-made. Generally oxidised but some sherds have an unoxidised core. A 'catch-all' fabric group for oxidised sandy coarsewares.

Fabric Q105 Hard, moderately fine-grained fabric with moderate to common microscopic quartz/mica, moderate quartz < 0.5 mm, rare to sparse crushed flint 0.5–3 mm across and rare iron oxides < 0.5 mm. Wheel-made. Oxidised, brownish–yellow in colour. Sand and flint tempered ware.

Fabric Q106 Hard, moderately fine-grained, slightly soapy fabric containing moderate to common quartz < 0.5 mm and moderate crushed shell 0.25–5 mm long. Manufacturing technology uncertain. Exterior surface smoothed. Unoxidised; mid grey–brown in colour. Sand and shell-tempered ware.

Fabric S100 Hard, slightly soapy fabric with common, poorly-sorted crushed shell < 4 mm, and rare quartz and iron oxides < 0.5 mm. Manufacturing technology uncertain. Exterior surface smoothed. Unoxidised; dark grey with paler surfaces. Shell-tempered ware.

Amphora

Two amphora body sherds were recovered (Table 7). Both are from Dressel 20 amphorae (Fabric 256), which were generally used to transport olive oil from southern Spain across the western provinces of the Roman Empire from the 1st to early 3rd century AD and possibly beyond (Peacock and Williams 1986, 136). Dressel 20 is perhaps the most common amphora type in Roman Britain, but only rims or stamped fragments can be more precisely dated.

Pottery dating

Most features did not produce enough chronologically diagnostic pottery to permit them to be assigned anything more than a general Romano-British date. These include pits 186, 216, and 249; ditches 260 and 275; robbed foundation trench 196; terrace 213, and hollow 282.

However, one group of early Roman (mid 1st–2nd century AD) pottery was identified from ditch 115. This included the Savernake ware base sherd, the rim of a large grog-tempered storage jar (Fig. 15: 3) and the wide-mouthed necked jar, with a girth groove, in a grey sandy fabric (Fig. 15: 1). In addition, a Black Burnished ware sherd has the acute-angled lattice decoration typical of 1st–2nd-century AD jar forms (Davies and Seager Smith 1993, 231), and the presence of white-slipped red wares (Fabric Q102), Dressel 20 amphora and predominance of grog-tempered wares, measured against the absence of characteristically late fabrics such as the Oxfordshire and New Forest wares, is also indicative of an early Romano-Britsh date.

Other early groups might include those from cut 110 over wall foundation trench 102, and pit 124. A samian Dr.35 rim and a base from a small white-slipped (Fabric Q102) vessel were found in pit 124 and Black Burnished ware was represented by only one sherd. Grog-tempered ware occurred in both features. Similarly, a layer over ditch 120 and pit 158 contain sherds dated from the mid 2nd century AD onwards (Fig. 15: 5) but without the characteristic later 3rd–4th-century AD elements. The small quantities of material hamper the precise dating of these features but cut 110 and pit 124 can perhaps be tentatively assigned to the 1st–2nd centuries AD and pit 158 and the layer over ditch 120 to the mid 2nd–3rd centuries AD.

Later Roman (from the late 3rd–4th century AD) groups proved easier to recognise. The first of these, from ditch 96, includes Oxfordshire red colour-coated ware (Young 1977, type C51) and a brown colour-coated ware beaker base, in addition to a possible sherd (Fig. 15: 7) of the coarse oxidised ware produced in this region (ibid., 185). The Black Burnished wares include everted rim jars with obtuse-angled lattice decoration beneath an incised groove (Fig. 15: 6), which date from the later 3rd–4th century AD (Davies and Seager Smith 1993, 231, type 3). Grog-tempered wares are absent. More tentatively assigned to this period were pit 231 and ditch 164 from which only small quantities of material were recovered (Table 7).

The latest material on the site, perhaps indicating the continuation of the settlement into the late 4th or even 5th century AD, was recovered from pit 225 (Fig. 15: 8–15) and ditch 253 (Fig. 15: 16 and 17). The collection from pit 225 includes a local copy of a comparatively uncommon BB1 form (Fig. 15: 12) which probably dates from the later 4th–5th century AD (Keely 1986, fig. 109, 155), as well as the three typical late Roman Black Burnished ware types (Fig. 15: 9, 11, and 14), and Oxfordshire red and brown colour-coated wares (Fig. 15: 13). Similarly late Roman elements from ditch 253 include the horizontally rilled greyware body sherd and the shell-tempered sherds, both are paralleled in 4th–5th-century groups at nearby sites (Wedlake 1982; Keely 1986; Seager Smith forthcoming). New Forest and Oxfordshire wares, including the Oxfordshire mor-

tarium base, were also represented but Black Burnished wares are absent from this group.

Conclusions

While the characteristic 1st–2nd-century AD finewares produced in north Wiltshire, including moulded imitation samian, colour-coated ware, and lead-glazed wares (Anderson 1979, fig. 1, 10–13) are absent and only one sherd of Savernake ware was identified, at least one group of 1st–2nd-century AD pottery was present, indicating a likely origin for the site in the early Romano-British period. Samian represents the only unequivocal early Roman import, the Trier-type Rhenish ware and Dressel 20 amphora being imported over long periods from the mid 1st–3rd century AD. Imported mortaria are also absent, the only vessel of this class being derived from the Oxfordshire region.

Continuity of activity into the later 2nd and 3rd centuries AD is less well attested by the ceramics, although this may be merely a result of the small size of the assemblage, as well as of problems with 3rd-century-ceramic chronology. The importance of Black Burnished ware at the site suggests activity after the expansion of this industry in AD 120 (Gillam 1976, 58). Later Romano-British occupation is indicated by the vessel forms of both the Black Burnished and the local grey wares (Fig. 15: 6–11 and 14–17) which are dominanted by typical later 3rd–4th-century AD types. British finewares from the New Forest and Oxfordshire regions dominate the finewares present. The presence of later 4th–5th-century elements amongst the coarsewares is indicated by the presence of the round-bodied jar/bowl (Fig. 15: 12), the horizontally rilled greyware sherd and the shell-tempered fabrics.

The overall pottery assemblage from the site contains the usual range of fabrics and forms typical of rural sites in southern England and is broadly comparable with other sites in Wiltshire (Wedlake 1982; Rigby 1982 a and b; Keely 1986; Mepham 1993; Seager Smith forthcoming; Seager Smith in prep.).

Environmental Analysis: Romano-British

Colluvial and alluvial sequences in the Winterbourne valley, *by Michael J. Allen*

A column of 13 contiguous samples was taken through the coarse mixed colluvial and alluvial deposits on the terrace edge at chainage 1186 m. Samples were taken for molluscan analysis at 0.10 m intervals throughout the sequence (sample series number 1057). The sequence of deposits comprised weathered chalk overlain initially by 0.4 m of grey silty alluvium and then by 0.8 m of silty colluvial sequences. The distinction between these two facies was made in the field and is important in determining the local palaeo-landscape, river valley, and floodplain or the dry chalkland, to which mollusc data refers, although this is determined to some extent by the data itself.

The interface between the two deposits displayed evidence of mixing. The sequence was described in the

Table 9 Mollusca from Winterbourne alluvial edge terrace

Alluvial edge terrace ?Roman (series 1057)

MOLLUSCA	1058	1059	1060	1061	1062	1063	1064	1065	1066	1067	1068	1069	1070
Context	705	704	704	703	703	703	702	702	701	700	700	700	700
Depth (cm)	130–140	120–130	110–120	100–110	90–100	80–90	70–80	60–70	50–60	40–50	30–40	20–30	10–20
Wt (g)	2000	2000	2000	2000	2000	2000	2000	2000	2000	2000	2000	2000	2000
Terrestrial													
Pomatias elegans (Müller)	–	1	–	–	–	+	+	3	1	1	–	–	–
Carychium tridentatum (Risso)	–	–	–	1	1	3	9	–	–	–	–	–	–
Carychium spp.	–	–	–	–	–	1	4	1	–	–	–	–	–
Catinella arenaria (Bouchard-Chantereaux)	–	2	–	2	–	–	–	–	–	–	–	–	–
Succinia spp.	–	–	–	–	–	–	1	–	–	–	–	–	–
Cochlicopa lubrica (Müller)	1	–	–	–	2	–	2	–	–	–	–	1	1
Cochlicopa spp.	–	5	3	–	7	7	8	3	1	2	6	7	7
Vertigo pygmaea (Draparnaud)	–	–	1	–	–	1	2	1	1	2	5	–	2
Vertigo spp.	–	–	–	–	–	–	–	–	–	–	–	1	–
Pupilla muscorum (Linnaeus)	3	24	9	39	21	11	7	–	6	3	–	1	–
Vallonia costata (Müller)	4	19	14	15	27	40	59	43	28	74	89	61	52
Vallonia excentrica Sterki	–	7	3	7	17	31	29	29	25	61	44	36	32
Punctum pygmaeum (Draparnaud)	–	9	4	4	5	4	1	–	–	–	–	–	–
Vitrina pellucida (Müller)	1	5	4	–	4	3	2	–	–	–	1	–	–
Vitrea crystallina (Müller)	–	–	–	–	2	1	–	–	–	–	–	–	–
Vitrea contracta (Westerlund)	–	–	–	–	1	6	6	–	–	–	–	–	–
Nesovitrea hammonis (Ström)	–	–	–	–	–	–	–	–	–	–	1	–	–
Aegopinella nitidula (Draparnaud)	–	–	–	–	–	2	3	–	–	–	–	–	–
Oxychilus cellarius (Müller)	–	–	–	–	1	2	1	2	–	–	–	–	–
Limacidae	22	12	7	29	28	22	48	43	37	31	18	43	74
Euconulus fulvus (Müller)	–	–	1	–	–	–	–	–	–	–	–	–	–
Cecilioides acicula (Müller)	–	21	35	62	125	234	148	52	23	12	6	3	4
Clausilia bidentata (Ström)	–	–	–	–	–	3	1	2	4	–	–	–	3
Candidula intersecta (Poiret)	–	–	–	–	–	–	–	–	–	–	2	–	–

Table 9 Continued

Alluvial edge terrace ?Roman (series 1057)

Sample	1058	1059	1060	1061	1062	1063	1064	1065	1066	1067	1068	1069	1070
Context	705	704	704	703	703	702	702		701	700	700	700	700
Depth (cm)	130–140	120–130	110–120	100–110	90–100	80–90	70–80	60–70	50–60	40–50	30–40	20–30	10–20
Wt (g)	2000	2000	2000	2000	2000	2000	2000	2000	2000	2000	2000	2000	2000
MOLLUSCA contd.													
Candidula gigaxii (L. Pfeiffer)	–	–	–	–	–	–	–	–	–	–	2	–	–
Helicella itala (Linnaeus)	–	4	11	13	17	14	16	41	34	11	5	18	18
Trichia hispida (Linnaeus)	–	8	10	15	20	34	66	30	18	83	105	93	90
Arianta arbustorum (Linnaeus)	–	–	–	–	–	–	–	–	–	–	+	–	–
Cepaea / Arianta spp.	–	–	1	–	–	1	3	–	2	1	–	1	1
Freshwater/Brackish-water species													
Lymnaea peregra (Müller)	1	–	–	–	1	–	1	–	–	–	–	–	–
Lymnaea truncatula (Müller)	–	3	–	1	1	–	–	–	–	1	1	1	–
Ansius leucostoma (Millet)	–	–	1	–	–	1	1	3	3	2	3	3	3
Pisidium obtusale (Lamarck)	–	–	–	1	–	–	–	–	–	–	–	–	–
Taxa	6	11	13	10	14	18	18	12	12	11	13	11	10
Shannon Index	1.06	2.16	2.24	1.87	2.24	2.30	2.18	1.88	1.95	1.63	1.60	1.71	1.71
TOTAL	32	100	69	127	155	187	270	201	160	271	273	266	283

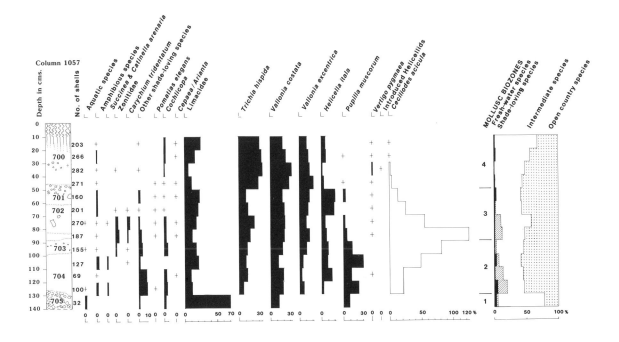

Figure 16   Winterbourne valley mollusc histogram

field following archaeological context notation, in line with standard pedological description, and is provided below.

Topsoil
0 0.45 m (700)   typical brown calcareous earth of very dark greyish–brown (10YR 3/2) silty loam with occasional small chalk and flint pieces. Samples 1071–1067.

Colluvium
0.45–0.6 m (701)   brown (10YR 4/3) silty loam with common small and medium chalk pieces. Samples 1067 and 1066.

Colluvium
0.6–0.85 m (702)   brown (10YR 4/3) silty clay loam with occasional chalk and flint fragments. Samples 1065–1063.

Alluvium
0.85–1.0 m (703)   light grey (10YR 7/3) with patches of brown (10YR 5/3) silty clay loam with rare chalk pieces. Samples 1063 and 1062.

Alluvium
1.0–1.3 m (704)   light grey (10YR 7/2) stonefree calcareous silt. Samples 1061–1059.

Chalk rubble
1.3–1.4 m (705)   white (10YR 8/2) chalk rubble; Lateglacial coombe deposits.

Sample 1058
This sequence is described in four local mollusc biozones, which are illustrated in a standard histogram (Fig. 16). The data is presented in Table 9.

Biozone 1 (1.3–1.4 m)
The basal coombe deposits produced few shells, but the assemblage is dominated by Limacidae with *Helicella*

itala and *Vallonia costata*. It is closely comparable with Late Devensian assemblages on the North Downs (Kerney 1963) and is typical of Kerney's (1977) mollusc biozone 'z' and indicates cold, open, moist conditions. The presence of *Lymnaea peregra* might indicate water draining through the valley.

Biozone 2 (0.9–1.3 m)
This zone contains broadly equal proportions of Limacidae, *Vallonia costata,* and *Trichia hispida.* Open country species (*Helicella itala* and *Pupilla muscorum*) are present throughout in low numbers and aquatic, amphibious, and shade-loving species occur in low numbers and show minor fluctuations.

The alluvium here indicates inundation of a dry, open floodplain. The colluvial or *in situ* component of the assemblage suggests open dry grassland. The initial zone 2i may represent a combination of long (shade-loving species) and dry grasses with some bare soil (*Pupilla muscorum*), with occasional localised wetter habitats due to the stream edges and possible seasonal inundation. An episode of dry floodplain (zone 2ii) is indicated by the temporary absence of amphibious and slum species and minor decline in Limacidae during which the local vegetation was allowed to grow affording more local shade.

Biozone 3 (0.5 – 0.9 m)
The sediments distinctly show a colluvial component indicating local activity, probably tillage, on the adjacent chalk slopes (cf Allen 1988). The mollusc assemblage reflects this in the rise of *Helicella itala*. However, the occurrence of amphibious species, almost absent in the upper alluvium, reflects the damper environments on the river edge.

Biozone 4 (0 – 0.5 m)
A local grassland in the river valley and arable on the chalk slopes, with occasional inundation, may account for the primarily colluvial nature of the sediments and *Trichia hispida* with *Vallonia costata*. The presence of Introduced Helicellids indicates a medieval or post-medieval date for this sediment sequence.

Discussion
The sediment sequence is largely Roman and post-Roman, indicating a hiatus, truncation, or lack of deposition of prehistoric deposit in the valley. The occurrence of the post-Pleistocene deposits can be seen to be indirectly anthropogenic, in that appreciable sediment deposition occurs during the Roman period for which there is significant archaeological evidence for settlement and farming activity. Fluctuations in the local floodplain environment reflect the local sediment patterns and the presence of hillwash in this location may not necessarily mean it is ubiquitous. Nevertheless, the picture is one of an open floodplain, possibly open pasture with cultivation of the local slopes. Increased colluviation in the medieval (or post-medieval) period may reflect larger areas under the plough locally, or that the soils had become more susceptible to local erosion due to continued tillage. However, it is evident that it is unlikely the sediment record is complete and significant episodes of activity may have been lost from it.

Animal bone from the Winterbourne Romano-British settlement,
by Mary Iles
A total of 1007 fragments of bone was recovered from both hand retrieved and sieved material from Romano-British contexts, of which 443 (44.0%) were identified to species and element (Table 10). The remainder were classified as cattle/horse size, sheep/goat/pig size, or unidentifiable.

Amphibians
The assemblage of identified species is dominated by bones from amphibians. Only the mandible and the pelvis were identified to frog or toad. From the recovered pelves, a minimum number of 15 individuals were identified as frog and two as toad and, from the mandibles, 11 for frog and two for toad. The amphibian bones probably represent accidental pit fall victims.

Mammals
Cattle dominate the meat bearing animals in both the sieved and unsieved material, followed by sheep. Dog and horse are also represented in small quantities.

Table 10 animal bone from Winterbourne Romano-British settlement

	Pits		Ditches		Wall Trenches	Total
	Hand	Sieved	Hand	Sieved	Hand	
Cattle	26	–	7	2	2	37
Sheep/goat	10	1	5	3	–	19
Horse	3	–	1	–	–	4
Dog	4	6	–	–	–	10
Domestic fowl	*28	7	–	–	–	35
Other bird	–	**10	–	–	–	10
Amphibian	–	258	–	–	–	258
Hare	–	–	–	–	1	1
Rodent	–	58	–	–	–	58
Fish	–	11	–	–	–	11
Sub-total	71	351	13	5	3	443
Cattle/horse size	23	–	4	5	–	32
Sheep/goat/pig size	18	5	–	2	–	25
Unidentifiable	8	454	6	39	–	507
Total	120	810	23	51	3	1007

*   All the bones come from one individual
** Nine bones come from one skeleton

Unusually pig is totally absent, although this may be the result of poor preservation or the small sample size. None of the rodent bones recovered could be identified to species.

Bird
An almost complete skeleton of a domestic chicken was recovered from pit 158. None of the bones showed any evidence of butchery. This and the completeness of the skeleton suggests that it was put into the pit intact, rather than being deposited as part of domestic food waste. Nine of the ten remaining bird bones recovered in the sieved material closely match wren (*Troglodytes* sp.). These bones probably also come from one individual. The remaining bird bone closely matches swift (*Apus* sp).

Fish
Of the 11 fish bones recovered from the sieved material, five vertebrae were identified as common eel (*Anguilla anguilla*).

Conclusion
The small sample size means that it is impossible to draw any wider conclusions about the assemblage. A significant proportion of the cattle bones are foot or ankle bones. Such a pattern may indicate primary butchery waste.

Unfortunately, the presence of amphibian, rodent, and bird bones in the pits cannot be used as indicators of the local environment. All the species represented could come from owl pellets. If these bones are the result of owl pellets being incorporated into the pit fill then they may represent a wider catchment area. The presence of amphibian bones in the pits may also indicate that they were left open at least for a short period of time, and that the frogs (or toads) present on the floodplain were attracted to the damp environment at the bottom of the pit.

Charred plant remains from the Winterbourne Romano-British settlement,
by Robert G. Scaife
Samples were examined from pits 124, 158, and 225, robbed wall foundations 129 and 134 of Building II, and ditches 96 and 144. Substantial quantities of cereal caryopses and cereal chaff were recovered but with few weed seeds. A dark charcoal layer, 228 in pit 225 and a charcoal layer 137 in the robbed wall foundation trench 134 (Fig. 11) produced the greatest numbers of identifiable cereal remains.

From Table 11, it is clear that *Triticum spelta* L. (spelt wheat) formed the most important constituent of all of the assemblages examined. This is based on identification of chaff rather than grain. The fills of pit 225 and the robbed wall foundation 134 contained substantial numbers of well preserved glume bases and spikelet forks which were easily identifiable to *Triticum spelta*. Feature 134 also had associated palaea, lemma, internodes, and some awn fragments.

The caryopses of *T. spelta* and *T. dicoccum* are in general difficult to separate because of their similar morphology. Features such as 'pear drop' shape in *T.*

dicoccum Schubl. (Jacomet 1987) were not sufficiently pronounced to allow satisfactory division between taxa. Furthermore, levels of grain preservation necessitated separation into categories of *T.* cf *spelta* type, and even *Triticum* indeterminable. In some samples, numerous caryopses fragments were recovered. These were especially prevalent in pit 225 where there were in excess of 200 fragments.

Compared to the importance of spelt, there are relatively few records of other cereal types found. Two caryopses of *Triticum aestivum* type (bread wheat including *T. aestivum* and *T. compactum*) were recovered from the richer contexts in pit 225 and robbed foundation trench 134. A single definite caryopsis of *Hordeum* sp. (likely *H. vulgare*) was identified from pit 225, although a small number of possible grains was recovered from robbed wall foundation trenches 129 and 134. The second most important cereal category comprised *Avena* (oats), but in many cases difficulty was experienced in separating this from *Bromus* (rye brome) because of removal of the surface/testa. These are recorded as *Avena/Bromus* type, the remains of which were again largely recorded from pit 225 and the robbed wall foundation 134.

As noted above, relatively small numbers of charred seeds were encountered in the analyses. These, however, include weeds typically associated with agriculture and disturbed ground: *Chenopodium* cf album, *Medicago* sp., *Vicia\Lathyrus*, *Rumex* sp., and cf *Centaurea*. A single mineralised seed of *Sambucus nigra* was recovered from pit 225. Other plant remains recorded include occasional *Corylus avellana* nut fragments and *Rosa/Crataegus* thorn. The latter are in accord with evidence presented by Rowena Gale who has examined the charcoals from this site.

Discussion
The charred crop assemblage is diagnostic and typical of the period. The Romano-British contexts have produced assemblages of grain and chaff, comprising largely spelt wheat (*Triticum spelta* L.) identified from numerous glume bases and spikelet forks. This is not unexpected since, although emmer had been the predominant wheat crop throughout Britain, by the Early Iron Age, regional variations had developed. In southern Britain there developed an undoubted predilection for spelt wheat from the first millennium (Helbaek 1952; Murphy 1977; Jones 1981); spelt cultivation became widely practised and became pronounced during the Romano-British period. Jessen and Helbaek (1944) and Helbaek (1952) recorded Early Iron Age spelt at Fifield Bavant and Little Solisbury and subsequently many Iron Age/Romano-British sites have been found to contain similar assemblages. It has been suggested (Jones 1981) that *Triticum spelta* and *T. aestivum* were more suited to heavier soils. Carruthers (in Butterworth and Lobb 1992) also notes the possible occurrence of spelt on heavier soils at Burghfield, Berkshire and it is possible that spelt may have been cultivated on the lower valley sides and possibly river clay/alluvial zone. Whilst it is more conceivable that cultivation was taking place locally, it must also be considered that cultivation was practised on another farmstead. There is some evidence that spelt was harvested and transported as

Table 11 charred plant remains from the Winterbourne Romano-British settlement

	Pits			Robbed Wall Foundations		Ditches	
Context no	124	158	225	129	134	96	164
GRAIN							
Triticum aestivum type	–	–	1	–	1	–	1
Triticum cf *aestivum* type	–	–	–	–	–	–	1
Triticum spelta type	1	–	22	–	39	2	6
Triticum cf *spelta* type	–	–	1	–	–	2	1
Triticum indet.	–	–	24	4	108	1	7
Hordeum sp.	–	–	1	–	–	–	1
cf *Hordeum*	–	–	2	1	4	–	–
Avena sp.	–	–	–	1	10	–	–
cf *Avena*	–	–	–	–	9	–	–
Bromus/Avena	–	–	6	–	27	1	–
Bromus secalinus	–	–	2	–	3	–	–
Indet. whole	–	6	33	6	–	–	3
Indet. frags	38	–	>215	–	*125	53	512
CHAFF							
gb. *Triticum spelta*	1	2	63	1	*459	–	46
gb. *Triticum* cf *spelta*	–	–	1	1	–	–	–
gb. *Triticum dicoccum*	–	–	1	–	1	–	–
gb indet. frags	2	–	53	–	–	–	25
sf. *Triticum spelta*	–	–	11	–	*296	–	–
sf. *Triticum dicoccum*	–	–	53	–	–	–	–
sf. indet.	2	–	1	6	–	–	51
int. *Triticum spelta*	–	–	–	–	*11	–	–
int. indet.	–	–	–	–	–	–	1
Palaea/lemma frags	–	–	–	–	+	–	–
culm nodes	–	–	–	–	+	–	1
Awns	–	–	–	–	+	–	–
Straw	–	–	–	–	+	–	–
SEEDS							
Sambucus nigra (mineralised)	–	–	1	–	–	–	–
Corylus avellana	–	–	2	–	–	–	3
Prunus/Crataegus thorn	–	–	1	–	–	–	–
Ranunculus a/r/b	–	–	–	–	1	–	–
Chenopodium cf *album*	–	–	–	–	1	–	1
Trifolium sp.	–	–	–	–	–	–	1
Medicago sp.	–	–	–	–	1	–	–
Vicia/Lathyrus	–	–	–	–	1	–	1
Rumex sp.	–	–	–	–	4	–	1
cf *Centaurea*	–	–	–	–	1	–	–
Anthriscus	–	–	–	–	1	–	–
Graminea/large	–	–	1	–	–	–	1
unidentified	–	1	3	–	–	–	2

* = 15 ml from 250 ml   gb = glume bases; sf. = spikelet forks; int. = internodes

whole ears of grain, stored in pits, and subsequently exhumed for use (Reynolds 1974).

The presence of substantial amounts of chaff debris does, however, imply that crop processing was being carried out locally. As spelt is a non-free threshing (hexaploid) variety, the grain has to be parched to facilitate release of the grain from the hull (Helbaek 1952). Thus, recovery of charred remains is usually interpreted as accidental burning or in the case of chaff debris, the destruction of waste material. Since the amount of chaff recovered here is sizeable in relation to the absolute numbers of grain found, the latter cause is suggested. The waste chaff material contains relatively few seeds and it seems that the waste chaff comes from a relatively late stage in the crop processing after extraneous weed material had been removed from the cereal heads after sieving/winnowing of the parched grain. The remaining chaff was perhaps dumped into the pits and foundation trenches and burnt along with other waste. Lesser numbers of grains found in other contexts may represent background 'noise'. The small number of other cereal grains of *Avena* and *Hordeum* may be considered as weeds of the spelt crop. It is also, however, possible that their remains have not been so fortuitously preserved since different processing techniques were used with these crops.

Charcoal from the Winterbourne Romano-British settlement, *by Rowena Gale*

A breakdown of the charcoal recovered from the Winterbourne Romano-British settlement is given in Table 12. Charcoal from ditch 96, situated slightly to the east of the other Romano-British features, included small fragments of ash (*Fraxinus*), oak (*Quercus*), and the Pomoideae. Charcoal recovered from the fills of pit 225 included fragments of oak (*Quercus*), ash (*Fraxinus*),

Table 12 charcoal from the Winterbourne Romano-British settlement

Context	no. / % within feature	Species
Ditch 96: primary fill 97	5	*Fraxinus* sp., ash
	2	*Quercus* sp., oak
	2	family Rosaceae, subfamily Pomoideae* (the sample comprised small fragments, mainly <3 mm in transverse section)
Pit 225: fill 228	12	*Quercus* sp., oak, stem
	11	*Fraxinus* sp., ash, stem
	9	*Corylus* sp., hazel
	5	family Rosaceae, subfamily Pomoideae*
	2	*Acer* sp. maple
	1	*Sambucus* sp., elder
	1	*Prunus*, cf P. spinosa (blackthorn)
Building II: layer 132 from robbed wall foundation trench 129	6	*Quercus* sp., oak, probably from a moderately wide stem
	4	*Corylus* sp., hazel (plus several fragments of unidentified bark and a large number of slivers of charcoal that were too narrow to identify)
Building II: layer 137 from robbed wall foundation trench 134	45%	*Quercus* sp., oak. The dimensions of one of the largest fragments suggested that it arose from a stem with a diameter of >5 cm. 12+ growth rings were observed on the incomplete transverse surface
	45%	*Fraxinus* sp., ash. The dimensions of one of the fragments suggested that it derived from a fairly wide stem with a diameter perhaps 10+ cm. The growth rings were mostly wide (some measuring 1 cm) and although measuring almost 4 cm in (incomplete) radial section only 4 annual rings were included
	8%	*Corylus* sp., hazel, stem (c. 2 cm diameter)
	2%	*Alder* sp., alder, stem (the sample included a large volume of charcoal fragments, many of which measured > 1 cm in the longest axis. All the fragments originated from roundwood).

* Family Rosaceae, subfamily Pomoideae includes *Crataegus* sp., hawthorn, *Malus* sp., apple, *Pyrus* sp., pear, and *sorbus* sp., rowan, whitebeam and wild service. These genera cannot be distinguished from each other by their anatomical structure.

hazel (*Corylus*), the Pomoideae, maple (*Acer*), elder (*Sambucus*), and (probably) blackthorn (*Prunus spinosa*). The range of species represented suggests typical downland vegetation of open scrub with blackthorn, hawthorn/ whitebeam, elder and hazel shrubs with taller species (oak, ash and maple) perhaps forming light woodland or isolated clumps of trees. It may be of interest to note that thorny species, such as blackthorn and hawthorn, have been used traditionally for hedges and barriers and, nowadays, old hedges established several centuries ago are frequently seen to include all the species named above. The wood/timber from these species (particularly oak, ash and hazel) is of economic value for structural, agricultural and domestic uses and as fuel. The origin of the charcoal deposited in the pit remains unknown but its presence in this context confirms that the contemporaneous environment supported a number of trees and shrubs, some of which grow only sparsely in the region today.

Two adjacent contexts from robbed wall foundation trenches 129 and 134, in Building II, produced charcoal. The large quantity of charcoal from layer 137 in feature 134 included fragments of roundwood large enough to estimate (very approximately) some minimum stem/trunk diameters. One piece of oak must have been at least 5 cm in diameter (12+ annual growth rings) whereas, an ash fragment suggested (by projection of the curve of the growth rings) a minimum diameter of 10 cm. The condition of the ash prevented any assessment of age but the widths of the growth rings observed were wide (*c.* 1 cm), indicating its origin from a fast growing tree. These fragments may represent the remains of a burnt structure, in which case it appears that poles or posts of oak and ash were used in combination with narrow roundwood or rods of hazel and alder (*Alnus*).

Despite the general paucity of charcoal, these samples are considered potentially important, since floristic information from sites of Romano-British occupation at Avebury and the surrounding areas has rarely been available previously and little is known of the contemporaneous environment. The identification of the charcoal compliments existing knowledge of the region and has provided a base-line on which to found evidence from future excavations.

Discussion

Although, by its narrow focus, the evidence from the pipe trench provides very limited evidence as to the nature of the Winterbourne Romano-British settlement, it does fill in important details about a period relatively under-represented in the archaeological record of the Avebury area. It also places earlier isolated and unconnected finds in the vicinity of Silbury Hill within the context of an identifiable settlement site.

In the case of all the buildings, no more than two walls were identified, with the result that no inferences can be confidently drawn as to the buildings' sizes or shapes. However, the well-constructed wall footings of mortared chalk and sandstone blocks and the evidence of burnt timber structures, combined with the large, undressed sarsen blocks found both in the foundation trenches and the backfill of the original pipe trench, suggest that the buildings may have been substantial stone and timber structures. Only one feature yielded fragments of Roman brick and, although pieces of flat worked sandstone, most of which were found close to the Roman Road, may have had a structural origin, they are more likely to have been used as roofing tiles or, in those with a polished surface, as floor tiles. The absence of ceramic roofing tiles implies the use either of such stone tiles or of organic materials to roof the buildings. The substantial nature of the buildings is hinted at by the fact that, when the Reverend Wilkinson was excavating in the vicinity of Silbury Hill in 1869, he noted irregularities in the ground in the area of either Building I or Building II, which he took to be the surviving surface indications of a building (Wilkinson 1869).

The pottery from Building I included four sherds of Central Gaulish samian dated to the early 2nd century AD, but lacked later forms, suggesting a possibly early date for the building. Perhaps significantly, ditch 115, a few metres to the west, produced the earliest pottery assemblage from the site. Building I was further distinguished by the lack of any signs of burning and full-scale stone robbing as was recorded in Buildings II, III, and IV. Although the precise location of the Roman Road at this point is not known, judging from its known alignments, passing Silbury Hill to the west and bisecting the 'Stukeley' barrow on Waden Hill to the east, it would appear to have run on a line very close to that of the pipe trench. The location and alignment of the Building I foundation trench, would place Building I very close, and at a right angle to the line of the road, although it was not possible to determine whether it pre- or post-dated the road.

What dating evidence there is from the pits and the ditches (ditches 115 and 120) supports the suggestion that there was a gradual spread of activity away from the vicinity of the Roman Road during the site's occupation. The pit closest to the road, pit 124, yielded pottery dated to late 1st to early 2nd century AD, while the pottery from pit 158 had a date range of mid 2nd–early 3rd century AD, and that from pit 225 continuing up to the late 4th and even 5th centuries AD.

While a number of the smaller ditches appear to have been field boundaries laid out in relation to the Winterbourne, the size of the wide ditch 164, which ran east–west through the site meeting the present course of the river at a right angle, indicates some other function, as does the possibility, suggested by the aerial photographic and geophysical evidence, that it extended over the south end of Waden Hill. The position of the ditch, cutting through the centre of the site, suggests that it may represent an early boundary to the settlement before the full extent of its northward expansion, with other sides possibly represented by the Roman Road and the Winterbourne.

Buildings I–V were recorded over a distance of 390 m. However, the occurrence of substantial quantities of domestic debris and building material from outside this area suggests a more extensive distribution of settlement activity. For instance, large quantities of worked stone, probably building material, as well as the only Roman ceramic building material from the Winterbourne site and a large undressed sarsen block, were recovered from the fills of ditch 96 some 55 m to the east of Building I, raising the possibility that there were other buildings, possibly fronting onto the Roman Road, extending the settlement to the east. Similarly, at the north end of the site, substantial quantities of material, including sandstone building material, were recovered from ditch 253, 65 m north-west of Building V, again implying the presence of some structural activity beyond the known distribution of buildings.

Because of the range of earlier finds in the vicinity, the area of settlement activity must be seen as extending beyond the Roman Road to the south and up to Silbury Hill to the west. This comprises an area of between 10 and 20 hectares, larger than would be expected for a simple rural agricultural settlement. The character of a settlement of this size, in a prominent roadside location, is not easy to define, particularly as it clearly developed from limited beginnings immediately adjacent to the road into a more extensive grouping of buildings, possibly representing a small village. In addition to its agricultural component, the site may also have had a local administrative and possibly commercial, function, roadside settlements often being used for the collection of *annona*, the corn tax. It is also possible that the presence of a major landmark at Silbury Hill may have encouraged travellers along the road to stop at this point, with the possible provision of refreshment or rest.

Although most of the pottery from the Winterbourne site is of late Roman date (3rd–4th centuries AD), the site does appear to span the entire Romano-British period. While the Roman Road close to which the earliest material from the site was found cannot be precisely dated, the west of England had been conquered and garrisoned by AD 47 and the road's construction is likely to have been completed by AD 60, providing a possible date for the initial settlement of the site.

It is also not possible to date the event represented by the burning and destruction particularly apparent with Building II and Building III, but occupation at the site into the later 4th–5th century is indicated by elements of the coarseware pottery, although the extent of the site during this period is not known. Although the New Forest and Oxfordshire kilns were still producing pottery into the early 5th century, the centralisation of administration and economic production had broken down completely soon after the Roman withdrawal from Britain in AD 410. However, farmsteads may have continued in use and the date for the final abandonment of the site is unknown. The degree to which there was continuity of rural settlement into the Saxon period is also unclear (Brown 1974). It does appear, however, that the abandonment of the Winterbourne site indicates a break in the settlement pattern, with the subsequent Saxon settlement at Avebury being one of a number of later settlements established in new locations on the valley floor.

The Romano-British settlement of Wiltshire was predominantly rural, comprising a large number of agricultural settlements varying from single family communities to villages (Leech 1976). Continuity with the Iron Age settlement pattern is shown by the fact that many of the Romano-British settlement sites on the chalk downs around Avebury are in the native tradition, with about a quarter of them on sites occupied in the Iron Age (Bonney 1968). There is also evidence for the reuse of Bronze Age field systems in the upper parts of the chalkland dry valleys, with the extensive re-establishment of arable land especially in the 1st and 2nd centuries AD. This pattern of unbroken settlement is clearly evident on the margins of the downland, such as on Overton and Fyfield Downs to the east, where fairly large Romano-British settlements, consisting of clusters or rows of structures in rectangular enclosures, were situated within abandoned Iron Age field systems, which in turn overlay Early Iron Age settlement (Bowen and Fowler 1962: Fowler 1967) and which, by AD 300, had been replaced by larger rectangular fields. The type of farming indicated by the floral and faunal evidence from the Winterbourne site is common on the chalklands of southern England, with large-scale cultivation of spelt and bread wheat and of oats, and it is tentatively suggested that these cereals were also cultivated on the heavier floodplain soils (Scaife above), with much of the crop processing being undertaken locally at the settlement. A mixed farming economy was practised and cattle and sheep were grazed, but pig does not seem to have been kept, possibly because there was no woodland for pannage.

Continuity with native traditions is also evident in the early Romano-British burial practices as revealed by the excavation of three tombs on Overton Down (Smith and Simpson 1964). Three small mounds, numbers 6, 6a, and 7, originally assumed to have been prehistoric in date, were sited in the north-east angle formed by the intersection of the Ridgeway and the Roman Road and aligned north–south, perhaps significantly on the ancient trackway rather than the Roman Road. The tombs, two of which had been opened by Colt Hoare, all had a similar form and can, therefore, all be assumed to be of similar date, although only No. 7 produced dating evidence. The practice of cremation suggests an early date for these tombs — up to *c.* AD 225, in contrast to the later Roman practice of inhumation as found adjacent to the Winterbourne site.

Some of the Romano-British settlements on Overton Down have produced evidence of unexpected wealth, including painted wall plaster, a number of bronze objects, and 63 coins, as well as of substantial construction with box tile, *tegula,* and *pila,* and sandstone roof tiles, suggesting that villas were not the sole form of wealthy and high status settlement (Hingley 1989). The position of the Winterbourne site, however, is closer to the siting and distribution of Roman villas in Wiltshire. While these are relatively few in number and limited to three main concentrations, most of the known villas are sited at low altitudes off the chalk, either on the lower hill slopes or in the valley bottoms (Bonney 1968). In 1922, a possible villa was found on the lower southern slopes of Windmill Hill, west-north-west of Avebury Trusloe at SU 0834 7000 when a small area of tessellated pavement with a chequer pattern was excavated by Kendall (1923, 359–61). Other finds included hexagonal stone roof tiles, bronze fittings, oyster shells, and pottery, including imitation samian. The only indication of the site was an amorphous raised area. About 1.5 km to the north-east, at SU 0841 7016, a second structure, with four chalk walls and a chalk floor, was recorded in 1976 by the Swindon Archaeological Society (SMR no. SU 07SE306).

While there are several possible villas further east along the Kennet valley, for instance at Fyfield House (SMR no. 16NW312), there is a danger of making inferences as to the nature of such sites with insufficient evidence (Scott 1993) and any statement as to the status of the Winterbourne site should await the collection of further evidence as to the full extent and nature of its buildings. Nonetheless, the apparent size and duration of the settlement and its location flanking the Roman Road, combined with the substantial construction of the buildings, the number of wells recorded in the area, and the wide range of finds retrieved both during this project and during earlier excavations, point to the fact that the Winterbourne site represents a major and significant focus of settlement within the Avebury area and the upper Kennet valley.

5. The Saxon and Medieval Periods

Archaeological Background

Saxon Period

Traces of Saxon settlement are known from a number of archaeological excavations to the south and south-west of Avebury village. It is possible that management of the Winterbourne floodplain during the Romano-British and Saxon periods led to the cessation of flooding and alluviation permitting continued settlement and cultivation of the valley floor. Excavations by R. Mount in 1985 at the north end of Butler's Field (SU 0979 6983), close to the line of the sewer trench, found two sherds of Saxon pottery (B20), one of 9th–11th century date from an Oxford kiln, the second, a grass-tempered ware of 5th–11th century date, and an uncalibrated radiocarbon date of 1160±80 AD (OxA-1120) from a cow bone also lies towards the end of the Saxon period (Mount 1991).

A number of excavations were also undertaken prior to the construction and later extension of the Avebury South Car Park, immediately to the east of Butler's Field, during the course of which post-built structures, interpreted as Saxon sunken huts, were recorded. Evidence of Saxon settlement in this area was first found during excavations by F. Vatcher in 1976 (B21), centred on SU 0997 6977, with sunken huts of two-post construction yielding glass beads and native grass-tempered pottery dated to the 5th or 6th centuries AD (SMR no. SU 06NE401). A further post-built structure in a large hollow (B22), interpreted by Borthwick (1985) as a Saxon sunken hut, was recorded during excavations by P. Harding in 1985, and in 1988, excavations by the Wiltshire Rescue Archaeology Project in 1988, found the remains of a sunken hut (B23) formed of six post-holes in a north–south alignment, and two aligned east–west, containing animal bone and grass-tempered pottery (Leah 1988).

The Saxons were generally pagan until the mid 7th century AD. A Christian church was built just outside the west side of the Avebury circle, probably in the 9th or 10th century AD. In the Church of St James, a number of Saxon features survive, including two round windows still visible high in the nave, along with a piece of a Saxon cross incorporated in the fabric of the nave. There is also a carved tub font dated c. AD 880–990, as well as some original plaster and typical long string-coursing (Taylor 1982). The description of the *Avreberie* church in the *Domesday* Book as *terra regis*, part of the demesne of *Chenete*, has led to the suggestion that it was a Saxon minster of regional importance and superior status, and of probable royal or magnate foundation (Gilchrist 1989).

Documentary sources, including Saxon charters and the *Domesday* Book, record the presence of a number of Saxon settlements along the upper Kennet valley — *Bachentune* (Beckhampton, A19), *Chenete* (Kennett, B24 and C4), *Ofaertune* (West Overton D3), *Uferantune* (East Overton), *Fifhide* (Fyfield), and *Lochrige*

(Lockeridge) — whose occupation, apart from periodic movements by the population onto the downs, is likely to have been more or less continuous (Fowler 1975). Many of the boundaries between these settlements, some of which may have been late Romano-British in origin (Bonney 1966), were set out with considerable precision and, being maintained by inheritance systems, are preserved as modern parish boundaries.

The antiquity of the *Ofaertune* tithing, for instance, is evident from two 10th century charters (Sawyer 1968, nos. 449 and 784). In the first, dated to AD 939, Athelston granted that part of the land which later became East Overton to Wulfswyth, a nun, who bestowed it to the Bishop of Winchester, so that by 1270 East Overton and neighbouring Fyfield were held by the Priory of St Swithun at Winchester. By the second charter, dated AD 972, Edgar bestowed West Overton to Elfled, also possibly a nun, and by the time of the *Domesday* Book, West Overton Manor was held by the Abbess of St Mary's at Wilton.

In delineating the boundaries of the granted land, the latter charter refers to a number of landmarks within or close to the study area (Brentnall 1939). The boundary starts at 'the Churchstead', the precise location of which is not known but which was probably sited near East Kennett Manor in the vicinity of the road to West Overton. While excavating foundations for an extension to the present Manor, two Anglo-Saxon loom weights (C5) were found (*Wiltshire Archaeological and Natural History Magazine (WAM)* 1928). The boundary then proceeded to 'the eldertree at Straetford', the point where the Ridgeway crossed the River Kennet, then continued past 'the seven barrows' on Overton Hill. Among the barrows on Overton Hill are the five pagan Saxon burials of 5th–6th century AD, found in secondary contexts in the Romano-British tomb No. 7 and the adjacent prehistoric barrow N. 6b (Smith and Simpson 1964; Eagles 1986). The practice in the Saxon period of marking land boundaries with burials, therefore suggests that the Ridgeway was a boundary from an early date in the Saxon period. There was also a Saxon burial on the top of Silbury Hill (VCH 1954, 36).

Medieval Period

Although the earliest reference to a village, as distinct from just a church, at Avebury is found in the Assize Roll of 1289, a number of excavations have produced evidence of extensive medieval settlement to the west and south-west of Avebury, dating from the 12th century (Fig. 17). A number of medieval features (B25) were recorded there by F. Vatcher during the original excavation of the sewer pipe trench, in the c. 50 m of trench south of the Avebury pumping station (c. SU 0980 6980). A sarsen wall foundation, c. 1 m wide aligned north–south, was interpreted as a medieval boundary wall. A stone hole, a ditch, and a burning pit containing 16 sherds, possibly indicating the former position of a

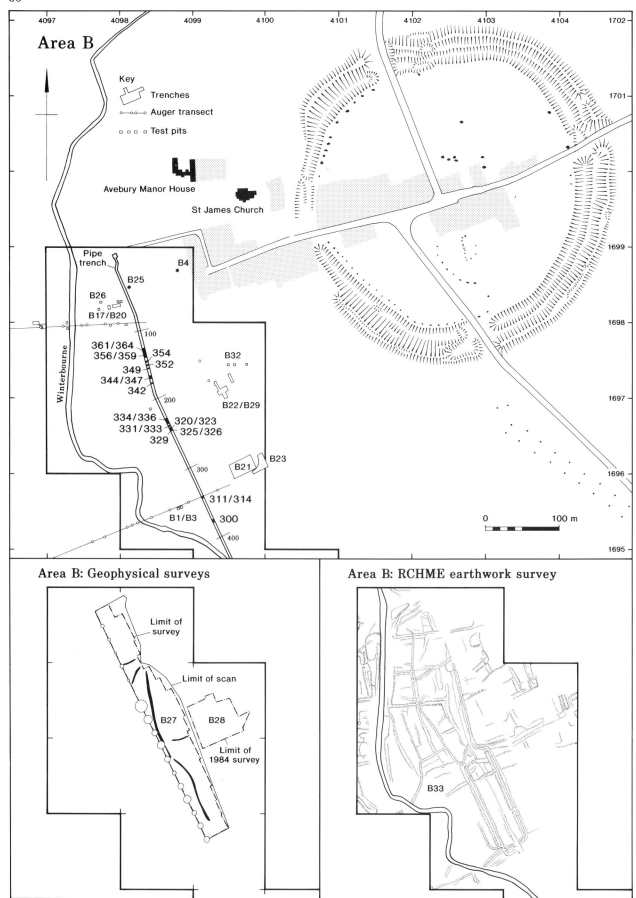

Figure 17 Medieval features, Butler's Field, Avebury. Area B surveys

sarsen stone, were recorded in a section and a chalk-based depression containing a brick fragment was recorded 'in the pumping station area' (Vatcher 1971a).

Medieval features and artefacts were also found in Butler's Field during excavations by R. Mount in 1985, close to the line of the sewer trench (B26). Trench J, at the north end of the field (SU 0979 6983), contained large quantities of daub, animal bone, and charcoal, and over 2200 sherds of medieval pottery associated with a ditch terminal, small pits, stake-holes, and gullies perhaps delineating plots or property boundaries dating to the mid 12th–late 13th century (Mount 1991, figure 12). Further finds were made in other test pits and auger holes dug as part of a series of palaeo-environmental studies between 1983 and 1986 (Evans et al. 1993). Layer 5 of Mount's 'medieval soil complex' represents settlement and cultivation on the dry valley floor from the mid 12th–late 13th century. This was followed by the abandonment of settlement in this locality, with two foci of settlement being established on slightly higher ground above the floodplain on either side of the Winterbourne, and Butler's Field being put under the plough. The earthworks of the shrunken medieval village at Avebury Trusloe, to the west, may represent more long term settlement commencing at a similar date, although this too eventually contracted in size in favour of Avebury village. Settlement within the Avebury Circle may date from the late 13th century, the earliest record of the village, which refers to the dyke of the Britons 'Waledich', dating to Assize Roll of 1289.

During the Stage 1 geophysical survey, strongly enhanced magnetic susceptibility readings (B27) were recorded in the central and southern part of Butler's Field (SU 0990 6960) (GSB 1992a, figure 6.1). Immediately to the east of Butler's Field, a geophysical survey was undertaken in 1984 prior to the northward extension of the Avebury South Car Park, in which magnetometer and resistivity surveys detected three or more substantial features, one c. 10 m across (B28) (David 1984). Subsequent excavations in 1985 by P. Harding (B29) identified a number of late medieval features, including a pit and a stone filled trench or ditch, possibly a wall foundation, yielding late medieval pottery (Borthwick 1985). To the north were ditches, a hollow-way and bank running 250 m to the south of, and parallel to, Avebury High Street. These may have served as the village boundary.

There is little archaeological evidence for continuity of settlement from the Saxon period into the medieval period. St James' Church, built in the 9th or 10th century AD, seems to have established a permanent ecclesiastical presence of some importance and was recorded in the *Domesday* Book in 1086 as having at least one resident priest, Rainbold (possibly the Chancellor of Edward I). By 1133 the parish church had been granted to Cirencester Abbey, the richest Augustinian abbey in England (it was on the lands of this estate, on the west side of the river, that Truslow Manor was later built).

In 1114, however, a Benedictine priory (one of two alien cells in England of the Benedictine Abbey of St George de Boscherville near Rouen) had been established on the site of what is now Avebury Manor, possibly to manage lands granted by William de Tancarville (Knowles 1956). In 1142 the priory was granted a license for its own chapel and a series of disputes arose between the two abbeys about the right to hold divine service in the monks' chapel and the payment of tithes. In the mid 13th century, tithes payable by the Benedictine priory show that the monks had up to 750 sheep and in Wiltshire by this time, sheep farming and wool marketing on the large lay and ecclesiastical estates were highly organised concerns. Ringwood (1987) suggests that there may have been a link between the Priory and Butler's Field, sheep bone dominating the bone assemblage from the medieval contexts from Mount's excavations. The priory was dissolved in 1391, and granted to Winchester College, and then in 1411 to Fotheringay College in Northamptonshire. In 1545 it was acquired by the Crown and sold the next year to Sir William Sharington. The earliest part of the present Avebury Manor was built in the 1550s.

Earthworks to the south of Village Street in Beckhampton, represent the remains of that village's medieval settlement (A20), the eastern edge of which extends into the south-west corner of the study corridor at SU 0900 6800 (SMR no. SU 06NE452) (Fig. 4). To the north-east of Beckhampton, two features are interpreted as medieval (or post-medieval) field boundaries. One consists of a straight ditch, 320 m long, running east-north-east to west-south-west parallel to the road (A21). It is visible in air photographs as a crop mark in a field on the north side of the A4361. Two associated ditches join it at right angles, one approximately 50 m long crossing it at the midpoint (SU 0915 6917), the other 75 m to the west, running 30 m north from it. The other feature, running at a right angle to the road on its south side, in the field known as The Paddock, is a well preserved bank (A22), approximately 2.5 m wide and 0.5 m high, running north-west to south-east at SU 0910 6903, the south-east end of which runs over the west side of Beckhampton barrow 4 (A4) (SMR no. SU 06NE834; RCHME 1992b).

To the east of Beckhampton, three parallel strip lynchets (A23), centred on SU 0912 6885, were identified from air photographs running east–west across the slope to the south of the barrow cemetery. Although they are not easily dated, this form of lynchet is almost certainly of medieval date. Further east, outside the study corridor, is a further series of seven parallel lynchets on the same alignment (RCHME) 1992b: RCHME) SU0969/6, 8 September 1934). Faint traces of two strip lynchets (B30) were also visible on air photographs on the south-west facing slope of Waden Hill, centred on SU 1060 6840. They measured just over 0.5 km in length, running north-west to south-east (RCHME) 1992b).

The Saxon settlements at East Kennett and West Kennett also continued into the medieval period, the areas of settlement impinging on the corridor of interest in West Kennett (B31) at SU 1000 6830 (SMR no. SU 16NW451) (Fig. 5), and at East Kennett (C6) at SU 1170

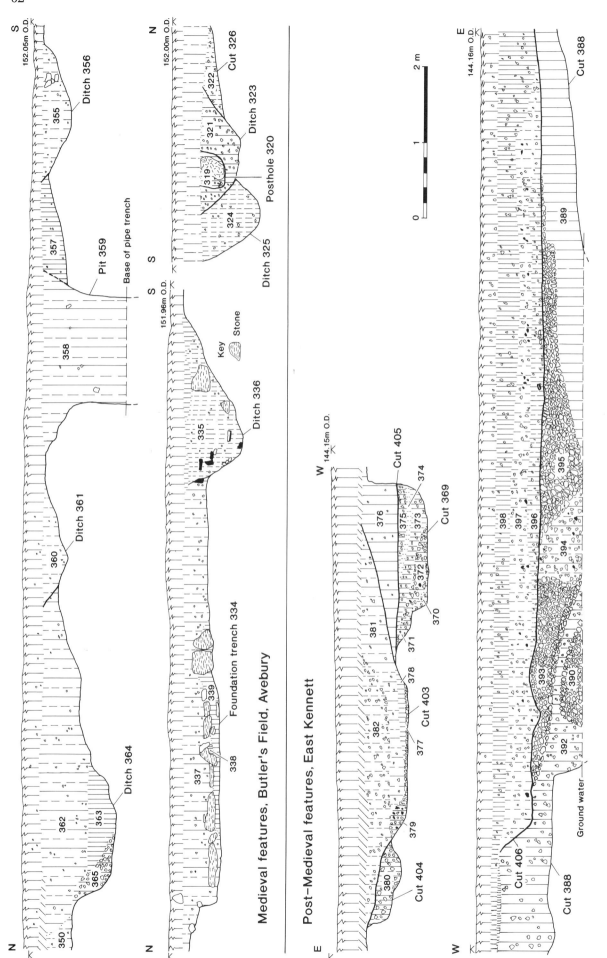

Medieval features, Butler's Field, Avebury

Post-Medieval features, East Kennett

Figure 18 Upper panel: medieval features from Butler's field, Avebury; lower panel: post-medieval features from East Kennett

6750 (SMR no. SU16NW450) (Fig. 21). A late medieval iron key (C.7) was found in 1925 in East Kennett in the vicinity of SU 115 677 (SMR no. SU 16NW462).

To the south-west of St Michael's Church, West Overton, there are extensive and well preserved earthworks (D4), most of which lie outside the study corridor at SU 1340 6810 (SMR no. SU 16NW411) (Fig. 6). These represent the remains of the medieval village of East Overton. A series of strip lynchets (D5), centred on SU 1345 6820, were faintly visible on aerial photographs, running east–west across Pound Field to the east of the village (RCHME) 1992b).

Results of the Watching Brief

Saxon Period

No features which could be assigned a Saxon date were recorded during the watching brief. However, a number of sherds of pottery, possibly Saxon in date, were recovered from three features, as follows:

Pound Field barrow ditch, West Overton

A single sherd (6 g) of possibly Saxon pottery was found in the fifth fill (3) of subdivision 1 of the ring-ditch (Fig. 6). This is a featureless body sherd in a vegetable-tempered fabric (Fabric V900), probably of local manufacture. Although the use of organic materials as temper is generally considered to be a characteristic feature of Early to Middle Saxon pottery (c. 5th–7th centuries AD), it is also commonly used in Middle to later Iron Age ceramics, as identified at Rucstalls Hill (Oliver and Applin 1979, 59–60), Brighton Hill South, near Basingstoke (Fasham et al. 1995), and Silchester (Timby 1985) in Hampshire, and at Riseley Farm, Swallowfield in Berkshire (Lobb and Morris forthcoming). The dating of this sherd is, therefore, uncertain; it contains less organic material than the Saxon sherds from Butler's Field (Fabric V400, see below) and the Fabric G1 sherds from the third fill of the Pound Field Barrow ditch indicate the potential for 1st millennium BC material in this area. However, the possibility that Fabric V900 sherd may be of Saxon date cannot be excluded as it occurs at a higher level than the Fabric G1 sherds in the ditch's stratigraphic sequence.

Fabric V900 Soft, irregularly fired fabric with oxidised surfaces and an unoxidised core; contains moderate to common quartz and muscovite mica <0.125 mm, sparse carbonised vegetable material or linear vesicles up to 3 mm across and rare iron oxides <0.5 mm. Handmade.

Fill 322, Butler's Field, Avebury

Three sherds of early to middle Saxon pottery, representing the earliest material recovered from Butler's Field, were found in the very dark greyish–brown silty clay fill 322 of cut 326, itself cut by the north side of ditch 323 (Fig. 18). These vegetable-tempered sherds (Fabric V400) were found in association with a glazed sandy ware jug sherd (Fabric Q400) of 13th–14th century AD. date. The precise position of this layer in the stratigraphic sequence is unclear (see description below), although it is likely that the Saxon sherds are residual in this context. The proximity of Saxon settlement identified in earlier excavations in the vicinity renders the occurrence of these sherds unsurprising.

Fabric V400 Soft, unoxidised fabric containing common to abundant microscopic quartz/mica < 0.125 mm, sparse carbonised vegetable material or elongated voids 605 mm long and rare iron oxides 601 mm. Handmade. Mid greyish–brown in colour. Source uncertain but probably local. Early/Middle Saxon.

Ditch 383, East Kennett

One sherd of vegetable-tempered pottery, weighing less than 1 g, was recovered during the processing of an environmental sample from the lowest visible fill (384) of this otherwise undated feature. As discussed above, the differences in vegetable-tempered pottery of Iron Age and Saxon date in this area are almost impossible to discern, especially in small featureless bodies. Nonetheless, the quantity of vegetable material in this sherd does suggest greater similarity to the Fabric V400 sherds from Butler's Field than to the Fabric V900 sherds from the Pound Field Barrow ditch.

Discussion

While the Winterbourne Romano-British site was occupied into the 5th century AD, no relationship between it and the origins of Saxon settlement in the Avebury area can be demonstrated. The absence of any unambiguous features of Saxon date and the very small number of finds from this period mean that the watching brief added little to present knowledge. The sherds of vegetable-tempered pottery from Butler's Field and from north of East Kennett Manor does little more than confirm the known presence of Saxon activity in these areas.

Medieval Period

Dated medieval features recorded in the pipe trench were limited to Butler's Field, Avebury, where they add to the known settlement on the south-west side of Avebury village. However, other features of probable medieval date, namely the strip lynchets visible at Beckhampton, Waden Hill, and West Overton, were also recorded during the course of the watching brief, although the lack of finds from them prevent certainty as to their date.

Butler's Field medieval settlement, Avebury

During the sewer pipe replacement, a number of features of medieval date, including pits, ditches, and a possible wall foundation trench were recorded over c.

110 m in the pipe trench in Butler's Field. Other undated features, including 14 ditches, may be of a comparable date.

Foundation Trench 334
None of the features recorded by Vatcher in the pipe trench near the Avebury pumping station could be conclusively identified during the watching brief. However, the sarsen wall foundation, interpreted by her as a medieval boundary wall, may be related to feature 334 (Fig. 18, Pl. 7), although at B.226–232 m (OD 151.7 m), it is some distance from the Avebury pumping station, the general location mentioned by Vatcher.

The feature was 5.7 m long, truncated by ditch 336 at its south end, and up to 0.42 m deep with a steep side at the north end and a flat base. Its primary fill, 339, was a light brownish–grey silty clay, containing fragments of charcoal towards its north end. Contained within it, and spread over 3.2 m from the north end, were bedded a number of laid sarsen stones up to 0.5 m long and 0.15 m thick (338), possibly forming the foundation of a wall. They were sealed by a layer of grey silt loam (337) containing a single sherd of 13th–14th-century pottery. The orientation of this feature could not be determined, although if aligned north–south, like Vatcher's 1 m wide foundation, this would account for

its elongated section, the pipe trench at this point running north-north-west.

Pit 359
A single pit (1.4 m wide) was recorded in the east side of the pipe trench at B.137–9 m (OD 151.8 m) (Fig. 18). It had vertical sides, apart from shallow lips on either side giving a width at the top of *c.* 2.4 m. It was over 1.3 m deep continuing below the base of the pipe trench. It contained a grey silt loam, fill 358, containing charcoal and pottery of 13th–14th century date.

Ditch 325 and Cut 326
Ditch 325 (Fig. 18) was recorded running east to west at B.242 m (OD 151.6 m). It was at least 1.1 m wide and 0.8 m deep with a steep U-shaped profile and was filled with a greyish–brown silty clay (324) containing worked flint, slag, and sherds of 13th–14th-century pottery. The north side of the ditch was truncated by a later undated ditch 323, to the north of which was a layer of very dark greyish–brown silty clay 322, also cut by ditch 323. This layer filled cut 326, which measured 0.3 m deep and at least 1.2 m wide with a shallow sloping north side, containing pottery of a similar date as well as residual sherds of Saxon date (*see* above) and charcoal. It is possible that cut 326 represents the shallow upper lip to

Plate 7   Medieval foundation trench 334, in Butler's Field, Avebury

the north side of ditch 325. However, any stratigraphical relationship between the two cuts is masked in the section by the later ditch 323.

Ditch 336
Truncating the south end of foundation trench 334, at B.232–4 m (OD 151.8 m), was a ditch 2.3 m wide and 0.8 m deep with a U-shaped profile steeper on its north side than its south (Fig. 18). Its fill, 335, was a very dark grey silty loam containing a number of large pieces of sarsen, as well as animal bone, a sandstone roof tile and sherds of 13th–14th-century pottery. Charred plant remains were analysed from this feature.

Ditch 361
This shallow V-shaped ditch, recorded at B.135–6 m (OD 151.8 m), was 1.3 m wide and 0.31 m deep and filled with a grey silty loam, 360, containing pottery of 13th–14th century date (Fig. 18). Its north side cut the upper fill of ditch 364 (below).

Ditch 364
This ditch was recorded at B.130–5 m (OD 151.8 m) (Fig. 18). It was c. 4 m wide at the top, with a steep side to the north and a very shallow irregular side to the south, cut at the southern edge by ditch 361. It was 0.8 m deep with a flattish base, with its primary fill 365 of greyish–brown silty loam, 0.35 m thick and containing some large chalk fragments, lying against the north side. This was overlain towards the base of the cut by 0.36 m thick layer of light brownish–grey silty clay, 363. The upper ditch fill (362, 0.65 m thick) consisted of a layer of grey silty loam and was indistinguishable from a layer of alluvial silt, 350, 0.35 m thick, which extended beyond the north side ditch.

Undated ditch 383, East Kennett
This substantial ditch, aligned north–south, was recorded north-west of East Kennett Manor at C.343–8 m (OD 143.3 m). It extended below the base of the pipe trench and was 6 m wide with shallow sides and over 1 m deep. The lowest visible fills on either side were layers of flint gravel in a brown silty clay matrix with frequent flecks of chalk. That on the west side (385) was 0.2 m thick, while that on the east side (384) was 0.5 m thick. These were overlain in the centre of the cut by a layer of greyish–brown silty clay (386). Filling the upper part of the ditch and extending beyond its sides, was a 0.82 m thick layer of very dark greyish–brown silt loam (387) containing a number of large sarsen stones. This also extended over the post-medieval feature 406 to the west.

Bulk soil samples for environmental analysis were taken from layers 384, 386, and 387, two of which produced sherds of pottery. One sherd of vegetable-tempered pottery, of either Iron Age or Saxon date, from layer 384 has already been discussed above under un-associated Saxon finds. However, the small size of this sherd makes it likely to be residual and the charred plant remains from the ditch (see below) are comparable

with medieval or post-medieval assemblages. Two other sherds derived from the layer sealing the ditch, layer 387. One, weighing less than 1 g, is probably of Romano-British date (Fabric E101 or Q100—see fabrics for the Winterbourne Romano-British settlement listed above), while the other (10 g) is a featureless coarseware body of Minety ware (Fabric E423) of 14th–15th century date. However, the clear post-medieval date of feature 406, also sealed by layer 387, indicates that these latter sherds, at least, are residual and, therefore, provide no evidence as to the date of this ditch. Nevertheless, the plant remains (see below) and the proximity of the East Kennett medieval settlement, suggest that this feature is not earlier than medieval and is probably associated with the medieval settlement (Fig. 21). The samples also yielded numerous fragments of animal bone.

Strip lynchets

Beckhampton
A negative lynchet, 40, was recorded at A.102–7 m (OD 163.8 m–164.1 m) and consisted of a terrace 6 m long, shallowing to its north (uphill) side and with a 0.4 m deep hollow to the south. It contained a series of layers of brown silt loam containing a variable amount of chalk (contexts 41–4) filling it from up-slope. The lynchet is in the vicinity of the groups of strip lynchets identified in air photographs (A23) (Fig. 4), and, although its position is some 40 m north of the most northerly of the western group, it is likely that it forms part of this group, the full extent of which may not have been visible in the air photographs.

Waden Hill
Both of the strip lynchets visible on air photogaphs (B30) (Fig. 4) were detected as negative lynchets in the pipe trench. Measuring some 400 m long, and recorded in the pipe trench at B.1191–8 m (OD 167.9 m), was negative lynchet 72, corresponding to the eastern (uphill) of the two lynchets, immediately to the east of the 'Stukeley' barrow. It consisted of a shallow, flat-based terrace, 72 (Fig. 7; Pl. 2), with a moderately steep uphill side at the east end and measured 5 m wide and up to 0.66 m deep. Its primary fill, 67, on the base of the cut, was a 0.11 m thick layer of pale brown silt. This was overlain by a layer of dark yellowish–brown silt loam (70) filling the east end of the cut and thinning out at c. 2 m from that end. Over this was a layer of dark brown silt loam (69), 0.3 m thick, thinning towards the downhill end. The upper fill of lynchet 68 was marginally stonier and extended downhill to seal the fill of the ring-ditch.

Negative lynchet 92, corresponded to the western (downhill) lynchet, measuring c. 700 m long with its southern end crossing the pipe trench at B.1885–90 m (OD 158.5 m). It was visible as a shallow terrace (cut 92), up to 0.5 m deep, sloping down to the west. Its primary fill (93) was a 0.1 m thick layer of light yellowish–brown silt loam, which was overlain by brown silt loam up to 0.5 m thick (95). These were overlain by a layer of hillwash, 96, which started at the uphill edge of the cut and continued over the lynchet, becoming deeper towards the bottom of the hill.

West Overton
Negative lynchet 20 (Fig. 7) straddled the north-western section 8 of the Pound Field barrow ring-ditch and corresponded to the second most northerly of the strip lynchets visible in the air photographs (D5) (Fig. 6). It was recorded in the pipe trench as a negative lynchet, at between approximately D.96–107 m. It appeared as a shallow terrace cutting into the ditch's upper fills. The primary fill in the base of the feature was a dark yellowish–brown loam (13), 0.17 m thick, containing a high proportion of chalk rubble, possibly eroded barrow material. Overlying this was a layer of dark yellowish–brown silty loam, 14, also containing some chalk, which was thickest (0.5 m) over the ditch. This layer extended beyond both the ditch and the terrace on both sides, as a thin layer reaching close to the centre of the ring-ditch and for some 5 m downhill.

Medieval Finds, by Rachael Seager Smith

Worked stone
Two fragmentary stone objects were found in the pipe trench in Butler's Field. Pieces of a medium-grained, calcareous white sandstone roof tile were found in ditch 336. A hole had been drilled through it close to the original peg hole, possibly indicating its repair and reuse after initial damage. The second stone fragment, a piece of flat medium to coarse-grained sandstone, c. 0.22 m thick, was found in pit 359 and is also likely to be part of a stone roof tile or other building stone. Both pieces were found in association with pottery of 13th–14th century AD date and are likely to derive from medieval activity in the area.

Pottery
A total of 30 sherds (306 g) of medieval pottery was recovered from Butler's Field (plus 3 Saxon sherds). It was recorded according to the standard Wessex Archaeology guidelines for the analysis of pottery (Morris 1992), using the same procedures and descriptive terminology as described for the Romano-British pottery above. In total, four fabric types, together with a range of sandy coarseware fabrics of unknown source (here considered as a single group for convenience), were recognised. These fabrics are listed below and their quantification (number and weight of sherds) by feature and context is summarised in Table 13.

All the sherds were comparatively small and few vessel forms were recognisable. These comprise four rim sherds from cooking-pots in Minety, Newbury 'B' (Fig. 19: 1) and Newbury 'C' wares and a bung-hole (Fig. 19: 2) from a Minety ware cistern or bung-hole pot (Musty 1973, fig. 1, 9) from the alluvial deposit 350. Two body sherds, also of Newbury 'B' ware, have combed wavy line decoration. Three of the sandy ware sherds (Fabric Q400) have slip decoration beneath a lead-based glaze on the exterior surface and are probably derived from jugs. All the other sherds were from unidentified coarseware forms. The assemblage is of predominantly 13th–14th century date, with the exception of the two Minety ware sherds, which may continue into the early 15th century, and a late medieval glazed jug sherd from an unknown source.

Table 13 medieval pottery quantification by feature/layer and fabric type (no./weight in grams)

Feature	Layer	E422	E423	E442	E443	Q400	Total	Date
Cut 326	322	–	–	–	–	1/6	1/6	13th–14th century
Ditch 325	324	–	–	3/6	–	–	3/6	13th–14th century
Ditch 336	335	1/3	–	1/6	–	3/6	5/15	13th–14th century
Trench 334	337	–	–	–	–	1/5	1/5	13th–14th century
Layer 350	–	–	2/83	11/110	–	–	13/193	13th –early 15th century
Layer 357	–	–	–	–	2/24	–	2/24	13th–14th century
Pit 359	358	2/18	–	–	–	2/18	4/36	13th–14th century
Ditch 361	360	–	–	1/21	–	–	1/21	13th–14th century
Total		3/21	2/83	16/143	2/24	7/35	30/306	

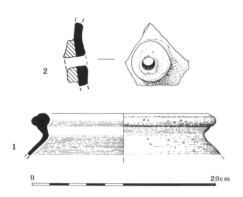

Figure 19   Medieval pottery

Fabric E422 Laverstock-type coarseware. Salisbury area of Wiltshire. 13th/14th century AD date (Musty *et al.* 1969).

Fabric E423 Minety ware. Minety area of north Wiltshire. 14th or 15th century AD. (Musty 1973).

Fabric E442 Newbury 'B' ware, identified at Bartholomew Street, Newbury and believed to be from a local source. 13th/14th century AD (Vince, in prep.).

Fabric E443 Newbury 'C' ware. identified at Bartholomew Street, Newbury and believed to be from a local source. 13th/14th century AD (Vince, forthcoming.).

Fabric Q400 'Catch-all' fabric group for sandy wares of unknown source. Hard or very hard, medium-grained fabrics generally containing moderate quartz < 0.5 mm and rare iron oxides of a similar size. The majority of sherds are also slightly calcareous containing rare, soft, white limestone fragments up to 1 mm long. Oxidised throughout or with an unoxidised core. Some sherds have a lead-based glaze and slip decoration on the exterior surface, 13th–15th century AD.

Environmental Analysis

Molluscan analysis in Butler's Field,
by Rosina Mount

A period of flooding and alluviation, recorded in Butler's Field, is datable by the artefacts and radiocarbon dates from the horizons below and above it to sometime between the Bronze Age and the medieval period. Analysis of the sample is considered within this section because of the proximity of the sampled alluvium to the

medieval settlement in Butler's Field. However, there is little datable evidence from the alluvium itself, though the recent find of a possible Romano-British coarseware sherd from the same context falls well within these limits.

Alluvium was sampled for Mollusca at a point near the edge of the floodplain where it was revealed by the pipeline trench. Unfortunately, the line of the trench only exposed a small length of alluvium, the true depth of which is uncertain as it was not reached by the trench, but was, however, in excess of 0.75 m. The aim of the molluscan analysis was to ascertain whether there were any detectable differences in local floodplain environment between this part of the floodplain and that closer to the present river which had previously been investigated by J.G. Evans and the author (Evans *et al.* 1993; Mount 1991).

Despite the fact that the preservation of shells was good, numbers of individuals were relatively low (Table 14). The 1984 series taken from a sample pit closer to the river at the south end of the field had approximately twice as many shells from half the sample weight of sediment. However, numbers were sufficient to enable environmental interpretation. Results were presented as a histogram (Fig. 20) of absolute numbers corrected to 1750 g of soil, as numbers were too low for a meaningful percentage histogram. The histogram can be divided into two local molluscan assemblage biozones.

Biozone 1 (0.72–1.22 m)
This is characterised by very low numbers of shells and is dominated by the aquatic/amphibious species *Lymnaea peregra, Anisus leucostoma,* and *Lymnaea truncatula.* Apart from *Trichia hispida,* terrestrial Mollusca are virtually absent until the top of the zone where new species appear and numbers begin to increase. This is the cause of the peak in assemblage diversity indicated by the Shannon index.

The alluvium indicates inundation of the floodplain by what was presumably overbank floodwater and there is, therefore, the possibility that some or all of the assemblage of zone 1 is allochthonous. However, the composition of the freshwater component indicates that it is possible that these species were actually living on the floodplain. According to Sparks's (1961) ecological groupings of aquatic Mollusca, *Anisus leucostoma* and *Lymnaea truncatula* are slum species, capable of tolerating small bodies of water subject to drying or stagnation. Both species were observed living on the floodplain at Port Meadow in the upper Thames basin, where they and other amphibious snails comprised most of the life and death assemblages of pasture land (Robinson 1988). *Lymnaea peregra* is a member of the catholic group, and will tolerate a wide range of conditions except the worst slums. In order to survive drought, it buries itself in mud until the return of water causes it to become active again (Ellis 1969). However, in the Thames basin, *L. peregra* was seen as unlikely to have lived on the floodplain (Robinson 1988). Alternatively, all three freshwater species may have originated from the river, washed on to the floodplain during the flooding episodes.

Table 14 land Mollusca from the alluvial sequence in Butler's Field

	1094	1095	1096	1097	1098	1099	1100	1101
Context	713							
Depth (cm)	112–122	102–112	92–102	82–92	72–82	66–72	56–66	48–56
Wt (g)	1600	1750	1750	1800	1750	1800	2000	2000
MOLLUSCA								
Terrestrial								
Pomatius elegans (Müller)	–	–	–	–	–	–	–	1
Carychium tridentatum (Risso)	–	–	–	–	–	–	5	2
Succinea spp.	–	–	–	1	–	–	1	–
Cochlicopa lubrica (Müller)	–	–	–	–	–	–	–	1
Cochlicopa lubricella (Porro)	–	–	–	–	–	–	1	–
Cochlicopa spp.	–	–	–	2	2	3	5	8
Vertigo pygmaea (Draparnaud)	–	–	–	–	1	2	–	5
Vertigo spp.	–	–	–	–	–	–	2	–
Pupilla muscorum (Linnaeus)	–	–	–	–	–	–	–	1
Vallonia costata (Müller)	–	–	–	1	3	4	13	13
Vallonia pulchella (Müller)	–	–	–	–	–	–	–	1
Vallonia excentrica Sterki	–	–	2	1	4	5	16	25
Vallonia spp.	–	1	–	1	11	17	49	104
Punctum pygmaeum (Draparnaud)	–	–	–	–	–	–	1	2
Discus rotundatus (Müller)	–	–	–	–	2	2	1	–
Vitrea spp.	–	–	–	–	1	1	–	–
Nesovitrea hammonis (Ström)	–	–	–	–	–	1	1	–
Aegopinella nitidula (Draparnaud)	–	–	–	–	2	1	1	1
Oxychilus cellarius (Müller)	–	–	–	–	2	3	3	2
Limacidae	1	–	1	11	9	19	19	27
Ceciloides acicula (Müller)	1	1	1	2	73	38	70	53
Clausilia bidentata (Ström)	–	1	–	–	2	3	–	–
Clausiliidae	–	–	–	–	–	–	1	1
Helicella itala (Linnaeus)	–	–	1	–	1	5	10	17

Table 14 continued

Sample	1094	1095	1096	1097	1098	1099	1100	1101
Context					713			
Depth (cm)	112–122	102–112	92–102	82–92	72–82	66–72	56–66	48–56
Wt (g)	1600	1750	1750	1800	1750	1800	2000	2000
MOLLUSCA contd								
Trichia hispida (Linnaeus)	3	8	9	17	36	33	90	123
Capaea hortensis (Müller)	–	–	–	–	–	1	–	–
Cepaea / Arianta spp.	1	–	–	–	–	–	1	4
Freshwater/Brackishwater species								
Lymnae peregra	5	1	3	–	5	4	–	–
Lymnaea truncatula	–	5	5	18	1	–	–	1
Anisus leucostoma	–	–	1	4	9	2	–	–
Arionidae	–	–	–	–	1	–	14	25
Taxa	4	5	7	8	16	16	16	17
Shannon index	1.17	1.23	1.54	1.64	2.14	2.20	1.88	1.81
Total	10	16	22	56	92	106	220	339

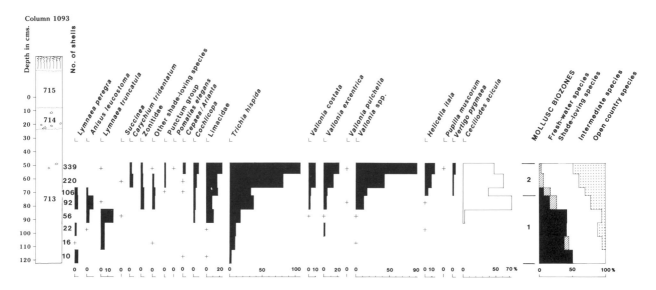

Figure 20   Mollusc histogram from Butler's Field, Avebury

A modern freshwater survey of the River Kennet (Mount 1991) revealed a similar fauna, dominated by *Lymnaea peregra* and *Anisus leucostoma*.

The environment of Zone 1 can, therefore, be interpreted as that of damp floodplain grasslands. Alluvium indicated flooding but this was probably seasonal. The aquatic species may have originated from the river but are all capable of surviving drought and are likely to have actively inhabited the floodplain for at least part of the year. Drier periods would have enabled the survival of *Trichia hispida* and *Vallonia excentrica*.

Biozone 2 (0.48– 0.72 m)

This is characterised by the disappearance of the freshwater species and a rapid increase in terrestrial species, most notably *Trichia hispida* and *Vallonia excentrica*, with *Helicella itala*, *Cochlicopa*, Limacidae and *Vertigo pymaea* also part of this low diversity assemblage. This is an impoverished fauna of grassland. However, the fact that flooding was still occurring is indicated by the lithology which is alluvium. It is unusual that allochthonous freshwater species were not introduced onto the floodplain during inundation. The flooding episodes must have been extremely short in duration and drying out rapid enough to ensure that conditions were not suitable for the aquatic species. It may be that the grassland management regime had altered. In the Thames valley, for example, it has been observed that pasture and hay meadow each have different and characteristic assemblages of aquatic and terrestrial Mollusca (Robinson 1988). Alternatively, the hydrological regime may have altered, perhaps with management of the river occurring for the first time.

In conclusion, the environment indicated is one of floodplain grasslands subject to seasonal flooding episodes. A gradual drying out of the floodplain through time is indicated, with the periods of standing water becoming shorter and therefore enabling the development of an entirely terrestrial molluscan fauna. From the investigation of deposits on other parts of the floodplain and the analysis of samples taken from the south end of Butler's Field, it is known that the period of alluviation is succeeded by the development of a terrestrial soil over the entire floodplain. Results from this new series indicate that the local environment was drier on this part of the floodplain, which is to be expected from its location. Sample series Av6 from towards the centre of the floodplain indicated that conditions remained wet enough for the survival of aquatic/amphibious species throughout the alluvium deposit, with the development of a terrestrial fauna only occurring once the flooding had ceased. In contrast, the floodplain edge would be the first to show the effects of a contraction in flooding from the river in the composition of its molluscan fauna.

Land Mollusca from the Waden Hill lynchet,
by Sarah F. Wyles and Michael J. Allen

Two spot samples were taken from negative lynchet 72 (Fig. 7) adjacent to the 'Stukeley' barrow which was sealed by ploughsoil and white chalk rubble (for methods and terminology *see* above).

Tertiary fill (69)	Dark brown (10YR 3/3) silt loam with under 1% chalk pieces up to 0.02 m.
Secondary fill (67)	Pale brown (10YR 6/3) silt with *c.* 2% chalk pieces up to 0.01 m.

Layer 69

The assemblage is dominated by the *Vallonias*, with other significant species being *Trichia hispida*, *Pupilla muscorum*, *Vertigo pygmaea*, and *Helicella itala*. The Introduced Helicellids and *Lymnaea truncatula* also occur. The shade-loving element, mainly the Zonatids and Punctum group, accounts for *c.* 10% of this zone.

Layer 67
This is characterised by the continued dominance of the *Vallonias*, but increasingly with *Pupilla muscorum*. *Helicella itala* and the shade-loving species, mainly the Zonatids, decline. There is a small increase in the Introduced Helicellids and *Helix aspersa*.

Interpretation
The samples from the negative lynchet (zone 5) postdate its creation and indicate a medieval environment of short grazed grassland, with the shade-loving species, and the Punctum group in particular, living in a localised mesic micro environment. In the upper fill, the assemblage indicates a more established grassland. A medieval or later date is confirmed by to the occurrence of the Introduced Helicellids in both samples, and the fauna probably represent long grassy verges at the edge of the medieval field against the barrow.

Animal bone from Butler's Field, *by Mary Iles*
A total of 546 bones was recovered from both hand retrieved and sieved material from medieval contexts of which 95 (17.4%) were identified to species and element (Table 15). However, only two (0.4%) came from the main domesticates. The remainder were classified as cattle/horse size, or unidentifiable.

Amphibians and fish
Three fish bones were recovered, one of which was from herring (*Clupea harengus*). This is in contrast to the Romano-British period, where the identified fish was eel (*Anguilla anguilla*). One frog bone was identified. The remainder could not be classified beyond amphibian. These are also likely to be pit fall victims, as is probably the case in the Romano-British assemblage.

Mammals
The sheep/goat bone recovered (a radius) showed no evidence of butchery. It is distally unfused and therefore comes from an individual less than 3.5 years of age. The presence of only two bones from the major domesticates makes the comparison with other medieval sites in the region invalid.

Charred plant remains from the medieval ditch in Butler's Field, *by Robert G. Scaife*
A single sample from ditch 336 in the Butler's Field medieval settlement (Table 16) produced identifiable charred plant remains. Numbers of charred remains were low and substantially lower than both the Romano-British and the undated (medieval or post-medieval) samples. Abraded caryopses were present, but no chaff of *Triticum* cf *aestivum* type (bread wheat) and barley; there was a high proportion of unidentified fragments. One vetch or tare (*Vicia/Lathyrus*) was the only charred non-cereal remain present.

Charred Plant Remains from ditch 383 at East Kennett, *by Robert G. Scaife*
Three samples from ditch 383 produced identifiable charred plant remains (Table 16). Overall numbers of charred remains were substantially lower than in the earlier Romano-British contexts (compare Table 11 with Table 16). The remains are, however, equally as diagnostic with typical medieval assemblages recorded. Caryopses of *Triticum aestivum* type (*T. aestivo-compactum*/hexaploid bread wheat) and T. cf. aestivum type were the predominant cereal form (predominantly contexts 386 and 387). Small numbers of other cereal types included *Hordeum* sp. (4 caryopses), *Avena* sp. and cf. *Avena* sp. (6 caryopses). Preservation was, in general, very poor with large numbers of fragmented and badly distorted caryopses. Chaff remains were present but were again badly degraded and fragmentary, with indications of having been abraded/weathered. Seeds remains were extremely sparse but included *Fallopia convolvulus* and *Galium aparine*.

Discussion
Although this ditch does not contain such well preserved or abundant cereal remains as those of the Romano-British contexts, the remains are typical of the medieval period, comprising *Triticum aestivum* type; that is, free threshing hexaploid bread wheat (*T. compactum* and *T. aestivum*). These cereal remains represent the cultivation of crops of very similar character to those used today in Britain. Unlike the spelt

Table 15 medieval animal bone from Butler's Field

Context	Pit 336 Fill 335		Alluvium 350	Total
	Hand	Sieve	Hand	
Cattle	–	–	1	1
Sheep/goat	1	–	–	1
Fish	–	3	–	3
Amphibian	–	67	–	67
Rodent	–	23	–	23
Sub-total	1	93	1	95
Unidentifiable	–	450	1	451
Total	1	543	2	546

Table 16 charred plant remains from medieval or post-medieval ditches

	Medieval ditch	Medieval or post-medieval ditch		
Feature no.	336	383	383	383
Context	335	384	387	386
Sample	1092	1102	1104	1103
GRAIN				
Triticum aestivum type	1	12	26	42
Triticum cf. *aestivum* type	–	–	20	6
Triticum spelta type	–	–	–	–
Triticum cf. *spelta* type	–	–	–	–
Triticum indet	4	3	3	6
Hordeum sp.	–	1	3	–
cf. *Hordeum*	1	–	–	–
Avena sp.	–	–	1	1
cf. *Avena*	–	1	3	–
Bromus / *Avena*	–	–	–	–
Bromus secalinus	–	–	1	–
Indet. whole	–	–	–	–
Indet. frags	89	91	399	261
CHAFF				
gb. *Triticum spelta*	–	–	–	–
gb. *Triticum* cf. *spelta*	–	–	–	–
gb. *Triticum dicoccum*	–	–	–	–
gb. indet. frags	–	–	4	–
sf. *Triticum spelta*	–	–	–	–
sf. *Tr-iticum dicoccum*	–	–	–	–
sf. indet.	–	–	27	48
int. *Triticum spelta*	–	–	3	–
Int. indet.	–	–	1	–
Palea/lemma frags	–	–	–	–
CHAFF contd.				
Culm nodes	–	–	1	–
Awns	–	**	–	–
Straw	–	–	–	–
SEEDS				
Sambucus nigra (mineralised)	–	–	–	–
Corylus avellana (nut frags)	–	–	–	–
Prunus / *Crataegus* (thorn)	–	–	–	–
Ranuculus a/r/b	–	–	–	–
Chenopodium cf. *album*	–	–	–	–
cf. *Pisum*	–	–	–	–
Trifolium sp.	–	–	6	–
Medicago sp.	–	–	–	–
Vicia / *Lathyrus*	1	–	–	–
Rumex sp.	–	–	–	–
Cirsium sp.	–	–	–	–
cf. *Centaurea*	–	–	–	–
Taraxacum officinale	–	–	–	–
Anthriscus	–	–	–	–
Graminae/large	–	–	1	–
Graminae/small	–	–	–	–
Unidentified	–	–	–	–
Galium aparine	–	–	1	–
Fallopia convolvulus	–	–	1	–

gb. = glume base

wheat of the Romano-British contexts, it seems likely that this bread wheat was being grown locally because of the presence of chaff debris indicating 'on-site' crop processing. As with spelt, cultivation may have been on heavier clay and alluvial soils. The few weed seeds present indicate that the crops had already been 'cleaned' before the grain was burnt accidentally or deliberately.

In conclusion, the charred plant remains are comparable with medieval or post-medieval assemblages and the predominance of hexaploid bread wheat and the small numbers of spelt wheat indicate that the remains at least are not earlier than the Romano-British period and are unlikely to be of Saxon date. In this respect the charred plant remains are typical of medieval but also post-medieval assemblages and therefore the occurrence of the Saxon sherd is most likely to be residual and the ditch is considered to be of medieval or post-medieval date.

Discussion

There is little evidence that the settlement which established itself on the western side of the Avebury Circle in the Saxon period continued in occupation into the medieval period, and the form of the early medieval settlement at Avebury remains unclear. The results of the watching brief confirm the presence of medieval settlement activity in Butler's Field as previously indicated by Mount's 1985 excavations (Mount 1991). The nature of the watching brief, however, meant that only a small sample of artefactual and environmental material was collected, with only eight of the 21 features providing dating evidence. Therefore, while the watching brief extended the area of known settlement towards the south of Butler's Field, it provided only a limited amount of new information as to the nature of the settlement. The medieval pottery recovered from features cut by the pipe trench is no earlier than the 13th century, a date that falls within the end of the range of dates suggested by the larger pottery assemblage, and by the radiocarbon dates, from Mount's excavations.

The pipe trench also provided disparate evidence of the medieval environment. The alluvial and colluvial sequences from the valley floor in Butler's Field indicated a floodplain grassland with seasonal (winter or spring) flooding in areas adjacent to the medieval settlement, while further down the Winterbourne, colluvial deposits indicate colluviation on the valley floor over alluvium. This increased colluviation may reflect larger areas under the plough locally, or that the soils had become more susceptible to local erosion due to continued tillage. The hillwash is typical of continual ploughing attrition and rill erosion from long-term arable fields (cf. Allen 1991). No major catastrophic erosion episodes (gravel fans) were noticed in the colluvial sequences which may indicate that the soils were not exhaustively tilled or that conditions requiring such erosion did not occur. Cultivation on Waden Hill, as at Beckhampton and West Overton, is indicated by the presence of medieval lynchets. The sediment and lynchet formation itself is testimony to that, but the molluscan evidence suggests grassland. This superficially conflicting evidence may suggest a grassy field boundary, or that downland pasture existed too.

6. The Post-Medieval Period

Archaeological Background

While post-medieval pottery was found in features during excavations by P. Harding in 1985 in advance of the car park extension at Avebury (B32) (Borthwick 1985) (Fig. 17), the most visible manifestation of post-medieval activity outside the immediate areas of settlement are those surviving channels and earthworks which relate to the water meadow management of the Kennet and Winterbourne valley floors. There is a complex of earthworks on both sides of the Winterbourne in Butler's Field, Avebury (B33) (RCHME) Earthwork Survey of Avebury and Avebury Truslow), some of which were also detected by the geophysical survey (B27) (GSB 1992a, 1.3 and 1.7). Air photographs reveal further evidence of abandoned water meadow channels between the A4361 trunk road and Swallowhead Springs south of the A4 trunk road (B34), and on the south side of the River Kennet (C8) (Fig. 21), just east of the line of the Ridgeway in East Kennett. These are likely to be dated to the late 18th and early 19th centuries (RCHME 1992b, page 12–13).

Air photographs have revealed a series of parallel strips (D6) in an area called the Blacksmith's Garden to the north of St Michael's Church, West Overton (Fig. 6). These are probably the result of post-medieval cultivation (RCHME 1992b).

Results of the Watching Brief

The only dated post-medieval features were recorded in the East Kennett section of the pipeline. Two wide features of uncertain character, both having more than one phase and showing evidence of recutting, were recorded on the north side of East Kennett Manor, and may relate to the Manor.

East Kennett Manor

Feature 369/403/405

A complex feature comprising three phases with a combined width of 6 m, was recorded at 450–6 m (OD 143.7 m). The earliest component, cut 369, was situated at the west end of the feature (Fig. 18; Pl. 8). It was 0.85 m deep with a vertical western side curving at the base to meet a flat base 1.6 m wide. Its east side was stepped in profile and rose 0.45 m from the base, at which level it was truncated by cut 405 (Fig. 18). The original cut, possibly a ditch, was filled with a series of distinct layers sloping in from the east side, all containing a high proportion of flint gravel. The primary fills, lying against the east side, were a brown sandy silt at the base (370) and a very dark greyish–brown silt loam at the top (371). These were overlain by a 0.24 m thick layer of light yellowish–brown sandy silt, 372, filling the base of the cut and containing post-medieval brick. Over this were layers of very dark greyish–brown silty clay, 373, dark yellowish–brown silt loam (374), and dark brown silt loam (375).

These fills were all truncated, 0.4 m from the base of the cut, by the level base of cut 405. This second cut shared its vertical western side with 369 but was itself truncated at its east side by a third cut, so that its original width could not be determined. It was, however, at least 2.4 m wide and 0.4 m deep with a single homogeneous fill of brown/dark brown silt loam (376) containing a high proportion of very fine flint gravel.

Ditch 403, the final cut in the sequence, truncating both cut 405 and a natural feature 404 to the east, was 5.4 m wide and 0.65 m deep. The sides, both of which had a similar profile, were very shallow and straight, dipping to moderately steep 0.2 m from the flat 1.7 m wide base. The primary fill, 377, in the base of the cut was a 0.04 m thick layer of dark greyish–brown silty clay with a high proportion of flint gravel. This was overlain on the west side by a 0.1m thick layer of dark yellowish–brown sandy silt (378), and on the east by a 0.2 m thick layer of brown silty clay (379) containing patches of unmixed chalky flint gravel, and a piece of post-medieval brick. Overlying these basal layers were two layers of silt loam, the lower dark brown layer 381 up to 0.4 m thick sloping in from the west side, the upper brown/dark brown layer 382 representing the top fill of the ditch.

Because only the south side of the original pipe trench was fully exposed at this point, it was not possible to determine the alignment of this feature and it is possible that not all its component parts had the same orientation. The elongated profile of ditch 403 in particular may represent a simple V-shaped ditch crossing the trench at a shallow angle.

Feature 388/406

A two phase feature was recorded on the northern edge of East Kennett medieval settlement (Fig. 21) at 327–39 (OD 143.9 m). Because only the north side of the original pipe trench was exposed at this point its alignment could not be determined. The first phase, 388 (Fig. 18), for which there was no direct dating evidence, was truncated by a subsequent post-medieval cut 406.

Cut 388 was at least 11 m long and extended below the base of the pipe trench so that only the upper 0.8 m of its fills could be recorded. To the west its side had an irregular stepped profile, steep at the top before levelling onto a 2.5 m wide flat terrace at a depth of 0.4 m, then sloping steeply down below the base of the pipe trench. The east side in contrast was very shallow and relatively straight. The primary fill against the east side was a layer of dark greyish–brown clay (389) 0.47 m thick. On the west side the cut was filled with a series of layers apparently dumped from the west. The lowest visible of these, 390, consisted of a pile of clean chalk rubble (0.5–2.5 m) tipped from the west side of the cut. This was sealed by a layer of very dark greyish–brown silty clay (392) up to 0.75 m thick, covering all of the west side and

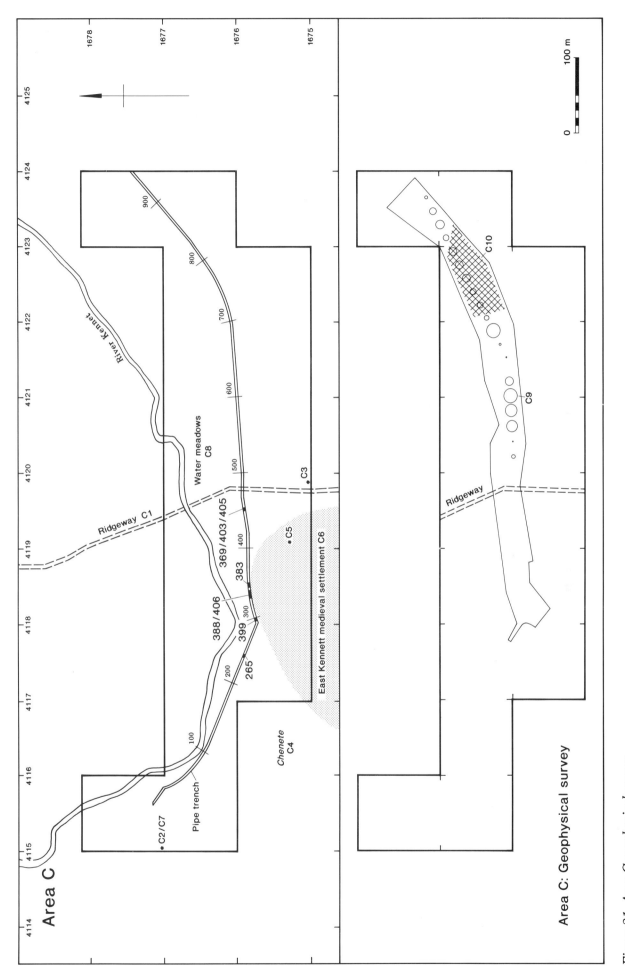

Figure 21 Area C geophysical survey

Plate 8   Post-medieval feature 369/403/405, north of East Kennett Manor

thinning to 0.15 m where it dipped below the base of the pipe trench in the centre of the cut. This in turn was overlain by three layers of dumped chalk rubble, each c. 0.5 m thick, the uppermost extending across to the east side of the cut. The lower and upper layers, (contexts 393 and 395), consisted of clean chalk, the middle layer, 394, consisting of chalk in a pale brown silty clay matrix. All the layers, with the exception being the lowest dump of chalk, 390, were truncated by a subsequent cut, 406.

The second phase, cut 406, was at least 10 m long with a straight, moderately steep side to the west and a flat base rising at a very shallow angle to the east. Its primary fill (396) was a 0.2 m thick layer of very dark greyish–brown silty clay containing a very large quantity of animal bone and a sherd of 13th–14th-century medieval pottery. A total of 30 fragments of animal bone was recovered from this layer, of which six, five horse bones and a single cattle bone, were identified to species. A further 15 fragments were of horse/cattle size, the rest being unidentified. Two of the pieces showed signs of butchery and much of the material appeared to have been deliberately broken up and spread along the base of the feature, but the very small size of the assemblage precludes any meaningful interpretation. Sealing this layer, and filling the rest of the cut, was a stony layer of brown sandy clay (397), containing a considerable quantity of broken late medieval and post-medieval brick The feature was sealed by a layer of very dark

brown silt loam (398, 0.6 m thick) which extended beyond the feature in both directions.

Post-Medieval Finds,
by Rachael Seager Smith

Ceramic building material
Ten pieces (874 g) of ceramic building material were recovered from the East Kennett Manor area. Two fragments (87 g) were found in fill 372 of cut 369. One of these (CBM Fabric 6) is derived from a post-medieval roof tile, the other (CBM Fabric 7), is probably from a brick of medieval or post-medieval date. The remaining pieces, from the upper fill 397 of feature 406, consisted of one fragment of post-medieval roof tile (CBM Fabric 6), a featureless fragment in CBM Fabric 7, and six brick fragments (CBM Fabric 8) also of later medieval or post-medieval date.

CBM Fabric 6   Very hard, dense fabric, moderate to common microscopic quartz/mica, rare iron oxides <0.5 mm, rare off-white or cream grog/clay pellets <2 mm. Generally oxidised, although some examples have a grey core. Moulding sand visible on edges, with one flat surface where these are preserved.

CBM Fabric 7   Hard, fine-grained fabric, moderate microscopic quartz/mica, sparse poorly-sorted iron oxides, 0.5–5 mm across, rare limestone particles <2 mm. Oxidised; brick red in colour. Less 'lumpy' but otherwise visually similar to CBM Fabric 8 below.

CBM Fabric 8   Hard fabric, very lumpy appearance, moderate to common microscopic quartz/mica, < 0.125 mm, moderate sub-rounded quartz 0.25–0.5 mm, and sparse iron oxides up to 5 mm across. Poorly- prepared clay leaving irregular streaks and lumps of pale buff clay in otherwise deep reddish–brown matrix.

Pottery

One sherd (10 g) of medieval pottery was found in the primary fill (396) of feature 406. The sherd, a small fragment from the rim of a cooking pot of a form very similar to type 19 (Fig. 19: 1), is of Newbury 'B' ware (Fabric E442) and is of 13th–14th century AD date. Its close association to large quantities of post-medieval brick indicate that it is residual.

Discussion

A manor house at East Kennett is shown on the 1773 map of Wiltshire by Andrews and Dury. However, the present Manor, a square red brick building in the late Georgian style, with a large service courtyard north of the house, is of early 19th century date, with barns, dovecote, and stables of 18th and 19th century dates. It is possible that the post-medieval features recorded in the pipe trench to the north of the manor, including the apparent filling in of wide hollows, related to the earlier occupation of the manor site and the creation of the meadow between it and the river.

7. Undated Features

Because of the likelihood that some of the undated features, particularly those from within the vicinity of identifiable sites, are contemporary with dated features from those sites, they are described by area or under those sites' headings. This applies both to the results of the desk-based study and geophysical surveys and of the watching brief. It should be borne in mind, however, that they may be unrelated to those sites.

Beckhampton

Desk-Based Study Data

The air photographic survey identified a number of linear features in the vicinity of the Beckhampton barrow cemetery (RCHME 1992b) (Fig. 4). Two parallel ditches (A24), centered on SU 0911 6887, were identified running north–south, approximately 30 m apart, both curving slightly to the west. The western ditch is approximately 90 m long, the eastern approximately 125 m. To the south they cross the medieval strip lynchets. In addition, between the upper two strip lynchets, two short lengths of approximately parallel ditch (A25), centered on SU 0920 2889 running east–west, were faintly visible.

None of the above features and no other undatable features, were recorded in the Beckhampton section of the pipe trench during the course of the watching brief.

Butler's Field, Avebury

Results of the Watching Brief

Twelve undated ditches were recorded among the medieval features in Butler's Field, as well as a single post-hole. Some of these may also be of medieval date, or they may be related to the post-medieval water meadow system (Fig. 10).

Ditch 314
At B.339–42 (OD 151.2 m) the fills of a natural hollow were cut by a ditch visible in both sides of the pipe trench. It was 2.5 m wide and 0.45 m deep with a shallow V-shaped profile. The primary fill, 315, lying against the south side of the cut, was a 0.10 m thick layer of brown/dark brown clay containing frequent pieces of chalk. The main fill (316) was a dark yellowish–brown silty clay, the upper part of which on the north side was completely stone-free (317). The whole feature was covered by a layer of dark greyish–brown silty clay (318), 0.45 m thick.

Ditch 323 and post-hole 320
A ditch was recorded at B.241 m (OD 151.6 m), cutting on its south side medieval ditch 325 and on its north side, layer 322 (*see* above). It was 1.7 m wide and 0.5 m

deep with a shallow V-shaped profile and an irregular base. It was filled with a brown silty clay (321) containing fragments of charcoal. A post-hole (cut 320), 0.45 m wide and 0.32 m deep, was cut into the ditch fill and this was filled with a brown silty clay, 319, containing a large sarsen packing stone.

Ditch 329
This ditch was recorded at B.238–41 m (OD 151.8 m). It was 2.25 m wide and 0.46 m deep, with steep sides and a concave base. Its primary fill (328) was a greyish–brown silty loam, 0.31 m thick. This was overlain by a layer of light grey silty loam (327) containing a few large flint nodules, although it was not clear whether this was a fill or constituted backfill material pressed into the sides of the existing pipe trench.

Ditch 331
Two features, interpreted as two intercutting ditches, were recorded at B.236–7 m (OD 151.7 m). This later ditch, truncating the south side of ditch 333 (below) was 1.42 m wide and 0.26 m deep with a shallow U-shaped profile. Its fill (330) was a pale brown silty clay loam, containing at its base on the north side, a lens of redeposited chalk.

Ditch 333
Ditch 333, truncated on the south side by ditch 331, was 0.53 m wide and 0.46 m deep with steep sides and a concave base. It was filled with brown silty clay loam, 332.

Ditch 342
This ditch, at B.174 m (OD 151.9 m), was 0.8 m wide and 0.38 m deep with a shallow, approximately V-shaped profile and a concave base. Its fill, 314, was a light brownish–grey silty loam containing animal bone.

Ditch 344
Cutting the southern edge of ditch 347, at B.169–71 m (OD 151.8 m), was a ditch 2.1 m wide and 0.54 m deep, with a shallow V-shaped profile and a concave base. It was filled with a light brownish–grey silty loam (343) with occasional chalk fragments increasing towards the base.

Ditch 347
Immediately to the north of ditch 344, at B.167–9 m (OD 152.0 m), and truncated by it on its south side, this ditch was at least 2.3 m wide and 0.5 m deep with an irregular shallow profile. Its primary fill (345), lying on the base and south side of the cut, was a yellowish–brown silty loam, 0.13 m thick. This was overlain by a light brownish–grey silty loam (346) with occasional chalk fragments increasing towards the base.

Ditch 349
A small steep sided U-shaped cut was sited at B.161 m (OD 151.9 m). It was 0.5 m wide and 0.35 m deep and

contained a light brownish–grey silty loam (348), with occasional chalk fragments increasing towards the base.

Ditch 352
This ditch, at B.154–6 m (OD 151.8), was 1.4 m wide and 0.68 m deep with a very steep south side, a moderately steep north side and a concave base. It had a greyish–brown silty loam fill, 351, with a spread of chalk fragments up to 0.3 m thick against the south side.

Ditch 354
This ditch, at B.149–51 m (OD 151.8 m), was 2.2 m wide and 0.9 m deep, with an irregular V-shaped profile, the sides being steep at the top and shallow at the base. Its fill, 353, from which animal bone was recovered, was a grey silty loam with chalk pieces concentrated against the sides and base.

Ditch 356
The ditch at B.140–2 m (OD 151.8 m) was 1.35 m wide and 0.36 m deep and filled with a grey silty loam (356) containing fragments of charcoal.

Winterbourne Romano-British Site

Desk-Based Study Data

An area of geophysical anomalies (Fig. 9) (B35), centered on SU 1015 6890, detected by magnetometer scan, is situated next to a footbridge and may be an area of recent dumping.

Results of the Watching Brief

A number of features, yielding no direct dating evidence, were recorded in the pipe trench within the distribution of Romano-British features which define the extent of the Winterbourne Romano-British settlement (Fig. 10). In all cases, where there was hillwash in the section, the features were sealed by it, indicating a Romano-British or earlier date. As no prehistoric features were recorded in this area, it is likely that at least some of these undated features are contemporary with the settlement and they have, therefore, been described under that section (above). These are ditches 120, 221, 233/236, 242, 269, 270, and 401 and hollow 282.

In addition, between the most northerly dated Romano-British feature, ditch 402 (B.797 m), and the A4361 trunk road (B.370), which bounds the south side of Butler's field, a further four features (ditches 288, 290, 293, and 294), all undated, were recorded. Some of these may also be Romano-British, but because they lie beyond the known extent of the Winterbourne settlement, they are described in this section.

Ditch 288
This feature, possibly a wide, shallow ditch running approximately north-east to south-west, was recorded crossing the pipe trench at B.679–83 m (OD 152.5 m), although its alignment could not be precisely determined. On the east side of the pipe trench, the southern end of the feature was obscured in section by the existing backfill. However, it was at least 4 m wide and 0.35 m deep with a very shallow profile. It contained a single fill, 289, consisting of brown silt loam, from which a fragment of flat polished sandstone (Table 6), animal bone, and the round flat head of an undatable tack or nail were recovered.

Ditch 290
A ditch, aligned east–west, was recorded crossing the pipe trench at B.627–8 m (OD 152.3 m). It was 1.4 m wide and 0.6 m deep with a moderately steep U-shaped profile. It was filled with two layers of dark yellowish–brown clay loam. The primary fill, 291, filling the base and the north side of the cut, was 0.38 m thick and less stony than the upper fill 292, which contained a considerable amount of chalk.

Ditch 293 and Ditch 294
Crossing the pipe trench at B.612–5 m (OD 152.0 m) were two ditches which ran parallel and adjacent to each other, aligned east–west. Ditch 293 to the south (1.1 m wide and 0.83 m deep) had a steep V-shaped profile and a single brown/dark brown silt loam fill (297). Ditch 294 was 1.2 m wide and 0.52 m deep, also with a V-shaped profile, steep on the south side and shallow to the north. Its primary fill, 295, was a brown clay loam 0.12 m thick. This was overlain by brown/dark brown silt loam, 296, indistinguishable from 297 but containing a very small featureless fragment of ceramic building material of unknown date.

Waden Hill to West Kennett

Desk-Based Study Data

During the excavation of the original pipe trench, a burial (B36) was found at the south end of Waden Hill, at SU 1070 6838, cut lengthways by the trench. It was excavated by F. Vatcher (SMR no. SU 16NW559). Because of this and other nearby finds, a magnetometer survey of the area was undertaken in addition to the magnetometer scan (Fig. 9). During the course of the full geophysical survey, a number of features of unknown date were detected.

- A group of three or four short linear features (B37) running approximately north–south, was detected by the magnetometer survey centred on SU 1062 6837 (GSB 1992a, figure 3.2) (*see* ditch 88 below).

- A single weak but broad circular anomaly (B38) detected by the magnetometer survey at SU 1049 6840, possibly a form of burial monument or a massive shaft/pit (GSB 1992a, figure 3.2).

- A group of five geophysical anomalies (B39) was detected by the magnetometer survey, centred on SU 1070 6838, four to the west (*see* hollow 80 below) and one to the east of barrow B.7 (GSB 1992a, figure 3.2).

- A linear feature (B40), 30 m long running approximately east–west, possibly a ditch (see ditch 53 below), was detected by the magnetometer survey, at SU 1074 6838 (GSB 1992a, fig. 3.2). This is on a similar alignment to, and could possibly be an eastward extension of, the wide Romano-British ditch 164 in the Winterbourne Romano-British site.

- An area of geophysical anomalies (B41 and B42) was detected by magnetometer scan, centred on SU 1056 6840 and SU 1080 6840 respectively (Fig. 9) (GSB 1992a, figure 9.1).

- An area of high magnetic susceptibility values — (B43) — centred on SU 1070 6840, was recorded by the geophysical survey associated with features B37–B39 (GSB 1992a, figure 9.1).

- An area of high magnetic susceptibility readings (B44), to the north-west of Honeysuckle Cottage, West Kennett, centred on SU 1100 6842, was recorded by the geophysical survey (GSB 1992a, fig. 9.1).

An earthwork bank (B45) at SU 1091 6835, running north–south on the south side of the A4, towards the Manor House, West Kennett, was visible on aerial photographs but barely visible on the ground (RCHME 1992b).

Results of the Watching Brief

Of all the features recorded in the pipe trench on the western side of Waden Hill, only the ring-ditch section and the strip lynchets could be assigned a date. Some of the rest, however, were identifiable as features either detected in air photographs or by the magnetometer survey (Fig. 5).

Hollow 80
Immediately to the west of the Waden Hill ring-ditch, at B.1950–60 m (OD 165.3–166.3 m), was a wide feature described as a hollow (cut 80, 10 m wide and 0.95 m). It had a vertical western side and concave base. The eastern side is very shallow, rising up for 2 m before sloping down into another shallow depression and then continuing in a shallow rise to the eastern edge. The primary fill in the base of the cut was a thin layer of yellowish–brown silt (81). This was overlain by two stony layers deriving from the western (downhill) side of the cut. The lower of these (82) consisted of a white chalky silt up to 0.5 m thick, with the upper layer, 83, being a yellowish–brown silt loam 0.35 m thick. The remaining fills of the feature appear to have derived from the eastern (uphill) side. The primary fill in the shallow depression on the eastern side (84) consisted of a layer of chalk rubble (0.28 m thick) possibly material eroded from the adjacent round barrow. Overlying it and filling the rest of the cut, were three layers (contexts 85–7) with a combined thickness of up to 0.85 m. These consisted of dark brown to dark yellowish–brown silt loam containing small and decreasing quantities of chalk towards the top. The nature of this feature is not clear. However, it may correspond to one or more of the four geophysical anomalies detected immediately to the west of the ring-ditch (B39).

Ditch 48
A ditch was recorded at B.2021–2 m (OD 167.9 m) and measured 0.8 m wide and 0.5 m deep with a moderately steep V-shaped profile and a narrow flat base. It was filled with three layers (contexts 49–51) of very pale and light yellowish–brown silt, each containing considerable quantities of chalk. The feature was sealed by a layer of yellowish–brown stony silt (52), up to 0.3 m thick, which extended beyond the sides of the ditch in both directions.

Ditch 53
At B.2023–5 m (OD 168.1 m) layer 52 (see ditch 48 above) was cut to the east by ditch 53 which crossed the pipe trench at an angle. In section it was 2 m wide and 0.48 m deep with convex sides and a flat base and was filled with a pale brown silt loam (54). Both ditch 48 and ditch 53 were sealed by a 0.95 m thick layer of brown silt loam hillwash, 55, which had accumulated along the bottom edge of the field. The angle of ditch 53 identifies it as the linear feature, aligned west-north-west to east-south-east, detected by the magnetometer survey (B40).

Ditch 88
This ditch was recorded crossing the pipe trench at a right angle at B.1898–90 m (OD 159.3 m). It was 2 m wide and 0.7 m deep with moderately steep irregular sides, concave to the west and convex to the east. Its primary fills (contexts 89–90) filled the sides of the base but not the centre and consisted of light yellowish–brown stony silts. Filling the centre of the cut was a layer of brown silt loam, 0.37 m thick. The position of this feature corresponds to the linear feature, aligned north–south, which was detected by the magnetometer survey (B37).

East Kennett

Desk-based Study Data

An area of high magnetic susceptibility values (C9), centred on SU 1210 6760, was recorded by the geophysical survey in the field east of East Kennett Manor (GSB 1992a, figure 11.1) (Fig. 21). A large area of discrete geophysical anomalies (C10), centred on SU 1222 6761 south of the road between East Kennett and West Overton, was detected by magnetometer scan, corresponding with high magnetic susceptibility values (GSB 1992a, figure 11.1).

Results of the Watching Brief

Two undated features, and one of uncertain date, were recorded in the pipe trench in the vicinity of East Kennett Manor (Fig. 21).

Foundation 265

A stone foundation was recorded in the north side of the trench at C.240–2 m (OD 143.8 m), on the west side of the Manor, *c.* 15 m west of The Cottage. It was aligned along the north side of the road which runs east–west through East Kennett. The foundation, resting on natural gravels, was visible for a length of 2.7 m, and consisted of four large, shaped sarsen blocks averaging 0.55 m long and 0.3 m deep, with smaller sarsen fragments placed around them. No cut was visible and the stones were surrounded by a 0.4 m thick layer of dark greyish–brown clay loam, 266. This was overlain by a layer of very dark greyish–brown silt loam (267) 0.6 m thick.

Feature 399

This feature was sited at C.295–300 m (OD 144.4 m), at the entrance to the yard to the east of East Kennett Manor. It was at least 6 m wide, extending to the south-west under the road, and was 1.3 m deep with a vertical side to the north-east and a flat base. It had a homogeneous dark greyish–brown fill (400). Because the excavation for the pipe trench at this point was 3 m deep and cut into very soft ground, proper examination or recording of the feature was not possible.

8. Conclusions

The Contribution of Pipeline Archaeology to Our Understanding of the Environment, Farming, and Settlement Patterns of the Winterbourne and Kennet Valleys,

by Michael J. Allen
and Andrew B. Powell

Introduction

The very limited disturbance of archaeological deposits and the narrow sample transect through the Avebury landscape provided by the re-excavation of the sewer pipeline trench, has inevitably produced a biased sample of the archaeology of that landscape. Although the number of undated features means that no period can be completely discounted, the predominant valley floor location of the pipeline's route (60% of it below 155 m) emphasised the archaeology of those periods when settlement was valley based, at the expense of those when it was attracted primarily to the chalk downland areas.

The sample of archaeological deposits recorded, however, was important because the route of the pipeline, although determined primarily by engineering requirements and constraints, avoided all the known major archaeological sites and passed through an area which, because of the lack of other known sites, had not previously been considered to be an archaeological priority. Moreover, the two main bodies of archaeological and palaeo-environmental evidence recovered during the project relate to the Romano-British and medieval periods, both of which are poorly represented in this general area, and so differ from those encountered in most other projects undertaken in the region, such as the Marlborough Downs landscape project (Gingell 1992), large-scale fieldwalking (Holgate 1987; 1988), the research conducted by Cardiff University (Evans et al. 1988; 1993; Whittle 1993), and the recent synthesis of the Overton Down and Fyfield area by Peter Fowler (forthcoming and pers. comm.). These previous projects were specifically led by archaeological research objectives, with the locations of fieldwork and intervention being chosen by archaeologists, often on known or recognisable archaeological sites, in order to answer specific questions. Many of the topographical areas crossed by the sewer pipeline have not, therefore, been previously examined and would not normally have been selected as a focus for archaeological 'research'.

Constraints on the available sample locations imposed by the pipeline route and the limited quantity of data produced as a result of the need for minimal disturbance of archaeological deposits, negate the possibility of assessing, or reassessing, the entire Holocene and archaeological history of the valley. However, even with extremely limited exposure and disturbance of the archaeological deposits, the fieldwork and analyses provide some important contributions to our knowledge of the development and use of the Avebury landscape, and enable us to make very specific and pertinent statements in relation to the wider interpretations provided by other large-scale projects of palaeo- environmental and archaeological research. The narrative that follows, therefore, highlights points of particular interest and significance to these larger research projects, and these summaries are presented by period and theme.

Neolithic

The project found no evidence of Neolithic activity, despite the obvious wealth of ritual and funerary monuments in the area and the proximity of the pipeline route to some of the most impressive monuments of the period, such as Avebury and Silbury Hill. Although there is limited evidence for Neolithic settlement in the vicinity, Smith indicates that Neolithic pottery has been found on every site in the Avebury area, implying a dense pattern of settlement (Smith 1984). Even John Evans's limited excavations at West Overton, which were designed primarily to recover palaeo-environmental sequences and data, also found struck flints and Neolithic pottery (Whittle in Evans et al. 1990, 169–172). Although this may not indicate dense settlement, it certainly suggests prolonged activity, with possibly intermittent settlement in the area. It further suggests that much of this evidence might be expected to be situated in alluviated or colluviated valleys as 'post-Neolithic processes of erosion and deposition have undoubtedly made it difficult to recognise the full extent of Neolithic settlement patterns' (Smith 1984, 106). Indeed the possibility of non-permanent Neolithic settlements in the Kennet Valley floodplain was suggested by Holgate (1988) and the more recently discovered large complex Neolithic palisade enclosures are located on the floodplain adjacent to the present course of the river (Whittle 1993). In view of this, it is perhaps surprising that no evidence of Neolithic activity was recovered in the form of either features or artefacts. Nevertheless, it must be admitted that the nature of the fieldwork, as imposed by the method of the pipeline replacement, was never conducive to the recovery of ephemeral features or small stray finds (see below).

The lack of evidence, therefore, does nothing to contradict the existing general picture of a low permanent, but fluctuating and perhaps fairly mobile, population through the Neolithic that was responsible for the gradual and progressive removal of the woodland cover. Despite the long archaeological and antiquarian interest in the area, and the more recent fairly large-scale fieldwalking (Holgate 1987; 1988) and geophysical surveys (Ucko et al. 1991), no major domestic settlement sites have been identified. Nevertheless, if such sites do exist it is more likely that they were situated in low-lying positions, as with the West Kennett palisade enclosures, and are possibly buried by alluvium or colluvium.

Bronze Age

New evidence for Bronze Age activity was confined to the chalk areas above the valley floor where new and known barrows were recorded and sampled. The palaeo-environmental evidence only confirmed both previous analyses (cf Evans 1972) and preconceptions of the area, indicating that the downland immediately above the valley floor was cleared of extensive woodland and that prior to and immediately after the construction of the barrows, the area had been open grazed downland in prolonged pasture for sheep or cattle.

Surprisingly, the majority of the alluvial edge colluvium (sensu Bell 1981a) and footslope locations was not of Bronze Age date, despite the significant colluvial deposits of this date identified elsewhere in Wessex (Allen 1992), and in particular at Piggledene Bottom (Allen unpublished) and Down Born (Fowler pers. comm.). This may indicate that cultivation during this period did not occur extensively or uniformly. Erosion may also have been minimised by the creation of formal bounded field systems. Elsewhere colluvium has been attributed to earlier Bronze Age tillage, but on Overton Down the field systems with large lynchets which might minimise erosion were only evident in the later Bronze Age (Fowler pers. comm.).

It is certainly true, however, that the agricultural regime in the post-barrow construction and post-Bronze Age period, did not involve the ubiquitous manuring with domestic and midden rubbish which would have resulted in pottery being strewn across the landscape. In the ditch fills of the 'Stukeley' barrow on Waden Hill, for instance, the consistent accidental incorporation of freshwater shells (Figure 6 and Table 4) may indicate manuring and mulching with vegetation from the Kennet floodplain. Here the exploitation of the local ecology can be paralleled by the suggestion of similar activities in the Dorchester landscape (Allen 1994, 359; Allen in Smith et al. forthcoming), at Balksbury, Hampshire (Allen 1995) and similar exploitation is seen in the collection of seaweed as a manure in the Bronze Age at Gwithian, Cornwall (Megaw 1976), and other coastal sites (Bell 1981b).

Iron Age

There is little evidence of Iron Age activity within the study corridor, a pattern confirmed by the lack of evidence during the fieldwork. This is perhaps surprising in view of the Iron Age settlement (at Overton Down) and extensive traces of 'Celtic' and Romano-British field systems on the nearby downland. The lack of evidence from the pipeline is also of interest as, although the Kennet Valley is on the edge of the major distribution of Iron Age votive deposits in water contexts (Wait 1985,

fig. 2.13), this is perhaps the type of location where such evidence might be recovered (Fitzpatrick 1984, 178–83).

Romano-British

The pipeline produced evidence of five separate stone built Romano-British buildings (farms) in the Kennet Valley below Silbury Hill, in an area where John Evans had previously recorded a Romano-British grave (Evans 1966). The lack of plans of these buildings, and of larger groups of datable finds associated with them, prevent both their certain dating within the Romano-British period and any determination of their function. Nevertheless, pottery indicates some sporadic activity occurring in the mid 1st–2nd century AD and the 3rd–4th centuries AD. The charred plant remains are conclusive evidence that spelt wheat and oats, and also less certainly bread wheat and barley, had been cultivated and processed locally. This may enable us to suggest that some of these buildings may be Romano-British farms, in which case it is especially noteworthy to find stone built domestic buildings of the earlier Romano-British period in this area, but does perhaps again reinforce the topographic location of these buildings, all of which were buried by subsequent colluvial and alluvial sediments. In many respects the presence of these buildings is important because of the general paucity of such evidence in the immediate vicinity, but this also reinforces Fowler's hypothesis of a major burst of activity in the downland at this time, in contrast to the Iron Age. In the later Romano-British period (3rd–4th century), Peter Fowler suggests that there seems to be an economy based on cattle (pers. comm.) and certainly the majority of the small bone assemblage are cattle and therefore do not refute this suggestion.

The discovery of Romano-British buildings in the Kennet valley, buried beneath colluvium and alluvium, has wider implications both for the broader settlement patterns and the location of farmsteads and settlements, as well as for the archaeological methods employed in recording them (see below). While the siting of Romano-British settlements on Overton and Fyfield Downs displays some sort of continuity with the prehistoric landuse of the downs, the predominance, in the pipe trench, of archaeological features of Romano-British and post-Romano-British date reflects the culmination of a process of gravitation in settlement, starting in the Late Bronze Age, away from the high chalk downland towards lower altitudes and ultimately into the river valleys. The Winterbourne Romano-British settlement, therefore, represents this development and the start of permanent occupation in the river valleys. The evidence for Romano-British settlement in the Winterbourne valley is significant in that, despite major studies of this landscape (Evans et al. 1993; Bonney 1968), no major Romano-British occupation had been recorded. Romano-British farms and settlements, like many current farms, were situated on the edge of the valley floor. As a result, they have been buried by over

1 m of deposits and it is therefore likely that a large number of other sites of this date may be blanketed by such deposits elsewhere in the Winterbourne and Kennet valleys (cf Allen 1988). Other lowlying Romano-British buildings are present, such as that further up the Kennet valley south of Windmill Hill on a low bluff above the floodplain (Fig. 22).

Saxon

While there is no demonstrable link between the early 5th-century AD occupation of the Winterbourne site and the Saxon settlement at Avebury, which started in the 5th or 6th century AD, it was quite possible that there was continuous settlement close to the river, with both the valley floor and the Downs being exploited. More-over, on the basis of documentary sources referring to Saxon settlement and land division within many of the areas traversed by the study corridor, one might have expected the pipeline to have identified greater evidence than it did of activity during this period. However, the locations, all within residual contexts, of the few sherds of possibly Saxon pottery, constituting the sole finds of this period from the pipeline, provide little additional evidence to the known pattern of Saxon settlement. The three pottery sherds from a feature in Butler's Field reflect the known presence of Saxon settlement at Avebury, while that from East Kennett is in keeping with previous unassociated finds and, with references to Saxon settlement, both these contexts indicate the continuation of valley floor activity. The sherd from the Pound Field barrow at West Overton, on the other hand, if Saxon in date, might indicate agricultural activity above the valley floor.

Medieval

Evidence for medieval settlement was limited to Butler's Field in Avebury, though medieval settlements are recorded at a number of other locations along the Kennet valley floor. This may indicate the localised nature of that settlement, although the significant number of undated features from all areas of the pipeline, in particular in low lying areas along the Winterbourne and at East Kennet, could reflect more extensive settlement.

The wider exploitation of the landscape, however, is clearly shown by the presence of the negative lynchets (eg Waden Hill), which were encountered on the lower chalk slopes. The levels of cultivation indicated by these features, possibly with adjacent downland pasture and floodplain grazing on the valley floor, as at Avebury (Evans et al. 1993), point to intensive and organised agricultural activity. Such cultivation would have contributed significantly to the development of the modern landscape, with erosion of soils resulting in the accumulation of colluvium and alluvium on the lower slopes and floor of the Kennet valley floodplain. By the medieval period, therefore, a pattern was established of valley settlement, exploiting in an organised way, the full diversity of the Avebury landscape, a pattern which has continued until the present day.

Landscape Taphonomy

The pipe trench along the Kennet and Winterbourne valley demonstrates that both colluvial and alluvial deposits (or packets *sensu* Needham 1992) are highly localised within the valley. Taking careful account of the topography, it is evident that colluvial footslope and alluvial edge deposits are not uniform 'blankets', but are both varied and localised in their occurrence. This is also true of alluvial units and the sampled section of which should not necessarily be viewed as representative of the whole sequence over long stretches of the valley. Even within the extent of one alluvial layer the preservation of the palaeo-environmental evidence is far from uniform. For instance, at Butlers Field, although the trench traversed the entire field covering roughly 370 m, it did not reveal the detail or complete stratigraphy analysed by Rosina Mount (Mount 1991; Evans et al. 1993) at a point less than 20 m to the west (Fig. 20), though it was admittedly sited slightly higher up the floodplain. Even where the comparable unit was analysed by the same specialist, major differences in preservation, but not interpretation, of the palaeo-fauna were observed (compare Mount 1991; Evans et al. 1993, with Mount this volume, Chapter 5).

On a wider spectrum, although Evans et al. (1993, 190) indicated a cessation of alluviation (around Avebury) in the Romano-British period, alluviation is recorded from the pipe trench in the Winterbourne which is coincident with the newly discovered Romano-British settlement sites (Chapter 4) and the burial recorded by Evans in the colluvium of the Winterbourne bank (1966). The localised presence of alluvial deposits along the Winterbourne indicates variations as a result of the complex relationships between human activity and its impact on the soils, sediment loads, and deposition or erosion environments (Patton and Schumm 1981; Burrin and Scaife 1988). This activity was not clearance, the valley and downland being already open land, but cultivation. As a result of larger and possibly more formalised farming practices, initial soil erosion led to increased sediment loads and localised alluviation. Later erosion was direct, with hillwash deposited on the valley floor, rather than into the Winterbourne itself, and therefore redeposited as alluvium.

Settlement Patterns

The presence of localised but extensive colluvial footslope deposits and alluvial edge colluvium is not surprising, and the fact that these deposits have the potential for burying archaeological sites is well understood (Megaw and Simpson 1979; Bell 1983; Allen 1988). Although these previous authors have demonstrated the burial of archaeological sites, they have each tended to concentrate on the prehistoric implications of this (eg Allen 1994). The discoveries along the pipeline obviously demonstrate that we should not be so complacent in confining such implications primarily to the prehistoric epoch. The discovery of five Romano-British buildings was a surprise (but see below), despite the known

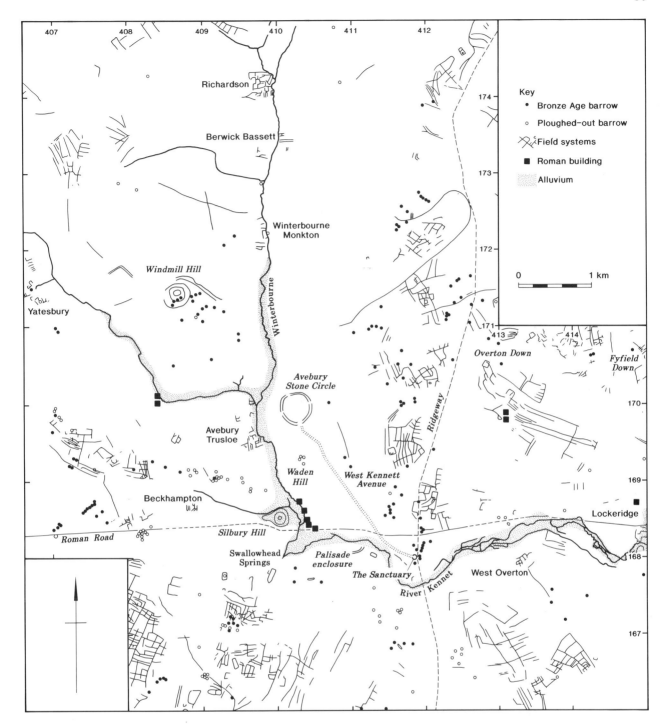

Figure 22   Archaeology of the Avebury area showing recently discovered sites (after Evans et al. 1993, fig. 1, with additions)

existence of the Roman Road. The concentration of nearly four centuries of activity in the valley at the base of the downs is significant in that this opens up new parameters for the discussion of Romano-British settlement patterns.

The reason that this Romano-British activity has not been discovered previously is that it was situated in the valley and, as a result, was sealed in places by over 1 m of alluvium and hillwash. It is likely that other Romano-

British sites in the local valleys are similarly blanketed by such deposits (cf. Allen 1988: 1994). More significantly the Romano-British buildings are stone built and are a form and status of building rarely encountered in the Avebury or, for that matter elsewhere in Wessex. Again, this has implications when considering wider issues of settlement patterns and the distribution and location of specific sites. It is not the place here to discuss those issues, or to attempt any reinterpretation of the

Romano-British landscape, but merely to highlight this fact so that other archaeologists attempting to do so may temper their interpretations with the information from these observations.

Appraisal of the Methods

The staged approach employed during this project, including initial discussions, archaeological assessment and follow up fieldwork, engineering mitigation, and finally construction and accompanying watching brief, allowed successful completion of the engineering project with minimum damage to the archaeological resource. It involved communication between the interested parties at all stages and demonstrated how planners, engineers, and archaeologists can work in unison to achieve their different, and potentially contradictory, objectives.

The results of the Stage 1 Assessment were essential to the formulation of an appropriate mitigation strategy. The desk-based study quantified the known archaeological resource of the area around the preferred route, while the air photographic and geophysical surveys (Pl. 9) gave an indication of some of the potential for additional archaeological remains.

However, as a consequence of a number of preconceptions about the Avebury landscape, this phase of the project did not achieve all that it might have, although these shortfalls are easier to recognise with the benefit of hindsight. First, the width of study corridor as defined by OS hectares, although necessarily arbitrary, had the effect of imposing a rather narrow vision on both the archaeology and the wider landscape. As a result, the selection of the areas for detailed magnetometer survey was based on the assumption, now realised to be mistaken, that the locations of previous archaeological finds inside the corridor were likely to be a reflection of the area's actual potential. Insufficient weight was given to the evidence within the wider archaeological landscape with, in some cases, individual unassociated finds within the corridor being afforded greater significance than potentially important evidence immediately outside, including not only major archaeological sites, such as Silbury Hill and Avebury, but also the accumulation, since the mid 19th century, of evidence for extensive Romano-British settlement next to the River Winterbourne.

While this had only a limited effect along most of the pipeline's route, it had a clear impact at the Winterbourne site, because, as well as demonstrating that there was unlikely to be any low-impact alternative to the preferred route, the data collected during the Stage 1 Assessment was to prove essential as a means of interpreting the archaeology revealed subsequently in the pipe trench. The location of the magnetometer survey along the Winterbourne was determined by the position of the Romano-British grave found eroding out of the bank of the river, but the survey was hampered in that area by the depth of colluvium. Although anomalies interpreted as pits were identified, the foundation trenches of Buildings III and IV and other substantial features were not. On the other hand, because no finds had previously been identified to the south of the burial, in the area adjacent to the main road (A4), this section

of the study corridor was not subject to a detailed survey. It was here, however, with substantially less depth of soil above the chalk, that such a survey could not only have identified specific archaeological features, including Buildings I and II, but could also have revealed their extent and plan, providing invaluable information as to the nature of the site. In the future, such a survey would seem to be a research priority for the understanding of this important site.

There was limited scope to project the archaeological finds within the trench into the wider landscape, a constraint emphasised by the mitigation measures adopted as a result of the Stage 1 Assessment. The lack of any topsoil stripping within the pipeline easement meant that archaeological features were visible only in section. Where linear features were visible in both sides of the trench, it was possible to ascertain their approximate alignments beyond the limits of the trench and, where features could be related to those detected in the air photographic and geophysical surveys, it was possible to relate the visible sections to their wider structure. However, in areas not covered by these surveys, or where the depth of the overlying soil prevented their detection, the sections constituted the totality of the evidence. As any excavation was limited to the cleaning of their sections prior to recording, approximately half of all the exposed features provided no direct dating evidence.

The preconceptions self-imposed during the Stage 1 Assessment, and the mitigation constraints imposed during the Stage 2 archaeological monitoring were more than compensated for by the fact that, in the end, a substantial amount of archaeological and environmental data was recovered from a major engineering project in an area of very high archaeological potential, with minimal disturbance to the archaeological resource. As far as the engineering works were concerned, the mitigation measure, involving the re-excavation of the original pipe trench and the removal of the existing pipe, did not add substantially to the amount of work required, the only additional work related to the continual setting up and moving of the over-pumping equipment, so that the operation of the existing sewer was not interrupted. The cost of textile sheeting to prevent soil contamination was largely offset by the lack of any need to strip the topsoil from the working easement.

During the fieldwork, it became very clear how far priorities had changed since the original pipe had been laid in the 1960s and to what extent an awareness had developed during that period of the value and fragility of the archaeological resource. At that time all the features had not only been cut through by the trench, but also exposed in plan within the stripped working easement. However, only a handful of them, two burials and a number of medieval features, had been recorded so that an opportunity to record the features in plan, not available during the recent work, was unfortunately missed. Although these developments within archaeology are reflected by Government guidance in Planning Policy Guideline Note 16, no specific guidance exists for the recording of archaeological features in World Heritage Sites, especially for works beyond the remit of planning control. That this level of valuable information could be added to the archaeological record, with

Plate 9   Conducting the geophysical survey at Pound Field, West Overton, with St Michael's church in the background

negligible disturbance to the archaeological resource, was therefore only achieved by Thames Water Utilities and Kennet District Council acting in the most responsible manner. Their initiatives ensured that, from the start, the engineering works were planned, modified, and ultimately undertaken in a way which was not only sympathetic to the needs of preserving that resource, but which also set an example for other developers undertaking similar projects.

The project offered the opportunity to examine an area of the landscape which had not previously been considered by archaeologists to be of high archaeological value. It has highlighted areas which need further academic attention and has demonstrated the biases in our archaeological knowledge which need to be comprehended when composing larger regional or sub-regional syntheses.

Conclusion

The examination of archaeological and environmental material from a narrow 4 km long corridor through the Avebury landscape has added substantially both to the archaeological record and to the environmental, land-scape, and landuse evidence, particularly of the Romano-British period. It has also drawn attention to a major bias in the landscape and archaeological record,

as compiled by previous archaeological work (see for instance Bowen and Fowler 1962, especially figure 1), providing a record of settlement located in the valleys, as predicted by Bell (1981) and Allen (1988; 1994). It is precisely because of the activity associated with and subsequent to those settlements, that they are buried under alluvial or colluvial sediments. The fact that these deposits have been shown to be highly localised, should ensure caution in interpreting their occurrence or non-occurrence as a regional phenomenon.

The addition of even limited evidence for Romano-British and medieval settlement and farming is signif-icant in what is traditionally viewed as a prehistoric landscape and provides a base-line for further archae-ological reconnaissance, excavation, and research. The most important discoveries resulting from the work are presented below.

- 1. The presence of the five Romano-British build-ings with masonry footings in an area with sparse evidence for Romano-British settlement has wider implications for our understanding of the Romano-British landscape and settlement pattern.

- 2. The burial of prehistoric to medieval sites by both colluvium and alluvium is likely to have a consid-erable effect on the known distribution of archaeological sites and on our interpretation of the use and development of that landscape.

- 3. That valley deposits (colluvial and alluvial) are discontinuous sediment packets and interpretations based on single locations are not wholly representative. The interpretation of the history of sedimentation and landuse must acknowledge this.

- 4. Although from its inception the project sought to assess and record objectively the impact of the engineering works on the archaeological resource, the strategy employed was still coloured by shared preconceptions about the archaeology of the Avebury area. The project has been a reminder, therefore, of the potential of any landscape, even one as heavily trod and closely examined as that around Avebury, to yield up the unexpected and so to expose our biases and confound our current theories.

Bibliography

Allen, M.J., 1988, 'Archaeological and environmental aspects of colluviation in south-east England', in Groenman-van Waateringe and Robinson, R. (eds), *Man-Made Soils*, Oxford, Brit. Archaeol. Rep. Int. Ser. 410, 67–92.

——, 1989, 'Land snails', in Fasham, P.J., Farwell, D.E. and Whinney, R.J.B., *The Archaeological Site at Easton Lane, Winchester*, Hampshire Fld Club and Archaeol. Soc. Monog. 6, 134–40.

——, 1990, 'The molluscan evidence', in Howard, S., 'A double ring ditched, Bronze Age barrow at Burford Farm, Pamphill', *Proc. Dorset Natur. Hist. Archaeol. Soc.* 111, 49–52.

——, 1991, 'Analysing the landscape: a geographical approach to archaeological problems', in Schofield, A.J. (ed.), *Interpreting Artefact Scatters; Contributions to Ploughzone Archaeology,* Oxbow Monog. 4, 39–57.

——, 1992, *Standard flotation procedures*, Salisbury, unpubl. Wessex Archaeology guideline no. 15.

——, 1994, *The land-use history of the southern English chalklands with an evaluation of the Beaker period using environmental data; colluvial deposits as environmental and cultural indicators*, unpubl. Ph.D. thesis, Univ. Southampton.

Anderson, A.S., 1979, *The Roman Pottery Industry in North Wiltshire*, Swindon Archaeol. Soc. Rep. 2.

Annable, F.K., 1962, 'A Romano-British pottery in Savernake Forest. Kilns 1–2', *Wiltshire Archaeol. Natur. Hist. Soc. Mag.* 58, 142–155.

Bell, M.G., 1981a, *Valley sediments as evidence of prehistoric land-use: a study based on dry valleys in south-east England*, unpubl. Ph.D. thesis, London Univ.

——, 1981b, 'Valley sediments and environmental change', in Jones, M. and Dimbleby, G.W. (eds), *Environment of Man; the Iron Age to Anglo-Saxon Period*, Oxford, Brit. Archaeol. Rep. 87, 75–91.

——, 1981c, 'Seaweed as a prehistoric resource', in Brothwell, D. and Dimbleby, G. (eds), *Environmental Aspects of Coasts and Islands*, Oxford, Brit. Archaeol. Rep. 94, 117–126.

Bonney, D., 1966, 'Pagan Saxon burials and boundaries in Wiltshire', *Wiltshire Archaeol. Natur. Hist. Soc. Mag.* 61, 25–30.

——, 1968, 'Iron Age and Romano-British settlement sites in Wiltshire: some geographical considerations', *Wiltshire Archaeol. Natur. Hist. Soc. Mag.* 63, 27–38.

Borthwick, A., 1985, *Avebury 1985: report of archaeological evaluation work undertaken by the Trust for Wessex Archaeology on behalf of Wiltshire County Council in advance of the planned extension to the southern car park at Avebury, Wiltshire, April–May 1985*, unpubl. report, Wiltshire County Council Library and Museum Service.

Bowen, H.C. and Fowler, P.J., 1962, 'The archaeology of Fyfield and Overton Downs, Wiltshire: (interim report)', *Wiltshire Archaeol. Natur. Hist. Soc. Mag.* 62, 98–115.

Branigan, K., 1976, 'Villa settlement in the West Country,' in Branigan, K. and Fowler, P.J. (eds), *The Roman West Country: Classical Culture and Celtic Society*, Newton Abbot, London: David and Charles, 120–141.

Brentnall, H.C., 1939, 'The Saxon bounds of Overton', *Rep. Marlborough College Natur. Hist. Soc.* 87, 116–36.

Brodribb, A.C.C., Hands, A.R. and Walker, D.R., 1971, *Excavations at Shakenoak Farm, near Wilcote, Oxfordshire*, vol. II, privately printed.

——, 1972, *Excavations at Shakenoak Farm, near Wilcote, Oxfordshire*, vol. III, privately printed.

Brodribb, G., 1987, *Roman Brick and Tile*, Gloucester.

Brooke, J.W., 1910, 'Excavation of a Roman well near Silbury Hill', *Wiltshire Archaeol. Natur. Hist. Soc. Mag.* 29, 166–171.

—— and Cunnington, B.H., 1896, 'Excavation of a Roman well near Silbury Hill', *Wiltshire Archaeol. Natur. Hist. Soc. Mag.* vol. XXIX, 373–5.

Brown, D., 1974, 'Problems of continuity', in Rowley, T. (ed.), *Anglo-Saxon Settlement and Landscape*, Oxford, Brit. Archaeol. Rep. 6, 16–19.

Burrin, P.J. and Scaife, R.G., 1988, 'Environmental thresholds, catastrophe theory and landscape sensitivity: their relevance to the impact of man on valley alluviation', in Bintliffe, J.L., Donaldson, D.A. and Grant, E.G. (eds), *Conceptual Issues in Environmental Archaeology*, Edinburgh, Edinburgh University Press, 211–232.

Carruthers, W.J., 1992, 'Plant remains', in Butterworth, C.A. and Lobb, S.J., *Excavations in the Burghfield Area, Berkshire: Developments in the Bronze Age and Saxon Landscapes*, Salisbury, Wessex Archaeol. Rep. 1, 149–158.

Clapham, A. R., Tutin, T.G. and Warburg, E. F., 1952, *Flora of the British Isles*, Cambridge, Cambridge University Press.

Clarke, G., 1979, *Pre Roman and Roman Winchester. Part II: the Roman Cemetery at Lankhills*, Oxford, Winchester Studies vol. 3.

Crummy, N., 1983, *The Roman Small Finds from Excavations in Colchester, 1971–79*, Colchester, Colchester Archaeol. Rep. 2.

90

Cunnington, M.E., 1932, 'Romano-British Wiltshire', *Wiltshire Archaeol. Natur. Hist. Soc. Mag.* 45, 166–216.

David, A., 1984, *Avebury car park: report on geophysical survey 1984*, unpubl. Ancient Monuments Laboratory Rep. 4449.

Davies, S.M. and Seager Smith, R.H., 1993, 'Black Burnished ware and other southern British coarsewares', in Woodward, P.J., Davies, S.M. and Graham, A.H., *Excavations at Greyhound Yard, Dorchester 1981–4*, Dorset Natur. Hist. Archaeol. Soc. Monog. 12, 229–284.

Eagles, B.N., 1986, 'Pagan Anglo-Saxon burials at West Overton', *Wiltshire Archaeol. Natur. Hist. Soc. Mag.* 80, 103–20.

Ellis A.E., 1969, *British Snails,* Oxford, Clarendon Press.

Evans, J.G., 1966, 'A Romano-British interment in the bank of the Winterbourne, near Avebury', *Wiltshire Archaeol. Natur. Hist. Soc. Mag.* 61, 97–8.

——, 1972, *Land Snails in Archaeology*, London, Seminar Press.

——, Limbrey, S., Maté I. and Mount, R., 1988, 'Environmental change and land-use history in a Wiltshire river valley in the last 14,000 years', in Barrett, J.C. and Kinnes, I. (eds), *The Archaeology of Context in the Neolithic and Bronze Age: Recent Trends,* Sheffield, Univ. Sheffield, 97–103.

——, ——, —— and —— 1993, 'An environmental history of the upper Kennet Valley, Wiltshire, for the last 10,000 years', *Proc. Prehist. Soc.* 59, 139–95.

Evans, M.V., 1985, *Boring holes near Avebury: the late Post-glacial history of the upper Kennet Valley,* unpubl. undergraduate thesis, Univ. Wales college of Cardiff.

Fasham, P.J., Keevill, G. with Coe, D., 1995, *Brighton Hill South (Hatch Warren): an Iron Age Farmstead and Deserted Medieval Village in Hampshire,* Salisbury, Wessex Archaeology Report 7.

Fitzpatrick, A.P., 1984, 'The deposition of La Tène Iron Age metalwork in watery contexts', in Cunliffe, B. and Miles, D., *Aspects of the Iron Age in Central Southern Britain*, Oxford, Univ. Oxford: Comm. Archaeol., Monog. 2., 178–90

Fleming, A., 1971, 'Territorial patterns in Bronze Age Wessex', *Proc. Prehist. Soc.* 37, 138–66.

Fowler, P.J., 1967, 'The archaeology of Fyfield and Overton Downs, Wiltshire: third interim report', *Wiltshire Archaeol. Natur. Hist. Mag. 62, 16–33.*

——, 1975, 'Continuity in the landscape? A summary of some local archaeology in Wiltshire, Somerset, and Gloucester', in Fowler, P.J. (ed.), *Recent Work in Rural Archaeology*, Bradford on Avon, Moonraker Press.

—— and Evans, J.G., 1967, 'Plough-marks, lynchets and early fields', *Proc. Prehist. Soc. 41*, 289–301.

Fulford, M.G., 1975, *New Forest Roman Pottery*, Oxford, Brit. Archaeol. Rep. 17.

Hingley, R., 1989, *Rural Settlement in Roman Britain,* London, Seaby.

Geophysical Surveys of Bradford, 1992a, *Report on geophysical survey: Kennet Valley Foul Sewer Improvements,* unpubl. client report no. 92/37.

——, 1992b, *Report on geophysical survey: Kennet Valley Foul Sewer Improvements survey II,* unpubl. client report no. 92/62.

Gilchrist, R., 1989, *Proof of evidence submitted on behalf of the Council for British Archaeology, Public Local Inquiry,* upubl. report.

Gillam, J.P., 1976, 'Coarse fumed ware in northern Britain and beyond', *Glasgow Archaeol. Journ.* 4, 58–80.

Gingell, C., 1992, *The Marlborough Downs: a Later Bronze Age Landscape and its Origins*, Devizes, Wiltshire Archaeol. Natur. Hist. Soc. Monog. 1.

Greene, K., 1978, 'Imported finewares in Britain to AD 250: a guide to identification', in Arthur, P. and Marsh, G. (eds), *Early Fine Wares in Roman Britain,* Oxford, Brit. Archaeol. Rep. 57, 15–30.

Helbaek, H., 1952, 'Early crops in southern England', *Proc. Prehist. Soc.* 18, 194–233.

Hodder, I., 1976, 'The distribution of Savernake ware', *Wiltshire Archaeol. Natur. Hist. Soc. Mag.* 69, 67–84.

Holgate, R., 1987, 'Neolithic settlement patterns at Avebury, Wiltshire', *Antiquity* 61, 259–63.

——, 1988, *Neolithic Settlement of the Thames Basin,* Oxford, Brit. Archaeol. Rep. 194.

Jacomet, S., 1987, *Prahistorische getreidefunde. Eine anleitung zur bestimmung prahistorischer gerstenund weizen-funde,* Publ. Botanisches Institut der Universitat Abteilung Pflanzensystematik un Geobotanik. Basel, Switzerland. 1st Edition.

Jessen, K. and Helbaek, H., 1944, 'Cereals in Great Britain and Ireland in prehistoric and early historic times', *Kgl. Dansk. Vidensk. Selsk. Biol. Skrifter, 3 No. 2,* Copenhagen, Denmark.

Jones, M.K., 1981, 'The development of crop husbandry', in Jones, M. and Dimbleby, G.W. (eds), *The Environment of Man: the Iron Age to the Anglo-Saxon Period,* Oxford, Brit. Archaeol. Rep. 87, 95–127.

Keely, J., 1986, 'The coarse pottery', in McWhirr, A., *Houses in Roman Cirencester,* Cirencester Excavations III, 158–165.

Kendall, 1923, *Wiltshire Archaeol. Natur. Hist. Mag.,* 359–61.

Kerney, M.P., 1963., 'Late-glacial deposits on the Chalk of south-east England', *Phil. Trans Roy. Soc.* B246, 203–54.

——, 1966, 'Snails and man in Britain', *J. Conchology* 26, 3–14.

——, 1976, *Atlas of the Non-Marine Mollusca of the British Isles,* Monks Wood, Institute of Terrestrial Ecology.

——, 1977, 'A proposed zonation scheme for Lateglacial and Postglacial deposits using land Mollusca', *J. Archaeol. Science* 4, 387–390.

Knowles, F., 1956, 'Avebury Manor', *Wiltshire Archaeol. Natur. Hist. Soc. Mag.* 56, 359–70.

Lawson, A.J., 1989, *Proof of evidence, West Kennett Farm Public Inquiry, August 1989*, Salisbury, unpubl. Wessex Archaeology report.

Leah, M.D., 1988, *Excavations in the car park, Avebury, level III archive report*, unpubl. Wiltshire Rescue Archaeology Project report.

Leech, R.H., 1976, 'Larger agricultural settlements in the West Country', in Brannigan and Fowler (eds), 142–161.

Limbrey, S., 1975, *Soils and Archaeology,* London, Academic Press.

Lobb, S.J., Mees, G. and Morris, E.L., 1986–90, 'Meales Farm, Sulhamstead: archaeological investigation of Romano-British and medieval features, 1985–87', *Berkshire Archaeol. J. 1986–90, Vol. 73, 55–65.*

MacGregor, A., 1985, *Bone, Antler, Ivory and Horn, the Technology of Skeletal Materials Since the Roman Period,* London, Croom Helm.

Macreth, D.F., 1986, 'Brooches,' in McWhirr, A., *Houses in Roman Cirencester*, Cirencester Excavations III, 104–106.

Malone, C., 1989, *English Heritage Book of Avebury,* London, B.T. Batsford/English Heritage.

Margary, I.D., 1955, *Roman Roads in Britain, Volume I,* London, Pheonix House.

Megaw, J.V.S., 1976, 'Gwithian, Cornwall: some notes on the evidence for Neolithic and Bronze Age settlement', in Burgess, C. and Miket, R. (eds), *Settlement and Economy in the Third and Second Millennia BC'*, Brit. Archaeol. Rep. 33, 51–66.

—— and Simpson, D.D.A., 1979, *Introduction to British Prehistory,* Leicester, Leicester University Press.

Mepham, L.N., 1993, 'The pottery', in Graham, A. and Newman, C., 'Recent excavations of Iron Age and Romano-British enclosures in the Avon Valley, Wiltshire', *Wiltshire Archaeol. Natur. Hist. Mag.* 86, 25–34.

Miles, D., 1978, 'The Roman pottery', in Parrington, M., *The Excavation of an Iron Age Settlement, Bronze Age Ring-Ditch and Roman Features at Ashville Trading Estate, Abingdon (Oxfordshire), 1974–76*, Counc. Brit. Archaeol. Res. Rep. 28, 74–78.

Morris, E.L., 1991, *Data levels guidelines: a structure for finds analysis*, Salisbury, unpubl. Wessex Archaeology guideline 2.

——, 1992, *The analysis of pottery*, Salisbury, unpubl. Wessex Archaeology guideline 4.

Mount, R.J., 1991, *An environmental history of the upper Kennet Valley, and some implications for human communities*, unpubl. Ph.D. thesis, Univ. Wales College of Cardiff, 1991.

Murphy, P.L., 1977, *Early agriculture and environment on the Hampshire chalklands: circa. 800 BC–AD 400*, unpubl. M.Phil. thesis, Univ. Southampton.

Musty, J., 1973, 'A preliminary account of a medieval pottery industry at Minety, north Wiltshire', *Wiltshire Archaeol. Natur. Hist. Mag.* 68, 79–88.

——, Algar, D.J. and Ewence, P.F., 1969, 'The medieval pottery kilns at Laverstock, near Salisbury, Wiltshire', *Archaeologia*, 102, 83–150.

Needham, S.P., 1992, 'Holocence alluviation and interstratified settlement evidence in the Thames valley at Runnymede Bridge', in Needham, S. and Macklin, M.G. (eds), *Alluvial Archaeology in Britain*, Oxford, Oxbow Monog. 27.

Oliver, M. and Applin, B., 1979, 'Excavation of an Iron Age and Romano-British settlement at Rucstalls Hill, Basingstoke, Hampshire 1972–5', *Proc. Hampshire Fld Club Archaeol. Soc.* 35, 41–92.

Patton, P.C. and Schumm, S.A., 1981, 'Ephemeral-stream processes: implications for studies of Quaternary valley fills', *Quaternary Research* 15, 24–43.

Peacock, D.P.S. and Williams, D.F., 1986, *Amphorae and the Roman Economy: an Introductory Guide*, London.

Royal Commission on Historical Monuments (England), 1992a, *West Kennett–East Kennett, archaeological survey in the vicinity of the Avebury World Heritage Site: air photographic transcription and analysis*, unpubl. RCHM(E) report.

——, 1992b, *Archaeological survey in and around the Avebury World Heritage Site: air photographic transcription and analysis*, unpubl. RCHM(E) report.

Rees, H., 1995, 'The Iron Age pottery' in Fasham and Keevill 1995, 64–65.

Reynolds, P.J., 1974, 'Experimental Iron Age storage pits: an interim report', *Proc. Prehist. Soc.* 40, 118–131.

Richards, J., 1990, *The Stonehenge Environs Project*, London, English Heritage Archaeol. Rep. 16.

Rigby, V., 1982a, 'The coarse pottery', in Watcher, J. and McWhirr, A., *Early Roman Occupation at Cirencester*, Cirencester Excavations 1, 153–200.

——, 1982b, 'The pottery', in McWhirr, A., Viner, L. and Wells, C., *Romano-British Cemeteries at Cirencester*, Cirencester Excavations II, 112–125.

92

Ringwood, V., 1987, *The animal bone from Avebury*, unpubl. BSc thesis, Univ. Wales College of Cardiff.

Robinson, M.A., 1988, 'Molluscan evidence for pasture and meadowland on the floodplain of the upper Thames basin', in Murphy, P. and French, C. (eds), *The Exploitation of the Wetlands*, Oxford, Brit. Archaeol. Rep. 186, 101–112.

Rogers, B. and Roddham, D., 1991, 'The excavation at Wellhead, Westbury 1959–1966', *Wiltshire Archaeol. Natur. Hist. Mag.* 84, 51–60.

Sanders, J., 1979, 'The Roman pottery', in Lambrick, G. and Robinson, M., *Iron Age and Roman Riverside Settlements at Farmoor, Oxfordshire*, Counc. Brit. Archaeol. Res. Rep. 32, 46–54.

Sawyer, P.H., 1968, *Anglo-Saxon Charters: an Annotated List and Bibliography*, London, Royal Historical Society Guides and Handbooks 8.

Scott, E., 1993, *A Gazetteer of Roman Villas in Britain*, Leicester, Leicester Archaeol. Monog. 1.

Smith, A.C., 1884, *Guide to the British and Roman Antiquities of the North Wiltshire Downs*, Marlborough Coll. Natur. Hist. Soc.

Smith, I.F. and Simpson, D.D.A., 1964, 'Excavation of three Roman tombs and a prehistoric pit on Overton Down', *Wiltshire Archaeol. Natur. Hist. Mag.* 59, 68–85.

Smith, R.W., 1984, 'The ecology of Neolithic farming systems as exemplified by the Avebury region of Wiltshire', *Proc. Prehist. Soc.* 50, 99–120.

Soffe, G., 1993, 'A barrow cemetery and other features recorded by air photography at Beckhampton, Avebury', *Wiltshire Archaeol. Natur. Hist. Soc. Mag.* 86, 142–157.

Sparks, B.W., 1961., 'The ecological interpretation of Quaternary non-marine Mollusca'., *Proc. Linn. Soc. Lond.* 172, 71–80.

Stukeley, W., 1743, *Abury: a Temple of the British Druids*, London.

Swan, V.G., 1975, 'Oare reconsidered and the origins of Savernake ware in Wiltshire', *Britannia*, 6, 36–51

Symonds, R.P., 1992, *Rhenish Ware: Fine, Dark Coloured Pottery from Gaul and Germany*, Oxford, Oxford Univ. Comm. Archaeol. Monog. 23.

Taylor, H.M., 1982, *Anglo-Saxon features in Avebury*, unpubl. St James' church guidebook, 2–4.

Timby, J., 1985, 'The pottery', in Fulford, M.G., *Guide to the Silchester Excavations — the Forum Basilica 1982–4*, Reading, Univ. Reading, 25–28.

Ucko, P.J., Hunter, M., Clark, A.J. and David, A., 1991, *Avebury Reconsidered: from the 1660s to the 1990s*, London, Univ. London, Institute of Archaeol.

Vatcher, F., 1971a, *Site file AV71, Site B, Marlborough–Ramsbury Drainage, Trusloe*, Avebury, unpubl. manuscript Alexander Keiller Museum.

——, 1971b, *Site File AV71, Site C, Paradise Garden*, unpubl. manuscript Alexander Keiller Museum, Avebury.

Wainwright, G.J., 1989, *Proof of evidence, Overton Hill Public Inquiry, August 1989*, unpubl. English Heritage report.

Wait, G.A., 1985, *Ritual and Religion in Iron Age Britain*, Oxford, Brit. Archaeol. Rep. 149.

Wedlake, W.J., 1982, *The Excavation of the Shrine of Appollo at Nettleton, Wiltshire, 1965–1971*, Rep. Res. Comm. Soc. Antiq. London 40.

Wessex Archaeology, 1992a, *Kennet valley foul sewer improvement: stage 1 archaeological assessment*, Salisbury, Wessex Archaeology unpubl. client report.

——, 1992b, *Kennet valley foul sewer improvement, stage 2: evaluation and monitoring: project design and costing*, Salisbury, Wessex Archaeology, unpubl. client report.

——, 1993a, *Kennet valley foul Sewer improvement: archaeological evaluation and monitoring, proposals for post-fieldwork analysis and reporting*, Salisbury, Wessex Archaeology unpubl. client report.

——, 1993b, *Mill Street, Wantage, Oxfordshire: archaeological site investigations*, Salisbury, Wessex Archaeology unpubl. client report.

——, 1993c, *Excavations at Maddington Farm, Shrewton near Salisbury*, Salisbury, Wessex Archaeology unpubl. client report.

Whittle, A., 1990, 'A model for the Mesolithic–Neolithic transition in the upper Kennet valley, north Wiltshire', *Proc. Prehist. Soc.* 56, 101–110.

——, 1991, 'A Late Neolithic complex at West Kennett, Wiltshire, England', *Antiquity* 65, 256–262.

——, 1993, 'The Neolithic of the Avebury area; sequence, environment, settlement and monuments', *Oxford J. Archaeol.*, 12, 29–54.

Wild, J.P., 1970, *Textile Manufacture in the Northern Roman Provinces*, Cambridge.

——, and Viner, L., 1986, 'Objects of bone and antler', in McWhirr, A., *Houses in Roman Cirencester*, Cirencester Excavations III, 114–115.

Wilkinson, Reverend, 1869, 'A report of diggings made in Silbury Hill and in the adjoining ground', *Wilts. Archaeol. Natur. Hist. Mag.* 11, 113–8.

Wiltshire Archaeology and Natural History Magizine, 1923, vol 42, 359–61, 'Roman pavement near Avebury,' in 'Notes', 356–73.

——, 1928, 'Pottery rings at East Kennett,' in 'Notes', 149, 260–70 (264).

——, 1990a, 'Wiltshire Archaeological Registers for 1987 and 1988', 83, 224–235.

Young, C.J., 1977, *Oxfordshire Roman Pottery*, Oxford, Brit. Archaeol. Rep. 43.

Index

by Lesley and Roy Adkins

Entries are largely in alphabetical order, but sub-entries follow a chronological order of entry where appropriate (for example, Middle Bronze Age, Late Iron Age). The following abbreviations have been used: EBA Early Bronze Age, BA Bronze Age, IA Iron Age, and RB Romano-British.

aerial/air photographs 10, 11, 12
    barrows 12
    ditches 78
    earthwork bank 80
    ring-ditch 13
    Roman Road 27
    strip lynchets 61, 63, 65, 66
air photographic survey 5, 7, 86
    Avebury to West Kennett (Area B) 9, Figs 5, 10
    Beckhampton barrow cemetery 26
    Beckhampton to Avebury (Area A) 8, Fig. 4
    West Overton to Lockeridge (Area D) Fig. 6
alder (charcoal) 33, Table 12
Alexander Keiller Museum 1, 5
alluvial deposits/sediments/silt 2, 3, 48–52, 65, 66, 83, 84, 87, 88, Table 9
alluviation 2, 59, 67, 70
alluvium 31, 67, 70, 73, 83, 84, 85, 87, Fig. 22
animal bones
    Romano-British 27, 31, 34, 35, 37, 38, 39, 52–3, 71, Table 10
    Saxon 59
    medieval 61, 65, 71, Table 15
    post-medieval 76
    undated 79
archive 19
Area A see Beckhampton to Avebury
Area B see Avebury to West Kennett
Area C see East Kennett to West Overton
Area D see West Overton to Lockeridge
arrowhead (flint) 9, 10
ash (charcoal) 32, 55, 56, Table 12
Ashville, Oxon (fired clay disc) 40
Avebury
    beads (Saxon) 59
    Benedictine priory 61
    boundary wall (medieval) 59, 64
    burning pit 59
    church (St James) 4, 59, 61, Fig. 17
    Circle/stone circle 13, 59, 61, 73, Figs 1, 2, 22
    ditches (medieval) 59, 61
    henge 3–4
    hollow-way (medieval) 61
    Manor/Manor House 61, Fig. 17
    pits (medieval) 61
    pottery
        Saxon 59
        medieval 59
        post-medieval 9, 74
    settlement
        Saxon 4, 9, 57, 59, 84
        medieval 4, 9, 59–61
    see also Butler's Field
Avebury Down barrows 4, Fig. 2
'Avebury soil' 2, 10
Avebury to West Kennett (Area B) 2, 10, Figs 1, 2, 17
    air photographic survey 9, Figs 5, 10

desk-based study 8–9
earthwork survey Fig. 17
geophysical surveys 8–9, Figs 5, 9, 17
SMR entries/sites 5, Table 1
Avebury Trusloe (medieval village earthworks) 61
Avenue see Beckhampton, West Kennett
axe (bronze, BA) 9, 13
axe hammer (BA) 8, 13

Bachentune 8, Fig. 4
banks
    on aerial photographs 80
    in The Paddock 8, 61
    see also earthworks
Barbury Castle hillfort 13
barrows
    on air photographs 12
    Avebury Down 4, Fig. 2
    bell barrows 12
    bowl barrows 12
    burials 12
    disc barrows 12, 13, 27
    mounds 12, 15, 16, 18, 24
    ploughed 11, 12, Fig. 22
    pond barrows 12
    saucer barrows 12
    as soil marks 11
    upstanding 12
    West Overton 8, 13
    see also Beckhampton, buried soil, Overton Hill/Down, Pound Field barrow, ring-ditches, 'Stukeley' barrow, Waden Hill
Bartholomew, Street, Newbury (medieval pottery) 67
beads (glass, Saxon) 59
Beaker pottery 4
Beckhampton 1, Figs 1, 22
    Avenue 3, 9, 10, 11
    barrow 1: 8, 12
    barrow 2: 8, 12
    barrow 3: 8, 12
    barrow 4: 8, 12, 15–18, 61
        bones (cattle) 16
        construction 26
        mollusca 18, 19, 24, Fig. 8, Table 3
        ring-ditch/ditch 12, 15–18, 19, 24, 26, Fig. 7, Table 3
        type 12
    barrow 5: 8, 12
    barrow 6: 8, 12
    barrow 7: 8, 12
    barrow 8: 8, 12
    barrow 10: 12, 13, 26
    barrow 11: 12–13, 26
    barrows/barrow cemetery 4, 5, 8, 11–13, 26, 61, 78
    chape (IA) 8, 13
    ditches (undated) 78
    earthworks (medieval) 4, 8, 61
    horseshoes (RB) 8, 30

lynchets/strip lynchets (medieval) 63, 65, 73, 78
    settlement (medieval) 4, 61, Fig. 4
Beckhampton to Avebury (Area A) 2, Figs 1, 2, 4
    air photographic survey 8, Fig. 4
    desk-based study 8
    geophysical survey 8, Fig. 4
    SMR entries/sites 5, Table 1
bell barrows 12
bird bones 52–3, Table 10
Blacksmith's Garden, West Overton 9
    cultivation strips 74, Fig. 6
boar bones 27
bones
    birds 52–3, Table 10
    boar 27
    cattle 16, 27, 52, 53, 76, 83, Tables 10, 15
    cow 59
    deer 27
    dog 52, Table 10
    fish 53, 71, Tables 10, 15
    horse 27, 52, 76, Table 10
    sheep 27, 52, 61
    sheep/goat 27, 71, Tables 10, 15
    see also animal bones
bone weaving tablets (RB) 35, 41, Fig. 14
boundaries see field boundaries
bowl barrows 12
bricks
    Roman 37, 39–40, 43, 56
    medieval 76
    post-medieval 74, 76–7
Brighton Hill South, Hants (IA pottery) 63
bronze
    axe (BA) 9, 13
    chisel (BA) 9, 13
    finger-ring (RB) 27
Bronze Age 11–13, 83
    axe 9, 13
    axe hammer 8, 13
    buried soil (possible) 7, 19, 24, Tables 2, 3
    chisel 9, 13
    cultivation 83
    dagger (copper alloy) 12
    environment 19, 24–6, 83
    field systems 57, 83
    flints 8, 13
    lynchets 83
    pottery 19
brooches (RB) 35, 40–1, Fig. 14
Building I (Romano-British) 27, 31, 32, 37, 56, 86, Figs 10, 11
    chalk walls 31
    destruction by fire 57
    mortar 31
    roofing tiles 31
    wall foundation trenches (robbed) 31, 33, 46, 56, Fig. 11
Building II (Romano-British) 27, 31–3, 34, 56, 86, Figs 10, 11, Plate 4
    chalk walls 31
    charcoal 31, 32, 56, Table 12
    destruction by fire 32
    mortar 31
    sarsen block 32
    wall foundation trenches (robbed) 31–2, 33, 40, 53, 56, Table 12, Plate 4
Building III (Romano-British) 32, 33, 34, 37, 56, Fig. 10
    destruction by fire 57
    wall foundation trenches (robbed) 33, 40, 86, Fig. 11
Building IV (Romano-British) 32, 33–4, 38, 56, Fig. 10
    floor (robbed) 33
    wall foundation trenches (robbed) 33, 38, 86, Fig. 11

Building V (Romano-British) 34, 35, 38, 39, 56, 57, Fig. 10
    wall foundation trench (robbed) 34, Fig. 11
buildings (Roman/Romano-British) 56, 58, 83, 84, 85, 87, Fig. 22
    see also Buildings I–V
building stone (RB) 34, 35, 37, 38, 41, 56, 57
Burghfield, Berks (spelt) 53
burials
    Romano-British 9, 27, 57, 59, 84
    Saxon 59
    secondary 12, 59
    Waden Hill 79
    see also barrows, grave
burial of sites see alluvium, colluvium
buried soil
    Bronze Age (?) 7, 19, 24, Tables 2, 3
    Butler's Field, Avebury 10
    Pound Field barrow 18, 19, 24, 26, Tables 2, 3
burning pits 10, 59
burnt flint 31, 37
butchery 52, 53, 71, 76
Butler's Field, Avebury 2, Fig. 17
    animal bones 61, 65, 71, 79, Table 15
    buried soil 10
    charred plant remains 65, 71
    ditches
        medieval 63, 64–5, 66, 71, 78, Fig. 18
        post-medieval 78
        undated 64, 78–9, Fig. 18
    earthworks 9
    excavations 59
    flints 9, 10
    flooding 67, 70
    geophysical survey 5, 61
    mollusca 67–70, Fig. 20, Table 14
    pits (medieval) 63, 64, 66, Fig. 18, Table 15
    post-hole (undated) 78, Fig. 18
    pottery
        Neolithic 10
        Romano-British 9, 30, 67
        Saxon 9, 59, 63, 64, 66, 84
        medieval 30, 63, 64, 65, 66–7, 73, Fig. 19, Table 13
    radiocarbon date 59
    roof tile 65, 66
    settlement (medieval) 61, 63–5, 67, 71, 73, 84
    sheep farming 61
    wall foundation trench (medieval) 63, 64, 65, Fig. 18, Plate 7

Caerleon museum (weaving tablets) 41
Calstone Down 27
cattle 26, 57, 83
    bones 16, 27, 52, 53, 76, 83, Tables 10, 15
causewayed enclosures 3
ceramic see bricks, fired clay, pottery
cereals see charred plant remains
chalk
    blocks (RB) 31, 33, 34, 56
    walls (RB) 31
chape (IA) 8, 13
charcoal 7
    alder 33, Table 12
    ash 32, 55, 56, Table 12
    Building II (RB) 31, 32, 56, Table 12
    Building III (RB) 33
    Building IV (RB) 33
    Butler's Field, Avebury 61, 78, 79
    ditches
        Romano-British 38, 55, Table 12
        medieval 64
        undated 78, 79

hazel 19, 33, 55, 56, Tables 2, 12
oak 19, 32, 55, 56, Tables 2, 12
pits
    Romano-British 34, 35, 53, 55–6, Table 12
    medieval 64
Pound Field barrow 18, 19, Table 2
wall foundation trenches
    Romano-British 53
    medieval 64
Winterbourne Romano-British settlement 31, 33, 34,
    55–6, Table 12
charred plant remains 7
    Butler's Field, Avebury 65, 71
    East Kennett 65, 71–3
    Winterbourne Romano-British settlement 53–5, 83,
        Table 11
    see also charcoal
charters (Saxon) 4, 9, 59
Chenete 8, 9, 59, Figs 5, 21
chisel (bronze, BA) 9, 13
church (Saxon) 4, 59, 61
Cirencester
    brooches (RB) 41
    pottery (RB) 46, 47
    weaving tablets 41
coins (Roman) 8, 27, 30, 57
Colchester, Essex
    brooches (RB) 41
    weaving tablet 41
colluvial deposits/sediments 48–52, 73, 83, 84, 87, 88
colluviation 52, 73
colluvium 83, 84, 86, 87
copper alloy
    brooch (RB) 35, 40–1, Fig. 14
    dagger (EBA) 12
    weaving tablets 41
cow bones 59
crop marks 5, 11, 61
crop processing 53, 55, 57, 73, 83
cultivation
    Neolithic 2, 3
    Bronze Age 83
    Iron Age 53
    Romano-British 53, 57, 83
    medieval 2, 61, 73, 84
    post-medieval 74
Cunnington, M.E. 27

dagger (copper alloy, EBA) 12
daub (medieval) 61
deer bones 27
desk-based study 1, 5, 6, 7, 8–9, 78, 79–80, 86
disc barrows 12, 13, 27
ditches
    Romano-British 7, 33, 35–9, 40, 41, 46, 47, 48, 53, 55,
        56, 57, 79, 80, Fig. 13, Tables 5, 6, 8, 10–12, Plate
        6
    medieval 7, 59, 61, 63, 64–5, 66, 71, 78, Fig. 18, Table
        16
    post-medieval 74, 78, Fig. 18
    undated 64, 65, 78–9, 80, Fig. 18
    of Roman Road 27, 37
    Silbury Hill 27
    see also ring-ditches
documentary sources 4, 59, 84
dog bones 52, Table 10
Domesday Book 8, 9, 59, 61
Down Born , Wiltshire (colluvial deposits) 83

earthworks
    medieval 4, 8, 9, 61, 63

post-medieval 2, 74
undated 80
survey 5, 74, Fig. 17
East Kennett Fig. 1
    axe (BA) 9, 13
    charred plant remains 65, 71–3
    chisel (BA) 9, 13
    ditch (undated) 65, 71–3
    flints (Neolithic) 9, 10
    geophysical survey 80
    key (medieval) 9, 63
    long barrow Fig. 2
    loom weights (Saxon) 9, 59
    Manor 2, 8, 9, 59, 63, 65, 74–7, 80–1, Plate 8
        house 77
    pottery
        Iron Age 13, 65
        Roman 65
        Saxon 63, 65, 73, 84
    settlement
        Saxon 61
        medieval 4, 9, 61–3, 65, Fig. 21
    stone foundation 81
    water meadows 9
East Kennett to West Overton (Area C) 2, Figs 1, 2
    desk-based study 9
    geophysical survey Fig. 21
    SMR entries/sites 5, Table 1
East Overton (medieval village earthworks) 63
enclosures *see* causewayed enclosure, henges, palisaded
    enclosures
environment 2
    Mesolithic 2
    Neolithic 2
    Bronze Age 19, 24–6, 83
    Romano-British 48–56
    medieval 67–73
    see also mollusca

Farmoor, Oxon (fired clay discs) 40
field boundaries 8, 56, 61, 73
fields/field systems 26, Fig. 22
    Bronze Age 57, 83
    Iron Age (Celtic) 13, 57, 83
    Romano-British 83
fieldwalking 13, 82, Fig. 4
Fifield Bavant (IA spelt) 53
finger-ring (RB) 27
fired clay 31, 37, 38, 40
fish bones 53, 71, Tables 10, 15
flints (worked) 64, 82, Fig. 4
    arrowheads 9, 10
    blade 18
    flakes 10, 27
    Mesolithic 9, 10
    Neolithic 9, 10
    Bronze Age 8, 13
    see also burnt flint
flooding/inundation 2, 26, 51, 59, 67, 70
floor tiles 43, 56
Folly Hill 2, 12
foundation trenches *see* wall foundation trenches
Fyfield Down Fig. 22
    settlement (RB) 57, 83
Fyfield House (RB villa) 58

geology 2
geophysical survey 1, 5–6, 7, 26, 27, 78, 82, 86
    Avebury to West Kennett (Area B) 8–9, Figs 5, 9, 17
    Beckhampton barrow cemetery 26
    Beckhampton to Avebury (Area A) 8, Fig. 4

96

Butler's Field, Avebury 5, 61
East Kennett 80
East Kennett to West Overton (Area C) Fig. 21
Pound Field, West Overton 13, Plate 9
'Stukeley' barrow (Waden Hill) 27
West Overton to Lockeridge (Area D) 9, Fig. 6
Winterbourne Romano-British settlement 33
    see also magnetometer surveys
glass beads (Saxon) 59
grave (RB) 9, 27
    see also burials
gullies (medieval) 61
Gwithian, Cornwall (seaweed manure) 83

hazel 26
    charcoal 19, 33, 55, 56, Tables 2, 12
henge see Avebury
hillforts (IA) 13
hillwash 27, 31, 33, 34, 35, 37, 38, 39, 52, 66, 80, 84, 85
hobnails (RB) 27, 35, 40
hollows
    Romano-British 39, 47, 79, Fig. 13, Table 8
    undated 80
hollow-way (medieval) 61
Honeysuckle Cottage, West Kennett 8, 80
hook (RB) 27
horse bones 27, 52, 76, Table 10
horseshoes (RB) 8, 30
Horslip long barrow 3

iron
    hobnails (RB) 27, 35, 40
    hook (RB) 27
    key (medieval) 9, 63
    nails (RB) 27, 31, 33, 34, 38, 39, 40
    shears (RB) 27
    styli (RB) 27
Iron Age 13, 83
    chape 8, 13
    cultivation 53
    fields/field systems (Celtic) 13, 57, 83
    hillforts 13
    pottery 13, 63, 65
    settlements 13, 57, 83

key (medieval) 9, 63
Knap Hill causewayed enclosure 3

Lankhills cemetery, Winchester (RB brooches) 41
leather(?, RB) 40
limestone (building stone) 41
Little Solisbury (IA spelt) 53
long barrows 3, Fig. 2
Long Stones 10, Fig. 2
loomweights (Saxon) 9, 59
lynchets/strip lynchets 8, 61, 80
    Bronze Age 83
    medieval 4, 9, 61, 63, 65–6, 70–1, 73, 78, 84, Fig. 7,
        Table 4, Plate 2
    undated 18, Fig. 7

magnetometer surveys 1, 5–6, 12, 13, 34, 61, 79–80, 86
    see also geophysical survey
Manor see Avebury, East Kennett
manuring 26, 83
Marlborough Downs 4
    barrows 26
    landscape project 82
    sarsen stones 4

medieval 59–62, 84
    animal bones 61, 65, 71, Table 15
    bricks 76
    burning pit 59
    charred plant remains 65
    colluviation 52
    cultivation 2, 61, 73, 84
    daub 61
    ditches 7, 59, 61, 63, 64–5, 66, 71, 78, Fig. 18, Table
        16
    earthworks 4, 8, 9, 61, 63
    environment 67–73
    field boundaries 8, 61, 73
    gullies 61
    hollow-way 61
    key 9, 63
    lynchets/strip lynchets 4, 61, 63, 65–6, 70–1, 73, 78,
        84, Fig. 7, Table 4, Plate 2
    pits 61, 63, 64, 66, Fig. 18, Table 15
    pottery 30, 59, 61, 63, 64, 65, 66–7, 73, 76, 77, Fig. 19,
        Table 13
    priory 61
    roof tile 65, 66
    settlements 67
        abandonment 61
        Avebury 4, 9, 59–61
        Beckhampton 61, Fig. 4
        Butler's Field, Avebury 61, 63–5, 67, 71, 73, 84
        East Kennett 9, 61–3, 65, Fig. 21
        West Kennett 8, 61–3, Fig. 5
        West Overton Fig. 6
    slag 64
    stake-holes 61
    wall foundation 59, 63, 64, 65, Fig. 18, Plate 7
Mesolithic 10
    environment 2
    flints 9, 10
Mildenhall, Wilts 4
    Roman Road 27
    Savernake ware 47
Mill Street, Wantage, Oxon (fired clay disc) 40
mitigation strategy 1, 6, 86
mollusca 7
    Beckhampton barrow 4: 18, 19, 24, Fig. 8, Table 3
    Butler's Field, Avebury 67–70, Fig. 20, Table 14
    Pound Field barrow, West Overton 19, 24, Table 3
    'Stukeley' barrow (Waden Hill) 18, 19, 24, 26, Fig. 8,
        Table 4
    Waden Hill 70–1, Table 4
    Winterbourne valley 48–52, Fig. 16, Table 9
mortar (RB) 31, 34
mounds (of barrows) 12, 15, 16, 18, 24

nails (RB) 27, 31, 33, 34, 38, 39, 40
Neolithic 10–11, 82–3
    alluviation 2
    cultivation 2, 3
    environment 2
    flints 9, 10
    land/woodland clearance 19, 82
    pottery 8, 10, 82
    settlement 82
    see also causewayed enclosure, long barrows, palisade
        enclosures, Silbury Hill
Nettleton, Wilts (RB pottery) 46, 47
North Farm, West Overton (Mesolithic flints) 10

oak 26
    charcoal 19, 32, 55, 56, Tables 2, 12

Ofaertune 9
Oldbury Castle hillfort 13
Overton Down Fig. 22
    field systems (BA) 83
    lynchets (BA) 83
    settlement 13, 57, 83
    tombs (RB) 57, 59
Overton Hill
    barrows/barrow cemetery 11, 12, 59
    burials (Saxon) 59
    Roman Road 27
    see also Down
    see also the Sanctuary
oyster shells (RB) 27, 34, 57

The Paddock bank 8, 61
palisade enclosures (West Kennett) 4, 8, 10, 83, Fig. 5
Paradise garden (buried sarsen) 10
Passmore, A.D. 10
petrological analysis (pottery) 19
pig 57
Piggledene Bottom, Wiltshire (colluvial deposits) 83
pits
    Romano-British 7, 27, 34–5, 40, 43, 46, 47, 48, 52, 53,
        55–6, Fig. 12, Tables 5, 6, 8, 10–12, Plate 5
    medieval 61, 63, 64, 66, Fig. 18, Table 15
    see also burning pits, rubbish pit
Planning Policy Guidance Note 16: 1, 86
plant remains *see* charred plant remains
ploughed-out barrows 11, 12, Fig. 22
pond barrows 12
post-hole (undated) 78, Fig. 18
post-medieval
    alluviation 2
    alluvium 31
    animal bone 76
    bricks 74, 76–7
    colluviation 52
    cultivation 74
    ditches 74, 78, Fig. 18
    field boundaries 61
    pottery 9, 74
    roof tile 76
    water meadows 9, 74, 78, Figs 10, 21
pottery
    Neolithic 8, 10, 82
    Beaker 4
    Bronze Age 19
    Iron Age 13, 63, 65
    Romano-British 9, 18, 27, 30–1, 33, 34, 35, 37, 38, 39,
        40, 41, 43–8, 56, 57, 65, 66, 83, Fig. 15
        amphora 47, 48
        Black Burnished ware 34, 46, 47, 48
        coarsewares 34, 35, 37, 46–7, 57, 67, Table 8
        colour-coated wares 46, 48
        dating 47–8
        decoration 43, 48
        fabrics 43, 46–7, 48, 65, Tables 7–8
        finewares 34, 35, 37, 43–6, 48, Table 8
        grey wares 46, 48
        kilns 46
        mortarium 27, 46, 48
        Rhenish ware 38, 46, 48
        samian 27, 31, 34, 43–6, 48, 56, 57
        Savernake ware 27, 47, 48
    Saxon 9, 19, 59, 63, 64, 65, 66, 73, 84
    medieval 30, 59, 61, 63, 64, 65, 66–7, 73, 76, 77, Fig.
        19, Table 13
    post-medieval 9, 74
    petrological analysis 19
Pound Field barrow, West Overton 9, 18–19, 31

buried soil 18, 19, 24, 26, Tables 2, 3
charcoal 18, 19, Table 2
geophysical survey 13
lynchet (undated) 18, Fig. 7
mollusca 19, 24, Table 3
mound 15, 24
pottery
    Bronze Age 18, 19
    Iron Age 13
    Saxon 13, 19, 63, 84
ring-ditch/ditch 12, 13, 18, 19, 63, 66, Fig. 7
Pound Field, West Overton 2, Plate 1
    geophysical survey 13, Plate 9
    strip lynchets 9, 63
priory (medieval) 61

querns (RB) 27

radiocarbon dates 59, 67, 73
recording system 7
Ridgeway 2, 9, 10, 57, 59, 74, Figs 1, 2, 21
ring-ditches/ditches 8, 12, 26
    on air photographs 13
    Beckhampton barrow 4: 12, 15–18, 19, 24, 26, Fig. 7,
        Table 3
    Pound Field barrow, West Overton 13, 18, 19, 63, 66,
        Fig. 7
    'Stukeley' barrow (Waden Hill) 13, 18, 19, 24, 26, 27,
        65, 83, Fig. 7, Table 4, Plate 2
    Waden Hill 8, 13, 80
    West Kennett 8
Riseley Farm, Swallowfield, Berks (IA pottery) 63
River Kennett 2, 26, 59, Figs 1, 2, 5, 21, 22, 67–70
Road, Roman 4, 9, 13, 27, 32, 34, 35, 37, 56, 57, 58, 84, Figs 1,
    2, 10, 22
robbing *see* wall foundation trenches
Roman
    coins 8, 27, 30, 57
    Road *see* separate entry
Romano-British 83–4
    animal bones 27, 31, 34, 35, 37, 38, 39, 52–3, 71, Table
        10
    bricks 37, 39–40, 43, 56
    brooches 35, 40–1, Fig. 14
    buildings 56, 58, 83, 84, 85, 87, Figs 2, 22
    Buildings I–V *see* separate entry
    building stone 34, 35, 37, 38, 41, 56, 57
    burials/graves 9, 27, 57, 59, 83, 84
    chalk blocks 31, 33, 34, 56
    charred plant remains 53–5, Table 11
    cultivation 53, 57, 83
    ditches 7, 33, 35–9, 40, 41, 46, 47, 48, 53, 55, 56, 57,
        79, 80, Fig. 13, Tables 5, 6, 8, 10–12, Plate 6
    environment 48–56
    field systems 83
    finger-ring 27
    fired clay 31, 37, 38, 40
    floor tiles 56
    hobnails 27, 35, 40
    hollow 39, 47, 79, Fig. 13, Table 8
    hook 27
    horseshoes 8, 30
    leather(?) 40
    limestone 41
    mortar 31, 34
    nails 27, 31, 33, 34, 38, 39, 40
    oyster shells 27, 34, 57
    pits 7, 27, 34–5, 40, 43, 46, 47, 48, 52, 53, 55–6, Fig.
        12, Tables 5, 6, 8, 10–12, Plate 5
    pottery *see* separate entry
    querns 27

roofing/roof tiles 27, 34, 43, 56, 57, Table 5
rubbish pit 27
sandstone 33, 35, 37, 38, 41–3, 56, Table 5
settlements 57, 83
    buried by deposits 84–6
shale 37
shears 27
shell 35, 37, 38
slag 37, 38
stone (worked) 41–3, 56, Tables 5, 6
styli 27
terrace 33, 47
tiles 27, 57
    see also roofing tile
trackway 38
villas 4, 57–8
wall foundation trenches *see* separate entry
weaving tablets 35, 41, Fig. 14
wells 27, 58, Fig. 10
whetstones 43
wood(?) 40
see also Winterbourne Romano-British settlement
roofing/roof tiles
    Romano-British 27, 31, 34, 43, 56, 57, Table 5
    medieval 65, 66
    post-medieval 76
round barrows *see* barrows
rubbish pit (RB) 27
Rucstalls Hill, Hants (IA pottery) 63

samian *see* pottery
the Sanctuary 3, 4, 10, Figs 2, 22
sandstone
    blocks 33
    building stone 34, 35, 37, 38, 41, 57
    floor tiles 43, 56
    roofing/roof tiles 34, 43, 56, 57, 65, 66, Table 5
    whetstones 43
sarsen blocks/stones 2, 4, 10, 61
    Building II (RB) 32
    Building III (RB) 33
    foundation (undated) 81
    ditches
        Romano-British 37, 56, Fig. 13
        medieval 65
        undated 65
    Paradise garden (buried) 10
    pit (RB) 35
    post-hole 78
    wall foundation trenches
        Romano-British 56
        medieval 64
saucer barrows 12
Saxon 59, 84
    animal bones 59
    beads (glass) 59
    burials 59
    charters 4, 9, 59
    church 4, 59, 61
    loomweights 9, 59
    pottery 9, 19, 59, 63, 64, 65, 66, 73, 84
    settlements 59
        Avebury 4, 9, 57, 59, 84
        East Kennett 61
        West Kennett 61
    sunken huts 59
Scheduled Monuments 2, 27
settlements
    Neolithic 82
    Iron Age 13, 57, 83
    Romano-British 57, 83

    buried by deposits 84–6
    see also Winterbourne Romano-British settlement
Saxon 59
    Avebury 4, 9, 57, 59, 84
    East Kennett 61
    West Kennett 61
medieval 67
    abandonment 61
    Avebury 4, 9, 59–61
    Beckhampton 4, 61, Fig. 4
    Butler's Field, Avebury 61, 63–5, 67, 71, 73, 84
    East Kennett 4, 9, 61–3, 65, Fig. 21
    West Kennett 8, 61–3, Fig. 5
    West Overton 4, Fig. 6
Shakenoak, Oxon (RB pottery) 47
shale (RB) 37
shears (RB) 27
sheep 26, 57, 83
    bones 27, 52, 61
    farming 61
sheep/goat bones 27, 71, Tables 10, 15
shell (RB) 35, 37, 38
Shrewton, Wilts (fired clay disc) 40
Silbury Hill 2, 3, 4, 31, 32, 82, Figs 1, 2, 10, 22, Plates 3, 4
    ditch 27
    Romano-British settlement/finds nearby 27, 57, Figs 9, 10
    Saxon burial 59
    timber palisade 4
    see also Winterbourne Romano-British settlement
Silchester, Hants (IA pottery) 63
slag 37, 38, 64
SMR entries/sites 5, 6, 12, 26, 30, 58, 59, 79, Table 1
soil erosion 84
soil marks 5, 11
soil samples 6, 7, 31, 65
South Street long barrow 3
Stage 1 Assessment 1, 2, 5–6, 8, 13, 27, 61, 86, Table 1
Stage 2 evaluation 1, 2, 6, 86
stake-holes (medieval) 61
stone
    worked (RB) 41–3, Tables 5, 6
    see also building stone, roofing tiles, sandstone
strip lynchets *see* lynchets
'Stukeley' barrow (Waden Hill) 8, 18, 65, 70
    construction 26
    disc barrow 27
    geophysical survey 27
    mollusca 18, 19, 24, 26, Fig. 8, Table 4
    pottery (Roman) 18
    ring-ditch/ditch 13, 18, 19, 24, 26, 27, 65, 83, Fig. 7, Table 4, Plate 2
    Roman Road nearby 56
Stukeley, William 10, 11, 13, 27
styli (RB) 27
sunken huts (Saxon) 59
surface artefact collection 6
Swallowhead Springs 2, 27, 74, Figs 2, 22

terrace (RB) 33, 47
tiles (RB) 27, 57
    see also roofing tiles
topsoil stripping 6, 86
trackways (RB) 38
    see also Ridgeway
Truslow Manor 61

undated
    animal bones 79
    ditches 64, 65, 78–9, 80, Fig. 18
    hollow 80

lynchets 18, Fig. 7
post-hole 78, Fig. 18

Vatcher, Faith 1, 10, 59–61, 64, 79
village earthworks (medieval) 61, 63
villas (RB) 4, 57–8

Waden Hill 2, 79–80, Figs 2, 9, 22
  barrows 4, 8, 13, 80, Fig. 10
  burial 79
  coins (Roman) 8, 30
  ditches (undated) 80
  hollow (undated) 80
  lynchets/strip lynchets (medieval) 9, 61, 63, 65–6,
    70–1, 73, 80, 84, Fig. 7, Table 4, Plate 2
  magnetometer survey 79–80
  mollusca 70–1
  pottery
    Neolithic 8, 10
    Romano-British 30
  ring-ditch 8, 13, 80
  see also 'Stukeley' barrow
wall foundation trenches/wall foundations
  Romano-British (robbed) 7, 31–4, 38, 40, 41, 46, 47,
    48, 53, 55, 56, 86, Fig. 11, Tables 10–12, Plate 4
  medieval 59, 63, 64, 65, Fig. 18, Plate 7
Wanborough, Wilts (RB pottery) 46, 47
Wansdyke 4
watching brief 1–2, 6–7, 8, 11, 12, 27, 86
  prehistoric results 15–26
  Romano-British results 30–56
  Saxon results 63
  medieval results 63–73
  post-medieval results 74–7
  undated results 78-9, 80–1
water meadows (post-medieval) 2, 9, 74, 78, Figs 10, 21
weaving tablets (RB) 35, 41, Fig. 14
wells (RB) 27, 58, Fig. 10
Westbury, Wilts (greyware kiln site, RB) 46
West Kennett 1, Fig. 1
  Avenue 3, 4, 10, 11, Figs 2, 22
  axe hammer (BA) 8
  coins (Roman) 8, 30
  earthwork bank 80
  long barrow 3, Fig. 2
  Manor House 80
  palisade enclosures 4, 8, 10, 83, Fig. 5
  ring-ditch 8
  settlement

    Saxon 61
    medieval 8, 61–3, Fig. 5
West Overton 1, Figs 1, 22
  barrows 8, 13
  earthworks (medieval) 4, 9
  environment 2
  lynchets/strip lynchets (medieval) 63, 66, 73
  Pound Field 2, Plate 1
  St Michael's Church 13, 18, 63, 74, Fig. 6
  settlement (medieval) 64, Fig. 6
West Overton to Lockeridge (Area D) 2, Figs 1, 2
  air photographic survey Fig. 6
  desk-based study 9
  geophysical survey 9, Fig. 6
  SMR entries/sites 5, Table 1
whetstones (RB) 43
Wilkinson, Reverend 27, 56
Windmill Hill 3, Figs 1, 2, 22
  causewayed enclosure 3
  villa (RB) 57
Winterbourne
  Romano-British settlement 2, 27, 31–58, 63, 65, Fig.
    12, Tables 10–12, Plates 3, 5
    charcoal 31, 33, 34, 55–6, Table 12
    charred plant remains 53–5, 83, Table 11
    dating 83
    ditches 79, 80
    function 57
    geophysical survey 33
    hollow 79
    magnetometer survey 34
    mortar 31, 33, 34
    pits 26, 33
    pottery 31, 34
    Saxon continuity 57
    size and function 56–7
    see also Buildings I–V
  river 2, 10, 27, 31, 33, 35, 37, 38, 39, 56, 61, Figs 1, 2,
    9, 17, 22, Plate 3
  valley
    alluvial deposits 48–52, Table 9
    colluvial deposits 48–52, 73
    mollusca 48–52, Fig. 16, Table 9
  water meadows 9
wood(?, RB) 40
woodland 2, 19, 56
  clearance 2, 26, 82, 83
World Heritage Sites 86
  Avebury 1, 2–3, Figs 1–2

Wessex Archaeology Reports

Wessex Archaeology Reports is a series of monographs established in 1992 as a vehicle for the publication of major reports on archaeological excavation and surveys undertaken in the Wessex area.

Copies of all reports and further details are available, post free within the UK, from:

Wessex Archaeology
Portway House
Old Sarum Park
Salisbury SP4 6EB
Tel   01722 326867
Fax   01722 337562

Reports available so far:

No. 1   Excavations in the Burghfield Area, Berkshire: Developments in the Bronze Age & Saxon Landscapes, *C.A. Butterworth & S.J. Lobb*
1992 ISBN 1–874350–01–9 £20.00, post free

No. 2   Excavations in the Town Centre of Trowbridge, 1977 & 1986–1988, *Alan H. Graham & Susan M. Davies*
1993 ISBN 1–874350–02–7 £18.00, post free

No. 3   Jennings Yard, Windsor: a Closed-Shaft Garderobe & Associated Medieval Structures, *John W. Hawkes & Michael J. Heaton*
1993 ISBN 1–874350–05–1, £15.00, post free

No. 4   Excavations at County Hall, Dorchester, Dorset, 1988: in the North-West Quarter of Durnovaria, *Roland J.C. Smith*
1993 ISBN 1–874350–08–06 £15.00, post free

No. 6   Early Settlement in Berkshire: Mesolithic–Roman Occupation in the Thames and Kennet Valleys, *I. Barnes, W.A. Boismier, R.M.J. Cleal, A.P. Fitzpatrick, and M.R. Roberts*
1995 ISBN 1–874350–12–4, £18.00, post free

No. 7   Brighton Hill South (Hatch Warren): an Iron Age Farmstead and Deserted Medieval Village in Hampshire, *P.J. Fasham and G. Keevill with D. Coe*
1995 ISBN 1–874350–13–2, £20.00, post free